Advance Prai

DIY Totemism is a must for anyone interested in nature spirit work. Lupa offers her readers a wonderful blend of practical material, direct experience, and sensible advice. Although written for animal spirit work, the exercises and ideas Lupa provides could easily be adapted for other nature spirit work as well. If you want to develop your own grounded, balanced practice in these realms, *DIY Totemism* is a great place to start. Buy this book, read it, enjoy it, share it. Highly recommended!

--Clare Vaughn, coauthor of *Learning Ritual Magic* and *Pagan Prayer Beads*

DIY Totemism is Lupa's newest foray into the world of animal magic and spirituality. She is a fine author and her care and expertise show on every page of this book. No armchair occultist, Lupa tackles difficult questions with experimentation and practical, down to earth advice. This excellent book will be a wonderful resource for anyone interested in the modern Neopagan practices of totemism, shamanistic work, and animism, developed within and for 21st century western culture. Lupa rightly points out that we have no need to appropriate the rituals or identities of other cultures in order to practice a valid totemistic path -- we have all we need for this work within our own relationships with spirit and our engagement with the natural world.

--Erynn Rowan Laurie, author of *Ogam: Weaving Word Wisdom*

I found this a wonderfully personal and immediate direct route into the heart of magical experience. Lupa is the finest animage whom I have ever met, and her book a perfect mixture of the deeply sensible and the deeply sensual.

--Dr. Ronald Hutton, author of *Triumph of the Moon*

An honest and personal doorway to the future of modern animal shamanism. I particularly enjoyed Lupa's innovative and open ended approach to animal oracle cards, giving you a greater range, freedom and responsibility than any other approach. - Christopher Penczak, author of *The Temple of Shamanic Witchcraft*

DIY Totemism: Your Personal Guide to Animal Totems

By Lupa

Megalithica Books
Stafford England

DIY Totemism: Your Personal Guide to Animal Totems
Lupa
© 2008 First edition

Cover Art: Pia Van Ravestein
Cover Design: Andy Bigwood
Editor: Taylor Ellwood
Copy Editor: innowen
Layout: Lupa

Set in Garamond and Kingthings Organica
Kingthings font care of Kevin King, font designer, http://mysite.wanadoo-members.co.uk/Kingthings/index.htm

Megalithica Books edition 2008
A Megalithica Books Edition
http://www.immanion-press.com
info@immanion-press.com
8 Rowley Grove
Stafford ST17 9BJ
UK

ISBN 978-1-905713-20-2

Dedication

To my lovely mate, Taylor, thank you for hanging in there with me through the tough times as well as the good ones; I love you, Tay. To the Animal Father, the totems, the skin spirits, and the other entities who have been aiding me in my path. May I learn to be as generous as all of you have been with me.

Acknowledgements

First, I thank Paleo for the guest essay, Ravenari for the art and guest essay, Taylor for the wonderful editing job, innowen for a great copy edit, and Storm, Andy and all the other awesome folks at Immanion Press/Megalithica Books for helping make a bunch of pixels into a book one more time. Many thanks to S. Kelley Harrell for the foreword, and all the wonderful folks who were willing to write up cover blurbs at such short notice! I also want to acknowledge all the folks who helped to field test the totem card deck, and a special thanks to those who were willing to share their results with the readers of this book. Finally, thank you to all the people, Paleo, Ravenari, and Taylor included, who gave me encouragement in both my work with animal magic, and the ongoing formation of therioshamanism.

Table of Contents

Foreword

Lacking the grounding structure of a unified tribal tradition has set up a challenging dynamic for the western seeker on an eclectic spiritual path. The yearning for a teacher amidst a collective history of religion forced upon divergent ethics and cultures, converging with New Age Aquarian consciousness, higher paradigms, and a contemporary focus on personal spirituality rather than rote belief has tested the resourcefulness of many a soulful sojourner. We have indeed observed a radical shift in the available apostles, from the beamed in satellite revivals of grassroots millionaire evangelists to the industry of the Now Age, in which daytime television is dominated by gurus. These are the same personalities whose teachings on ascension, wellbeing, and creating our own realities dot the shelves of every megabiblio chain in America. The market alone projects that concerns surrounding the soul's purpose and the heart's intent have open-book resolutions. If our consciousnesses can conceive it or our hearts grieve it, someone has composed a reference tidily summing the perfunctory steps to enlightenment. It would seem that we have merely traded one saviour for another, another someone to tell us how.

We are remembering as we stumble through the ecstatic discipline of liberating ourselves what tribal traditions have known from time immemorial: there is no external teacher. There are nemeses, witnesses, partners and advocates who spur our growth without the temple of ourselves, but the only true teacher lies within. It is that needy student in us all who teaches ourselves. There are no slideshows, no graphics, no indices. None other than ourselves and our relationship to the spiritual tribe of our making has our answers. We are self-taught, even in the realization of the tribe.

On the road to finding the voice of our spirit comes the resonance of the counsel inherent in All Things, if we choose to honor it as such. The presentation of one's personal experience traveling that road with spiritual allies is an extraordinary gift. By virtue of honoring the journey of another our inner teacher constructs the lessons for our growth. Cultivating an active relationship with our guiding totems is a bond rich for arousing such catharsis. Neither evading nor catering to conventional wisdom, the soul growth shared through Lupa's words in DIY Totemism is unapologetically frank and necessarily visceral. Her ability to present her knowledge of totems so that others can create their own relationship to them is inspiring, a needed lone howl sounding pack unity.

S. Kelley Harrell, author of *Gift of the Dreamtime*

Introduction

To the casual observer, "paganism"[1] and "occultism" are synonyms. Even among some of those who adopt either or both of these paths, the line is often blurred. However, with deeper examination the two words describe fairly distinct groups of people and philosophies in the modern magical community as a whole. Keep in mind, of course, that these are *generalizations*, but they are persistent trends at the time of this writing.

The pagan community is one that is primarily concerned with spirituality and religion. The focus is on revering deities and other entities and interacting with the Otherworld in a belief-based manner. While rituals may feature magic, their purpose tends to be primarily celebratory. Spells and other magical works may be performed, but generally speaking, magic is seen more as an auxiliary force to one's relationship to the Divine/Otherworld/etc.

Occultism, on the other hand, is much more focused on results-based magic and practicality. Magic is the main course of the occultist's feast, for the purpose of improving hirself internally and/or externally. For some occultists, particularly among Chaos magic, belief itself is a tool secondary to the main target of successful magic. Within older ceremonial traditions, magic is used to further the magician along hir own personal evolution. Some magicians even take a rather solipsistic view, believing that deities, spirits, and other entities and phenomena are solely derived from their own minds[2].

When my first book, *Fang and Fur, Blood and Bone: A Primal Guide to Animal Magic*, was originally published, Klint Finley, in his Technoccult blog, was kind enough to pass along the announcement. His opening sentence, though, reflects a common sentiment among occultists: "I've never put much thought towards animal magic before, even though animals have been so important to magical practices throughout the world and history".[3] It's not that the modern occult scene particularly dislikes animal magic, but it's not something that really gets discussed amid the talk of Kabbalah, Chaos magic, Lovecraft, and neurolinguistic programming.

Part of my intent with *Fang and Fur* was to create a bridge between the two philosophies. I wanted to offer something to the pagan community that promoted the idea of magic as a practice for its own sake

---

[1] By "paganism" I am referring specifically to the revival of pagan religions, particularly stemming from the mid-20th century, as opposed to paganism in a more general definition.
[2] Ellwood 2008
[3] Finley 2006

and that went beyond the usual dictionary treatment of the topic. For the occult community, I wrote it to demonstrate the potential that this particular paradigm has in both practical and metamorphic magic. Having come from a blended background magically, I created a syncretic system based on my experiences in both fields.

DIY Totemism: Your Personal Guide to Animal Totems is an expansion on that system. As with *Fang and Fur*, it's designed to get reader to rethink hir views, though this time the focus is specifically on animal totemism. Some of the chapters deal with new perspectives on totemism itself, while others involve subjects and practices that may be used in conjunction with totemism. My goal is for people to be able to create their own totemic systems, rather than being limited by what they think (or have been told) animal totems *should* be. Both books work well as companions to each other; some of the material in *Fang and Fur* comes into play at certain points in this book. However, don't feel that you have to have the earlier book to understand what's in the pages to come. I certainly won't complain if you have both books, but *DIY Totemism* also works nicely as a standalone volume.

I also want to encourage creative, independent thought on the part of the reader. Just like *Fang and Fur* this book does not include a totem animal dictionary. Why? Because it doesn't need one. What the totems tell me may not be what they tell you, and while I will use some anecdotes from my own experiences to illustrate my points, they shouldn't be taken as holy writ. Additionally, there are plenty of totem dictionaries in existence; I don't feel the need to add yet another one.

Instead, this book is designed to help you create your own totem animal dictionary and, if you so choose, your own tradition of working with totems. If you'll notice, the subtitle, *Your Personal Guide to Animal Totems*, emphasizes the fact that this is your journey that you are taking, and that you are creating your own dictionary based on your experiences. The material I cover, as well as the exercises at the ends of the chapters, provide ideas and methods for helping you determine which totems you'd like to work with, how to work with them, and how to literally do it yourself. The most effective magic is the magic you create yourself, or at least customize to your own needs. This is why there are so many religions, spiritualities, and types of magic out there; while some people look for a precrafted way of life that works for them, others prefer to forge their own path. Both ways are valid; however, in the realm of animal magic in general, totemism included, I believe there needs to be more information on trailblazing. The dictionary can be a useful way of organizing information on a totem, but all too often totemists only go so far as to consult previously published dictionaries, and never explore beyond that point.

This is neopagan totemism, not the totemic system of any particular indigenous culture, Native American or otherwise. It is based on my experience as a neopagan and magician coming from a middle-class American background; I make no pretensions of having an indigenous teacher who doesn't actually exist in physical reality, or the idea that I had a past life as a Native American (which supposedly makes one more legitimate when practicing anything remotely indigenous, at least according to some people). I disagree with the claim that modern American culture is devoid of spirit, or that neopaganism is a bunch of fluff compared to older traditions. I am a product of my time, and I don't try to escape that fact.

While the word "totem" is derived from the Ojibwe language[4], its definition has changed with appropriation and subsequent use. This is similar to the word "shaman", which no longer refers just to the ecstatics of the Evenk (formerly known as Tungus) people in Siberia; anthropologists in the early twentieth century appropriated the term to refer to any similar practitioner in other cultures[5]. I use the term totem primarily to describe archetypal beings that represent all of the qualities of a given species; while they have a connection to us internally, they also have their own individual existences independent of us. However, I also acknowledge that some people think of totems as individual animal spirits, or aspects of one's psyche. I realize that some people prefer to differentiate between "totems", "power animals", "animal spirit guides", "spirit familiars", etc., and the concepts have become rather blurred in neopagan practice. I have seen totems explained as archetypes, as individual spirits, and even as figments of the human psyche. While I primarily favor the archetypal theory mixed with some psychology, and I don't consider just any animal spirit to be a totem, I choose to use the term totem in an archetypal manner for the sake of simpler semantics in writing this book; you may apply the techniques in this work to your own conceptions.

As with my other writing on magic in general, I assume that my reader already has the basics of magic and totemism under hir belt. I'm not going to elaborate on 101-level magic when there are already authors who have done an excellent job thereof. After all, there's no such thing as one book that has it all, and by this point you should be used to doing research (The thrill of the Hunt, made manifest in the 21st century!). That

---

[4] Lupa 2006
[5] Vitebsky 1995

being said, I've done my best to explain my techniques thoroughly and in an easy to understand manner without watering the text down. Use them as inspiration for your own magic.

So here's my second offering of animal magic based on my ideas and experiences. Whether you consider yourself neopagan or occultist, witch, shaman, or magician, may you find it a useful springboard for your own exploration and practice!

Chapter One: Rant On! Some of the Problems with Neopagan Totemism

When most pagans and other magical folk think of animal magic, totemism is what first comes to mind. Popularized by totem animal dictionaries, decks of cards designed to help you find your totem, and even stones and jewelry with images of totems on them that serve as reminders of your sacred bond, it has a rather broad appeal in the magical community, particularly among pagans. Since I already elaborated upon the basics of totemism in *Fang and Fur, Blood and Bone*, I won't recycle my words here. If you need a basic guide to totemism I reference a number of them throughout this text and in appendix G.

For many people, totemism is primarily a spiritual pursuit. The totem is perceived to be a guide in beliefs and celebration. The close bond between the individual person and totem, however, is a wellspring of potential magical work, both practical and metamorphic, and I'll be relying heavily on it throughout this book.

As you probably gathered from the introduction, I believe that there are some areas for potential growth in animal magic in general. Keep in mind, of course, that these are colored by my own opinions—in fact, this entire book has a lot more of "me" in it than some of my other writing. At any rate, take everything I say with however much salt you like. I've yet to achieve perfection (though not for want of trying).

You may notice that a good bit of my material stems from my frustration with existing material on totemism and animal magic. I probably never would have become an author if I hadn't gotten fed up with the lack of variety in the extant literature (and thus *Fang and Fur* was born). The bulk of this chapter is a potpourri of topics related to totemism that I'd really like to see addressed more often.

But first...

What is Neopagan Totemism?

This book is about neopagan totemism. I use this term to differentiate between the bulk of totemism found in books by authors ranging from Ted Andrews to Jamie Sams and David Carson to Stephen Farmer, and even me; and traditional totemic systems found in indigenous cultures around the world. I also include reconstructions of the totemic systems of "dead" cultures, such as pre-Christian European ones, as neopagan, since regardless of how well you research them it's impossible to entirely separate that sort of reconstruction from the modern culture you live in. Some of the material in neopagan totemic literature, such as *The Medicine Cards* by Sams and Carson, is considered to be more New Age, but is used by many neopagans nonetheless.

Neopagan totemism is just that—the totemic system of new paganism. The neopagan community has spawned an incredible amount of material on nature-based religions, religions based on pre-Christian beliefs, and the practice of magic, in the past few decades. The form of animal totemism that has developed in this particular subcultural cauldron is my primary inspiration. It combines elements of traditional totemism, shamanic power animals, and individual spirit guides, to create a basic concept that is uniquely suited to the individualistic, decentralized American culture that a lot of pagans come from, as well as those cultures affected by the increase overall in individualization and globalization. It also reflects the fact that many pagans act as their own clergy, and almost none feel they require an intermediary between themselves and the spirit world. Thus the cultural organization and archetypal qualities of traditional totemism are married to the individual magical experience of the power animal, and filtered through the journey (or, much less often, qualities of the family, time, place, and circumstances of one's birth) used to find one's guardian animal spirit[6]. Totems, in a neopagan context, have become entities associated largely with the individual person rather than any particular group. They've also become, to an extent, part of the identities of those who work with them—how often have you heard someone in a discussion group, or seen someone online, ask "So, what's your totem?" and had the response "I'm a wolf totem", or "I'm a bear person"? For therianthropes, who feel that on some level of their being that they are some animal other than human, the totem may have a strong connection to the animal that they identify as (though this is not universal). All of this, and more, sets neopagan totemism far away from its roots in indigenous cultures.

This may seem heretical to some, or at least disappointing, but chances are pretty good that whatever you're getting in books—even if it's supposedly written by a Native American[7]--isn't pure traditional totemism from any culture. The exceptions are usually anthropological texts, but

---

[6] Lupa 2006

[7] Just because a person has Native Americans in one's family tree does not predispose one to knowing all about Native American cultures, especially when raised by a white family in suburbia with no tribal contacts. There are a number of neopagans and New Agers who make a huge deal about having such and such tribe in their backgrounds, but who show no apparent connection to the living cultures today. I myself am largely of European stock, including Czech, but I inherently know about as much about traditional Slavic paganism as a duck knows about the stock market.

even then they're either older texts that came from a more Eurocentric anthropology, or are in many cases based on those older texts, though more enlightened research techniques have become increasingly popular in recent years. Even with the best research, the researchers' fear of going native may affect hir interpretation of the material s/he gathers, giving an incomplete view. *Caveat emptor.*

Neopagan totemism is aimed at saying "Okay, maybe what we're doing isn't the same as what people were practicing thousands of years ago, and it's not exactly the same as what today's indigenous people believe, but it's still valid". It's also a living, evolving tradition that has a lot of room for growth and experimentation. Most importantly, though, it is based on whatever background the individual practitioner has, regardless of whether it's being raised in suburbia, or the inner city, or out in the middle of nowhere, and it makes no distinction as to cultural and racial background. It is about placing totemism in the context of your experiences, rather than trying to copy someone else's.

Let me say, though, that it should not be assumed that traditional totemic systems are static and stale. Just the opposite—many of the cultures they're from are still quite alive and evolving. And while I'm not directly involved with any of them, I would imagine there's certainly room for some personal interpretation and experience based on the lore that's learned. In fact, it's this vivacity that's part of the reason I've been developing my own version of neopagan totemism. I don't want to base my totemism on ideas that place living cultures firmly in the past and ignore the present issues facing the people within those cultures. The hyper-romanticized ideals applied to Native Americans and other indigenous peoples are all too often based on incomplete and outdated conceptions of those cultures, and perpetuated by people who are in denial of the reality. That being said, if you are an active member of such a culture and wish to integrate its practices and spirituality into your own form of neopagan totemism, go for it! Just understand that it will be its own entity, rather than strictly traditional (The only way I could see it being anything remotely traditional is if, for whatever impossible reason, every member of your indigenous culture decided to buy this book and collectively adopt the ideas therein, making it a part of their cultural heritage. Yeah, I'm not holding my breath, either.).

The rest of this book is designed as a tool for creating your own system of neopagan totemism. It allows you to draw from the information you find appropriate to your experience—without claiming someone else's culture as your own. It encourages honesty when speaking of your background and sources, reminding you that you don't have to exaggerate or even fabricate claims in order to be "legitimate". This, to me, is what separates neopagan totemism from plastic shamanism—the latter is about hiding one's "white" roots or making false claims about one's involvement with a particular culture, just to try to get attention or even make money off of the gullible.

One final advantage is that you get to negotiate your own relationships with the totems you work with, rather than automatically going by whatever such-and-such author says. This is why I've made this book partly a workbook for creating your totem animal dictionary, because your own experiences should be the basis of your practice. And this leads me to my first rant…[8]

Enough With the (Prefabricated) Totem Animal Dictionaries!

I've been practicing neopagan totemism since the mid 1990's. The first book I ever picked up on the topic was Ted Andrews' *Animal Speak*, an experience that I've shared with numerous people. It was a wonderful introduction to neopagan totemism—there were exercises for finding and working with your totem, as well as an extensive dictionary of the basic qualities of animals from around the world. Since then, I've seen that book referred to more than any other as an introductory text to animal totemism.

Ten years later I found myself in one of those huge chain book stores perusing titles on various pagan and occult topics. A brand new title on totemism caught my eye, and I couldn't resist picking it up. I am, after all, a bibliophile, and animal magic in general is one of those topics that if someone writes a book about it from any angle, I absolutely *must* read it or I'll die (Okay, I won't die, but you get the idea.).

I eagerly opened it up, scanned a couple of sections…and was sorely disappointed. *Yet another totem animal dictionary*. The format was almost exactly the same as Andrews' book: an introduction to the concept of totemism, a collection of exercises, and then the bulk of the book was dictionary. I spent the next half an hour looking through it, seeing if there was anything else in there and trying to decide whether I wanted to buy it or not, and ended up putting it back on the shelf.

I'm tired of prefabricated totem animal dictionaries, which is why I refuse to write one, at least for commercial purposes. The bulk of the books out there on animal magic in general tend to resemble each other

---

[8] Welcome to my opinions. I reserve the right to declare myself right. I also reserve the right to be wrong. Either is quite likely, including in the same instance. As with all opinions, your mileage may vary.

quite a bit. Either they're dictionaries of the meanings of a variety of animals, or (less frequently) they focus on one particular animal (and different books on the same animal end up repeating each other quite a bit). Even books that have more in-depth material often rely on the dictionary for filler (or so it would appear to this reader); if you took away the dictionary in some of these there would be maybe a hundred or so pages left, if that.

I can name a dozen of them just off the top of my head, and at the time of this writing I know there are at least a few more I haven't read yet. There are really only two books on totemism that I'm aware of that are specifically written for the neopagan crowd and show any real break from the dictionary format. *Animal Spirit* by Patricia Telesco and Rowan Hall does have some of the usual material, including a dictionary section, but also breaks into new territory as well. For example, it's the only book I'm aware of, other than this one and *Fang and Fur*, which deals with animal parts in magic in any detail. And Yasmine Galenorn's *Totem Magic* also has some unique takes on totems and animal spirits—and it lacks a dictionary!

Beyond that, you have to delve into the realms of mythology, psychology, and anthropology in order to find any new relevant material. Very little of it is practical, too; the only exception I can think of is *The Personal Totem Pole* by Eligio Stephen Gallegos. For those not familiar with it, the Personal Totem Pole blends psychotherapy, the seven primary chakras, and totems for each of the chakras. It's an ingenious system for personal growth and metamorphosis, and something that I highly recommend for anyone reading these words right now (yes, that means you!).

Don't get me wrong. Dictionaries do have their uses. If you're new to totemism, then totem animal dictionaries can help you get an idea of general traits and patterns associated with each animal. Additionally, many of the authors do include exercises that can help forge the bond between magician and totem. I have a collection of dictionaries that I keep around primarily for when I do totem animal workshops so people can research the animals they find after the meditation is done.

However, keep in mind that those definitions are what the totems told the author (or what the author researched in other books and sources), and your message may be very different. I haven't used dictionaries myself in years, simply because if a totem makes hirself known to me, I get the best results just asking hir what s/he has in mind. And honestly, totemism 101 is getting to be as overflogged as Wicca 101. We need to be expanding beyond this in our shared material.

It's a better idea to keep records of your personal experiences with different totems and compile a dictionary from the information. Then, if you need to find a totem for a specific purpose on short notice you'll already have some connections made. This is a good idea in general when dealing with totems, but in this case you'll have access to personalized information about even the most obscure critters you've worked with (and if you ever need money you can publish it down the line, as totem dictionaries never seem to go out of style…just kidding!).

Additionally, I've seen a lot of magicians and pagans, when confronted with an unusual totem, who immediately go online to forums and message boards and ask "Does anyone know what this animal means?" This is often a fruitless endeavor. Most respondents will parrot (no pun intended) whatever *Animal-Speak* or *Animal-Wise* says, assuming the animal is even in there. Barring totem animal dictionaries, people may fall back on mythology and folklore from various cultures. Almost no one comes up with any personal experiences. The querent may then feel like s/he's at a dead end. This, again, is why I am so adamant about doing the work yourself; rather than waiting around in hopes that someone might be able to hand you the answers you want, it's much better in my opinion to just find out for yourself. If you want to trade notes with others later on, that's fine. But no one can replace the results of working with the totem yourself. There is a real danger of becoming overly dependent on other peoples' definitions and experiences. If you've ever emailed me, or asked me after a workshop, about what I think about your experience with a specific totem, I've almost certainly told you to ask the totem hirself what s/he has to say to you. Get it straight from the horse's (or emu's, or sea snake's, or *Ornithorhynchus anatinus*[9]) mouth.

At the end of each chapter I have included exercises, an idea I snagged from my husband Taylor Ellwood's books. These exercises are designed to help you create your own dictionary. Chapter four is a particularly important chapter, as the card deck I've designed is capable of helping you get in touch with the totem of literally any species of animal. But don't stop with the cards. You can add biological information, mythology, research from other totem animal dictionaries, and other third-party source material (with the *caveat* that third party sources *should not* take precedence over your own experiences). Dreams, visions, and other personal experiences should also be added in. Just as a dream dictionary can't tell you what a specific symbol means to you, so a totem animal dictionary written by someone else can't tell you what a totem will teach you, the individual.

---

[9] Also known as the duck-billed platypus.

Plastic Shamanism, Cultural Appropriation and Escapism

As I established earlier, and in *Fang and Fur*, neopagan totemism blends a number of practices and beliefs from traditional totemic and related systems. From traditional group-based totemism we get archetypal (and often abstract) qualities for each animal, and the people who are within a certain totemic group may exhibit those qualities and/or associated values in turn. The concept of the personal animal guardian of the average person appeals to us in our more individual-based culture. The power animal of the shaman adds in the guidance during rituals and journeys as well as the most common form of guided meditation for finding your totem.

Unfortunately, this has contributed to a trend in the past several decades of cultural appropriation, particularly of Native American traditions. Arguably one of the earliest sources of "plastic shamanism" was Carlos Castaneda, who in the 1960s and 1970s published a series of books supposedly drawn from his experiences with don Juan Matus, a Yaqui shaman. Though for the first few years after his initial publication Castaneda went largely unchallenged, starting in the 1970s several authorities questioned the existence of don Juan, and pointed out numerous inconsistencies among his works[10].

Today, several decades after Castaneda claimed to have met his mentor, numerous members of various Native American tribes point out what they see as rampant theft of their cultural heritage by non-Native outsiders. In 1993 the Lakota Summit V saw the unveiling of a document titled the *Declaration of War Against Exploiters of Lakota Spirituality*. The complaints therein range from books written about pseudo-Lakota rituals to the sale of "sacred" pipes in flea markets. Both the non-Native and Native exploiters are targeted, and tribe members are discouraged from enabling appropriation[11]. Lisa Aldred's article, "Plastic Shamans and Astroturf Sun Dances", skewers such popular new age (or, as the jargon says, NuAge, rhymes with sewage) authors as Lynn Andrews and Mary Summer Rain[12]. The American Indian Movement presented a resolution in 1984 that protested the damaging actions of Sun Bear, Brooke Medicine Eagle (spelled "Ego" in the resolution) and Wallace Black Elk, among others[13]. Websites such as http://newagefraud.org/ and http://spiritways.org/plastic_medicine_men take great pains to describe exactly what the hallmarks of a wannabe are. Even some pagans have

---

[10] Anonymous 1973 and de Mille 1977
[11] Mesteth, Standing Elk and Swift Hawk 1993
[12] Aldred 2000
[13] American Indian Movement 1984

gotten in on the act; one exceptionally detailed web page features a European-American pagan discussing the plastic symbolism of a number of "Native American" tarot decks[14].

Specific to neopaganism, there have been a number of cases where people have taken pieces of indigenous cultural practices out of context and then represented them as genuine. This is different than syncretic approaches to magic and paganism, in which the practitioners at least admit where they've gotten their material and that it isn't the same as in its original context. Sarah M. Pike dedicates an entire chapter of her book *Earthly Bodies, Magical Selves* exploring cultural appropriation of both Native and non-Native cultures, specifically within the setting of pagan festivals[15].

Some neopagans (and New Agers) are trying so hard to emulate the traditional cultures in our totemism that we often forget that we have our own culture. I consider myself, culturally, to be a modern mainstream American, with a strong subcultural emphasis on the American neopagan and occult communities, among others. This is primarily what informs my conception of totemism, and magic in general. While I respect those who adopt the ideals of pre-Christian cultures such as Celtic or Norse societies, or modern indigenous paths, I believe that there is a strong attitude, particularly within the pagan community, that in order to be truly genuine pagans we have to look outside of modern American (or other postindustrial) culture for inspiration.

A lot of this is because many pagans (particularly Americans) are disillusioned by what they see as an overly materialistic setting, dominated by a religion (Christianity) that they may feel is spiritually empty and exists solely for power-grubbing. The proliferation of environmental abuse and social illnesses perpetuated by postindustrialism further causes some to feel that there's no redeeming quality to this junction of space and time. Some pagans may turn to the "noble savages" that they believe live entirely pure lives as a way of escaping from the negative aspects of the culture they are currently a part of. Pike observes, "Neopagans' desire to identify with other cultures is the inverse of distancing themselves from mundania and from Christianity...They seek to replace the past they have cast off with ritual objects, clothing, symbols, and ceremonies such as those of Tibetan Buddhists or Native Americans"[16]. Yet, she later adds, "Neopagans approach the cultures they most want to emulate with ambivalence. They are eager to claim these traditions as their own but at

---

[14] Cole 2004
[15] Pike 2001
[16] Pike 2001, p. 123-4

the same time want to remain autonomous from them"[17]. Pike specifically cites the often vastly different perspectives between various Native American cultures and neopagans on women participating in sweat lodges and other ceremonies during menstruation. While the former view it as a taboo, the latter may see this as an example of misogyny (though this doesn't include all pagans). Many pagans who draw from indigenous cultures are loathe to give up all elements of the "spiritually devoid, materialistic" culture they seek to escape.

Additionally, there's a certain amount of neophobia in paganism that stems from criticism of newer religions such as Wicca. Many pagans and nonpagans have fallen into the trap of believing that older = better, and specifically among some pagans if you can prove that your beliefs predate the current religious juggernaut, Christianity, you're automatically more legitimate than someone who "got their Wicca out of a book". Earlier in the neopagan community the older = better fallacy led to tenuous research, such as the idea that nine million Wiccans died during THE BURNING TIMES!!! (also known as the Inquisition) or that paleolithic Wiccans were following the Rede 50,000 years ago. These days it often means stereotyping recently created spiritual traditions as being inferior to older ones; witness the persistence of people who attempt, by any means (including poor scholarship) to prove they practice pre-Gardnerian British witchcraft, or who claim that having a grandmother who read tea leaves makes them part of a family tradition.

Yet this opposition to what is commonly perceived as "white culture", including the ever-increasing stream of "new stuff", disempowers people who could change that culture while being a part of it. While neopaganism isn't solely limited to those of Caucasian descent, it does have the very real potential to create change within the aforementioned "white culture". Deborah Root, in analyzing her experience with Karma, a white guy in beads and fringes who claims to be part of the Native Way, says, "[Karma] thinks he has to turn himself into a 'white-skinned Indian' because he cannot find a way to transform and locate power in his own tradition…And because Karma thinks white culture is one thing—the dead shopping-mall culture of our time—appropriation becomes his only escape"[18].

Granted, reconstructionists in Europe and elsewhere have shown that the cultures of predominantly Caucasian people haven't solely been limited to modern mainstream America. And, again, mainstream America certainly isn't limited to white people, though the depictions of it are

---

[17] Pike 2001, p. 147
[18] Root 1997, p. 229

almost universally focused on "white" culture. While race does not equal culture, certain generalizations may be made for the purpose of this discussion. The *stereotypical* white culture (with all its inaccuracies) is the "dead, shopping-mall culture" that Root describes, something that has been sucked dry of its spirituality and is wholly materialistic. While the reality is quite different, and mainstream America is much more diverse, people like Karma see this void as connected directly to their white skins and feel their only other option is to dive into the cultures of people of different races.

We can even take this a step further, and theorize that some, *not all*, people who embrace pre-Christian European religions are escaping into earlier cultures as a way of getting away from the Big Mac and Abercrombie and Fitch-infested mainstream media culture we have now. The issue of appropriation in regards to reconstructionist religions has come up, as in Erynn Rowan Laurie's exploration of Celtic Reconstructionism and modern Irish and other Celtic culture, "Dead Religions, Living Cultures: The Reconstructionist Research and Visionary Blues".[19] Outside of reconstructionist religions, there's an even more pronounced tendency towards escapism, complete with poorly-researched romanticization of various cultures, Celtic and Native American in particular. In fact, a large number of books on neopagan topics seem to want to take the reader back to a different time and place, far from the craziness and destruction of the modern mainstream American world. Having said all this, I want to make it quite clear that I don't believe everyone who draws from other cultures, whether recon or not, is an escapist; I am merely reporting trends that I have observed in *some* modern pagans and related subcultural trappings[20].

Speaking of subcultures, some people become disillusioned with perceived flaws in neopaganism and occultism, as if escaping from one religion to another means that you're entering Utopia. Whether the issue is with drama and petty interpersonal politics, or the existence of poor scholarship and "fluff", there are those who adopt an affectation of superiority by rather loudly distancing themselves from neopaganism and occultism at large, painting the rest of us dumb schmucks with the same broad brush. This doesn't mean that I think we need to excuse any stupidity that runs rampant in neopaganism and occultism, or that we should turn a blind eye to bad research presented as fact. But I do think

---

[19] Laurie 2008
[20] Laurie, on her personal spiritual blog, "Searching for Imbas", made a great post about the difference between feeling a connection to a culture other than the one you're currently a part of, and using that other culture as a form of escapism. The post is located at http://searchingforimbas.blogspot.com/2007/12/belonging.html.

there's sometimes the perception that because paganism isn't Christianity (a religion that many, though certainly not all, pagans feel is inadequate), that the newer religion should be free of all the usual mistakes that the older religion has made. The same goes for magicians who feel that because they perceive different ways to change reality, that they're somehow more "evolved". Unfortunately, this ignores the fact that regardless of what religion or system you put people in, human nature is still a fact of life, and there's no cure-all for it. I've seen hellacious flame wars among magicians who had supposedly crossed the Abyss, had used NLP and other techniques to change themselves for the better, achieved high degrees within magical orders, or otherwise were supposedly advanced beings. I've seen pagan elders participate not only in snarkfests, but "bunny hunts" in which a "fluffy bunny" pagan is chased all over the internet from forum to forum. Clearly while paganism and occultism can give people the tools for personal advancement, even the most advanced people may still fall prey to human error and habits. It doesn't make them bad people, and it doesn't mean paganism and occultism are useless. It simply means we need to have a more realistic expectation of what these beliefs and practices can do for us on their own.

The pagan and occult communities provide thriving modern subcultures that have their own contexts for magical practice. Even reconstructionist pagans will never be able to completely duplicate the cultures they're inspired by, and so to an extent are "neo" themselves. As several sociological studies of neopagan and occult subcultures have shown, particularly Pike's work, there is a modern magical culture that has differentiated itself to an extent from mainstream culture, but is still connected to it in some forms. It is completely false to say that modern postindustrial cultures completely lack magic, and ignorant to say that the magic that we do have is inherently inferior to other magical cultures past and present. Otherwise we may fall into the same trap as twentieth century academics who based their definitions of magic on indigenous cultural practices around the world, while denying that everything from the Golden Dawn to Wicca existed in "advanced" cultures[21].

There's nothing wrong in taking inspiration from other times and cultures, as long as you are honest with yourself and others about where you got your material from, and that you don't actually live in the past or around the world. Reconstructionists of various flavors do an excellent job living rebuilt spirituality and cultural practices to the best of their ability in this modern world, and while neopagans in general may create temporary autonomous zones at festivals, they also function well in "the

---

[21] See Ellwood 2008 for an elaboration on this idea.

real world". However, I strongly argue against the idea that there is nothing good about postindustrial cultures, or that the pagans and magicians therein are inferior to those of other times and places. If you use inspiration of other cultures to help improve the weaknesses of the one you *acknowledge you are a part of*, that's one thing. But if you're a Caucasian straight out of American suburbia attempting to "be more like the wonderful Indians because all white people suck" you're bordering on escapism, if not drowning in it. In my opinion, part of effective magic involves being consciously present in your environment; if you accept that you are where you are right now, then it's a lot easier to figure out how to get to where you want to be.

If you're really unhappy with whatever culture you're a part of, and the culture you'd like to be a part of still exists, then make plans to join it as best as you can. Just understand that you may not be welcomed with open arms, and that settling for a bunch of material taken out of context won't make you any more legitimate than before. And if you're a reconstructionist, do your best to recreate your chosen culture—but also understand that it won't be the same, and that you're still going to have to conform to some standards of whatever modern culture you reside in[22].

Breaking Out of the BINABM

Chances are good that if you know more than handful of pagans, you know somebody whose totem is Wolf (If not, hi, nice to meet you!). Wolf is quite possibly the most common totem in the pagan community, followed closely by Bear, Cougar (or another large cat), Deer, Eagle, Hawk, Raven and Coyote. In fact, I would wager that over three quarters of all primary totems that neopagans claim fall into the above list.

This isn't a bad thing in and of itself, though I've heard both pagans and nonpagans question whether Wolf is really that busy, or if people are just claiming the most visible, seemingly powerful totem animals. I have talked to or heard of folks with less common totems— Chicken, Stingray, and yes, even Dung Beetle (don't you know that's what the scarab beetle is?).

A totem may be of any species. If you see totems as archetypes, every species has a being that embodies all of its traits, as well as the human addition of lore and other subjective perceptions about that

---

[22] You may be interested in the anthology I edited. Talking About the Elephant: An Anthology of Neopagan Perspectives on Cultural Appropriation (November 2008) is a collection of essays on the impact that cultural borrowing by pagans has had on the cultures borrowed from, as well as the effects of mainstream culture taking from the neopagan community.

animal. And if you believe totems are animal spirits, then it's possible to meet with the spirit of any critter that exists (or, for that matter, has ever existed—more on that in chapter three).

With thousands upon thousands of species in numerous phyla worldwide, why is there such a concentration of lions, tigers and bears (oh my!)? The answer may be found in an acronym: BINABM. Big, Impressive, North American Birds and Mammals. (Or bye-nah-bum, if you'd rather just try and pronounce the acronym.) These six letters hold a plethora of potential explanations for the distribution of totems among neopagans (though it shouldn't be seen as holding the answers to every totemic relationship). Let's take a look at each one individually.

Big: Humans are visual creatures. The larger an animal is, the more likely it is that we'll notice it. And since in the grand scheme of things we're bigger than most other animals, there are a lot of species that go relatively unnoticed because they're "too small". Ask people to name some marsupials and almost everyone will be able to list at least half a dozen. Ask them to name some worms, and once many folks get past "earthworm" they're stuck. The animals we seem to connect with the most are large and noticeable.

Impressive: Not every large animal is flashy, though. People generally don't think much of cows or sheep, other than as food. Even wild animals like the razorback hog rarely find totemic devotees (though Celtophiles and Norse pagans may venerate the European boar). If you'll re-read the list above, you'll notice that most of the animals are carnivorous. Meat-eaters are at the top of the food chain, and we often fool ourselves into thinking the rest of Nature is inferior. Deer, on the other hand, is primarily noted for her gentleness (never mind how aggressive bucks can be during rutting season, or does when defending young!). Our totems often tend to be animals we can brag about, and in modern American culture, at least, it's the predators that are most admired.

North: While in recent years some authors and other totemists have tried expanding to global collections of totems, and there have been a couple of resources specific to Australian fauna, the bulk of totemic information is centered around animals of the Northern hemisphere. This is especially true for those totems that may not be so big and impressive; once again, people look to the familiar and easy to find, and it's easier to look out your own window than to do research on the microfauna of other continents a half a world and a hemisphere away. While there is something to be said for being familiar with the locals, there are plenty of other totems out there who would love to have someone to work with on a regular basis.

American: An additional bias is towards North American animals. A lot of this is because a good deal of the literature on neopagan totemism draws its information from sources (often questionable) on various Native American cultural conceptions of totemism[23]. In fact, if you ask a random person on the street, pagan or otherwise, where totems come from, they'll probably say "Oh, the Indians!" (and they're not talking about Indians from India).

Birds: If you have any doubt that birds (at least some of them) are considered to be cool, just look at the national avian emblem of the United States: the bald eagle. Along with being big and impressive, the eagle gets to soar high above everyone else (including chickens). Other common bird totems are similarly impressive: Hawk, Falcon, Peacock, Raven, Dove (give peace a chance!). There's nary a Pigeon, Parakeet, or Killdeer to be found.

Mammals: Even more common than birds are mammals. Humans are mammals, and perhaps we feel more kinship according to genetics. Still, as with birds, the impressive factor seeps in. Bear, Wolf, and Tiger will always trump Monkey, Mouse, and Manatee.

Now, does this mean that every person who has a Wolf totem can be explained by the above? I doubt it. Pia Van Ravestein, the cover artist for this book and someone I consider a good friend, has been working on compiling her own collection of information about the various teachings associated with totem animals through her interactions with them. One thing she has pointed out is the idea of Wolf being the teacher who takes on many students in the hopes that a few will really catch onto the material[24]. This may seem elitist, but think about it for a moment. Neopagans aren't the only ones who are crazy about wolves; go into any gift shop that has animal-themed statues, pictures, t-shirts and other items, and you'll no doubt find a bunch of wolves among them. Go to a tattoo parlor and check out their collection of flash art and photos of

---

[23] Incidentally, Ted Andrews, who is commonly mistaken as being a writer on Native American totemism, stated specifically in an interview that "In none of my books and none of the thousands of workshops on animals that I have taught over the years have I ever presented myself as Native American" (Hemachandra 2003, p. 5).
[24] Van Ravestein 2007

completed ink, and it'll be a rare studio that doesn't have at last one wolf in its collection.

But look at the reality of wolves. In the past couple of centuries humanity has managed to wipe out several species and subspecies of wolf entirely. The red wolf in the Southeast United States was culled to a population of 14 in the 1970s, and was saved from extinction only by careful breeding programs[25]. The grey wolf, while stronger in numbers, still faces threats from hunters, ranchers, and the politicians who cater to them.

I won't go into a spiel about how true pagans are environmentalists. However, I think a lot of people, pagans and otherwise, take the wolf (and other animals) for granted. We talk about how the wolf symbolizes freedom, social cooperation, and toughness. Yet how many of us have contributed money to the Defenders of Wildlife or other nonprofit groups that work for wolf reintroduction and habitat preservation? Or, failing that, how many have written letters to the Department of the Interior and other decision makers about the preservation of the Endangered Species Act or funding for reintroduction programs? If every person who had ever bought a statue or picture of a wolf took the same amount of money and gave it to such an organization, or donated it to a wolf sanctuary to pay for expenses, these groups—and, by extension, the animals and habitats they work to protect--would be in much better shape[26].

We ask so much of other species, taking their habitat, their bodies and their very existence in this world, and we give back comparatively little. If one of Wolf's lessons is that of freedom and appreciation of the wild, maybe it is true that not everyone who Wolf touches in some way, whether they're conscious of it or not, "gets it". Of course, it's also our decision as individuals to decide how we relate to the world around us, and what decisions to make.

For example, while I donate money to the Defenders, I also do use wolf fur and other parts (legally taken) in my artwork. Those of you who have read *Fang and Fur, Blood and Bone* already know my stance on animal parts. But for those who don't, in a nutshell my decision is to take the remains—fur, bones, teeth, etc.—and turn them into something other than a trophy on a wall or a status symbol on someone's shoulders. I create ritual tools, sacred jewelry, and totemic dance costumes, and go through a fairly elaborate purification ceremony for each completed work.

---

[25] Hook 1998

[26] I highly suggest that if you do make a donation to a nonprofit, and they offer you a "free" gift such as a backpack or t-shirt, see if you can opt out and let them use your entire donation for their work.

I then offer these for sale to the pagan community at large online and at events (as well as make some gifts) and invest some of the money back into the Defenders.

For some people, this may seem hypocritical. Believe me, I've questioned it quite a bit! But I have made my relationship with Wolf, and with other totems, in the manner that works best for us. Other people may choose a life completely free of animal-based products of any sort, or choose to only purchase secondhand animal remains such as coats.

And that's really the crux of the issue. It is up to each one of us to figure out what our relationships with our totems are. Nobody can truly judge the veracity of another person's spiritual experiences. On the other hand, there's always the possibility that some peoples' primary and secondary totems[27] are cases of mistaken identity. There may very well be situations in which a person has a Duck totem, but may assume that such a humble animal can't be a totem—so how about Hawk instead? Additionally, someone could have rather vague visions of an herbivorous creature with cloven hooves and horns, and make the automatic assumption "I must have seen a deer!", not even considering Gazelle or Muntjac. As for totems that we approach for help with specific problems, why limit yourself to well-known animals? Perhaps the one that's best suited to helping you is one you've never even heard of, let alone seen.

I want to encourage people to break out of the BINABM trap. You don't have to stop working with Bear if you don't want to. But with so many other potential experiences out there, maybe it's time to see who else is willing to speak to you.

Before I wrap up this chapter, though, I do have to give some of the writers on neopagan totemism credit on this particular topic. Ted Andrews really set the bar higher when he came out with two volumes that detailed not only the usual BINABM, but also delved into all sorts of critters from around the world. Several authors since then have followed suit, though occasionally it seems like a bit of a competition as to who can offer definitions for the most animals. Unfortunately, so much emphasis is often placed on the dictionary aspects that not much else is discussed.

---

[27] For those who don't have Fang and Fur, here's a quick lesson in definitions. A primary totem is what most people think of as "your" totem; s/he's the one who's with you for most or all of your life. Having more than one primary totem is possible, but relatively rare. A secondary totem is one that comes into your life for a specific period of time or to teach you a specific lesson; while a person may have many of these in a lifetime, it's not common to work with more than a few (less than half a dozen) at a time, simply because the lessons may be pretty intensely focused. Tertiary totems are ones that we specifically approach for help with particular issues, and our interaction with them rarely extends beyond that task. Any totem can be in any of these roles; I simply use these terms to describe the varying types of relationship we may have with totems.

Still, those who have offered their thoughts have contributed to the corpus of knowledge surrounding neopagan totemism, and while I may not agree with all of their contributions, I respect them.

I have some suggestions for expanding beyond the BINABM, but before you start looking to where you're going, let's take a look at where you've been—by starting at the source.

Journaling Exercises

1. If you have worked with totems before, which ones have you worked with? Did they fit the BINABM description?
2. What are your thoughts on cultural appropriation? How have you interacted with elements of other cultures?
3. If you have access to two or more totem dictionaries (see appendix G for examples), compare the material, both the basic information and exercises, and the dictionary portions. If you've worked with totems, how have your experiences compared to those of the authors?

Chapter Two: Starting at the Source

Indigenous, Historical, and Contemporary Sources

If you want to learn about Native American spirituality, go to the Native Americans (and be sure you know what tribe you're looking for). If you want to learn about the indigenous spirituality of Australia, talk to the people who have lived there for thousands of years. If you want to learn genuine Siberian shamanism, you'd better go to Siberia.

In other words, the most accurate information about a current culture is found within the culture itself.

This means that with each degree of separation from the original source, the information has a greater chance of being distorted. Most people's potential exposure to indigenous totemic lore, whether from current or extinct cultures, is through anthropological works. Getting information from, say, a Native American tribe, isn't as easy as walking up to some random person at a powwow and saying "Hi, can you tell me about animal totems?" This is especially true if you're like me and look like you just stepped out of central Europe. While it's not impossible for friendships and acquaintances to happen across cultural boundaries (and thankfully it happens all the time), many of the tribes in the Americas have had to deal for years with assorted forms of stupidity from white people in particular. While "twinkies" looking for spoonfed mysticism are generally more annoying than deadly, it hasn't been all that long since literal genocide was still common. In fact, some tribes, such as the Yanomami in the Amazon basin, are still murdered by outsiders; in 1993, Brazilian miners killed 20 Yanomami[28]. While it's doubtful the miners had any interest in Yanomami spirituality, it demonstrates that there may still be risk in contact with non-indigenous people.

That's actually one of the main reasons I've never really tried getting involved in any tribal culture, beyond going to the occasional powwow to watch the dancers; while I know a couple of folks who are registered members of their respective tribes, that doesn't mean I can just invite myself on in. Nor do I feel it's my right to exploit those friendships just to get something out of them. If the opportunity arises to be more than a powwow spectator, then I'll consider it, but it's not my main focus spiritually. My interests lie primarily within neopaganism; I'm generally more interested in learning about animal magic in general than in immersing myself in another culture. I can't tell you how to get an "in"

---

[28] Carson 1995

with a tribal culture, nor will I even pretend to try. All I can say is, if you want to find out more about Native American totemism(s), talk to the Native Americans. If you want to learn about genuine 100% European-American mutt neopagan totemism, keep reading.

So since I'm not willing to try and intrude on someone else's life without an invitation, my next best source is books written by people who were bolder (and/or better connected) than I. The most respected sources tend to be anthropological texts. Of course, the issue with these, particularly the older ones, is that there's a certain amount of bias. Until recently (and even still to an extent) anthropology was very heavily Eurocentric; everything was judged according to the values of American and European anthropologists. These days that particular bias has lessened, only to be replaced by academic bias, which decrees that the anthropologist must avoid "going native" at all costs. This mandatory distancing means that the anthropologist must always be, to an extent, an outsider, and keep a detached viewpoint of what's going on. Ellwood specifically critiques the actions of modern academics, who may end up exploiting the very people they study. This includes neopagans who allow researchers to observe them. One example in particular is Tanya Luhrmann, who studied neopagans through interacting with magical groups; not only did she present an inaccurate interpretation due to her conscious detachment, but she also angered some people by publishing oathbound material in her work.[29] This is similar to what's been done to indigenous people worldwide, who have rarely received any compensation for their information, which is often misrepresented in the end anyhow[30]. Because many anthropologists aren't willing to fully engage what they're studying, they can never truly grasp what it is they're working with; therefore they may display a destructive sort of insensitivity to subtle cultural and subcultural nuances.

Still, more recent anthropology can be an effective third-party source regarding traditional totemic systems. While a bit dated and still limited by biases and pigeonholes, Claude Levi-Strauss' *Totemism* is a foundational work on the topic, and a number of books have used it as a source. Levi-Strauss explored everything from totemic taboos to the function of totems and exogamy in cultures from Africa to Australia to North America. I'm also fond of Brian Morris' ethnographies regarding the tribal populations in Malawi in Africa. While the totemic and other spiritual information may primarily be found in *Animals and Ancestors*, his other work, *The Power of Animals* is also well worth reading as it explains

[29] Ellwood 2008
[30] See Coombe, Nason, and Roht-Arriaza in Ziff and Rao 1997

the day to day interaction between the people and the animals in this area, and gives excellent context for the more ethereal relationships.

Books on individual cultures may have information on totemic and related subjects. Anthropological texts, particularly more recent ones, are a good bet. Despite the abundance of books proclaiming information on "Native American spirituality" and "shamanism", it can be particularly tricky finding decent source material on Native American cultural practices. While there have been a number of books on related topics written by Native Americans[31] (or people claiming to be), a person's ancestry doesn't necessarily mean that s/he is active within the culture of hir tribe. Unfortunately, some people take advantage of the fact that many folks, once they hear "Well, I'm part (insert tribe here)", never ask questions beyond that point...

The New Age and Plastic Shamanism

Not all books are created equal. Starting in the 1960s, mainstream (primarily white) Americans, disillusioned by the environmental and social upheaval of the time, and seeing the primarily Christian-dominated society as spiritually and ethically devoid, started looking to Native American cultures for answers:

Many of us appropriated the most superficial and hackneyed marks of this romance— beads, feathers, fringe—as a means of displaying our opposition to our own cultural background...[which] for the most part had to do with political and social tensions within middle-class white society rather than with Native people...the images of Native people we mined for our countercultural costumes came directly from television and the movies, hardly sources set outside the mainstream bourgeois culture we set ourselves against[32].

Castaneda can be considered the granddaddy of New Age shamanism. An anthropology student at UCLA, he travelled to the deserts along the U.S.-Mexican border in search of a genuine shaman to study. There he supposed came across don Juan Matus (or Matos), a Yaqui shaman who taught him everything from healing to shapeshifting. An entire series of books was the result of his adventures—which in turn spawned a huge amount of criticism both from mainstream culture and Native American

---

[31] http://www.nativevoices.com/ has a wide selection of books on Native American cultures, though be aware that they also carry neopagan and New Age texts such as Ted Andrews' Animal-Speak. Also, check out http://www.oyate.org/ for further suggestions, particularly in regards to childrens' books and other educational resources.
[32] Root, 1997, p. 226-227

tribes. Even the Yaqui themselves grew so tired of "hippies" trying to find the "real" don Juan that they ended up coming up with tricks to get one over on the white people.[33] In the end, his work was shown to be fraudulent from a literal, anthropological sense. One of the earliest books to critique Castaneda, *Castaneda's Journey* by Richard de Mille, revealed that Castaneda's doctoral thesis was a draft of his third book *Journey to Ixtlan!*[34]

Soon numerous urban and suburban Americans were reading Castaneda's works, not just for interest's sake, but to attempt to learn "genuine" shamanism. By the 1980s a number of authors had written texts on a variety of shamanic topics. Some of these were less than stellar. Sams and Carson's *Medicine Cards* was joined by texts by Sun Bear, Mary Summer Rain, Brooke Medicine Eagle and Lynn Andrews. Some, such as Andrews and Summer Rain, have been criticized for their questionable (at best) connections to Native tribes.[35]

In 1990, Michael Harner published *The Way of the Shaman*, the foundational text for what is called core shamanism. In it, Harner stripped the cultural trappings away from shamanic techniques he had learned from several indigenous cultures and boiled them down to pure practicality[36]. Unlike earlier anthropologists, he embraced the practices he studied, rather than being in fear of "going native". Unfortunately, he didn't entirely divorce his material from cultural contexts, leaving a partial connection to the roots of the shamanic techniques he describes that may be misleading. Additionally, he only presents a partial perspective on what shamanism can entail, and presents altered techniques from a very small selection of tribes as being "universal"[37]. Harner's "core shamanism" has since caught on in a major way, teaching numerous "Westerners" that they, too, can be real shamans without any cultural context.

The totemic lore in this body of information also varies in quality. Some, such as *The Medicine Cards*, are heavily influenced by the New Age[38]; generalizations of "Native American spirituality" (as if the tribes are all monolithic in belief), and the "Native American medicine wheel" abound.

---

[33] Kelly 1991

[34] De Mille 1977

[35] Aldred 2000

[36] This is rather similar to what Peter J. Carroll and others did with Chaos magic.

[37] You can see a more detailed review with my thoughts on this book at

http://lupabitch.wordpress.com/2007/09/24/the-way-of-the-shaman-michael-harner/.

I've also discussed some of my personal misgivings with core shamanism in general at http://therioshamanism.com/2007/12/05/this-may-be-blasphemous-to-some/.

[38] The noble savage stereotype that finds all too much use, particularly by New Agers, can sometimes have some rather blatant (as well as more subtle) racist results. In The Medicine Cards book, Sams and Carson literally say that the "red race" (yes, they used that exact term) was descended directly from the people of Mu, a New Age land similar to Atlantis (Sams and Carson 1999, p. 201).

Unfortunately, because the authors often claim connections to various tribes, many readers assume that what they're teaching is "genuine Native American totemism", especially if the author talks about having Native blood, or being trained by someone of Native descent, *even if there's no direct involvement with the culture being drawn from.* There seems to be little critical thinking about the material, and instead "if it sounds good, it must be good" is the theme of the day. While I have no problem with working what is best for you, I find the amount of dishonesty and misleading language in some of the extant literature to be undesirable. See appendix G for more details on my critiques and praises for various books.

Neopagan Books and Workshops

Today, one can find works on numerous types of shamanism and shamanism-flavored neopaganism. *The Temple of Shamanic Witchcraft* by Christopher Penczak is joined by John Matthews' works on Celtic shamanism, and D.J. Conway's works *Falcon Feather and Valkyrie Sword* and *Advanced Celtic Shamanism.* Some of these purport to be reconstructions of old European shamanic traditions, while others draw from contemporary sources with varying degrees of quality. For example, Amber Wolfe's *In the Shadow of the Shaman* is a rather light mix of Wicca and a hodge podge of items from various Native American cultures. All of these books feature some material on working with totems and/or power animals. Even books that aren't specifically about shamanism may have lists of animals; both *City Magick* by Penczak, and *Urban Primitive* by Raven Kaldera and Tannin Schwartzstein include mini-dictionaries of totem animals for city-dwellers.

Neopagan books on totemism abound, though the best known are Ted Andrews' *Animal-Speak* and its sequel, *Animal-Wise.* Along with the works by Galenorn, Telesco and Hall mentioned earlier, there are also (Other examples). Much of the material in Timothy Roderick's *The Once Unknown Familiar* can also be applied to totems, particularly for those who work within the psychological model of magic. Numerous 101-level books on Wicca and neopaganism in general briefly touch on the topic of totems. I already ranted about the shortcomings I perceive in most of these books earlier, so I'll spare you the reprise (I figure your short-term memory is probably better than that!).

The neopagan community loves workshops. Some are taught by published authors, others by other experienced members of the community. Both pagan gatherings and bookstores frequently feature workshops lasting from an hour or two to several days. Generally speaking, the presenter works not only from books, but also from hir own experiences with totems. Many of them are introductory courses to give people the basics, and may include a guided journey for the purpose of finding one's (primary) totem. These are good for introductions to how each presenter interprets totems, though if you attend one and are curious, try asking the person where s/he got hir information from. The answers may surprise you, and may additionally give you further sources to research (or avoid!).

Occasionally you'll find a shop or an individual who offers periodic (weekly, biweekly or monthly) classes that explore the meanings of different totems. These are essentially vocal totem animal dictionaries, with additional input from attendees who may have their own experiences to share. If you're interested in finding out more about what individual people think about certain totems, this is an option.

You may also find workshops presented by people claiming to teach traditional (usually Native American) totemism. Be careful! Make sure you research the person presenting the workshop. If s/he has a website, check it out. See if s/he is a member of the tribe whose lore s/he's claiming to teach, or at least has a verifiable connection to a tribe member. Remember that just having Native blood does not make one an expert on your tribe's culture or spirituality!

UPG

UPG means, alternately, Unverified or Unsubstantiated Personal Gnosis. It originated in Asatru (Norse pagan, not Wiccan) community and related reconstructionist groups in the 1970s or 1980s. The term refers to inspired personal spiritual experiences that may not necessarily mesh with traditional cultural mythology, or material that is otherwise largely based on one's own experiences.[39] While I have some early inspiration from assorted sources, the vast majority of my personal path is composed of UPG.

UPG is gained through everything from meditation to magic to unexpected visions and meaningful dreams. It isn't inherently a bad thing, though, particularly if you're working within a traditional or reconstructionist context, its validity *for other people* may be questioned. For example, my first patron deity, Artemis, has often been associated with everything from unmarried women to the hatred of men (depending on who you're talking to). However, in my own UPG, gained through my conversations with her, I learned that in this day and age she isn't quite as worried about protecting women from men, since many men have learned

---

[39] Anonymous 2007-D

to treat women like actual people rather than chattel. Therefore, despite the claims of certain radical feminists, she never had a problem when I dated men who treated me well (though on the occasions when things got unhealthy she'd definitely let me know that the time had come to break things off). This is solely based on my UPG—in Greek mythology, the few times Artemis had anything to do with men, things generally went bad for the mere male mortals (I need only to mention Actaeon, I believe, to make my point). But from my personal experience, she's mellowed out in recent years, though she's still not happy about places where women are still treated like lesser beings.

The biggest danger with UPG is self-delusion. For example, a common motif among newbies (and sometimes not-so-newbies) in various magical communities is the Apocalyptic Destiny. This is a quest, often shared by a small group of people (usually less than a dozen) that states that the world is coming to an end soon, and that group is at the center of making sure that it either doesn't end, or transitions to its rebirth smoothly. While the participants may make use of convenient apocalyptic lore (such as that surrounding the year 2012), they spend quite a bit of time generating all sorts of UPG. Anything that sounds good is accepted as literal fact, both for themselves, and for everyone else.

Usually people grow out of this grandiose fantasy, though they may find a more grounded "cosmic purpose" to work with, one that's less focused on the ego and more on interactions with others in shared reality. But until then, they're a classic example of UPG gone wrong. Rather than questioning their experiences and visions, they instead not only accept them immediately, but will actually feed off each other's exuberance (and paranoia), creating a group egregore that continues to tell them stories of what they want to hear about themselves.

I'm careful to question my UPG. If I hear something in a vision, I hold onto that thought and wait to see if later experiences match up with it (keeping the power of suggestion and wishful thinking in mind). Additionally, if the UPG involves a known entity, such as a deity from an ancient culture, I'll research that entity to find out what the accepted "canon" surrounding hir is. If my UPG deviates quite a bit from the mythology, I may not necessarily throw it out entirely, but I'll be more cautious about integrating it into my path.

Occasionally I may have an experience that I have no doubt is true for me, but I'll still be cautious about applying it to anyone else. For example, recently a new deity came into my life. You know the cave painting in Les Trois Freres in France often known as the Sorcerer, a humanoid figure with branching stag's antlers, bear's paws, cat face, and wolf's tail? That image has always struck a deep part of my soul, though I didn't know why until recently, when the Paleolithic deity (not the same as the modern Horned God, Cernunnos, or Herne, by the way) associated with that image made himself known to me, and told me to call him the Animal Father. Now, I have absolutely no proof that he actually existed in Paleolithic times and that he isn't just a figment of my speculation (and that of such folks as Joseph Campbell, as well as a few fellow pagans who claim to have worked with him independently). I know, without a doubt, that this deity is 100% real to me. However, I don't assume that everyone will see things my way, and may very well question my experiences due to a lack of empirical data. This is one of those situations where I allow myself my UPG, but don't assume everyone else has to play along.

UPG can be incredibly useful for working with totems. When someone asks me about what such-and-such totem means, I tell them to go ask the totem themselves. That's UPG, especially if their results don't corroborate with what the dictionaries and myths say. However, keep in mind that UPG is Unverified *Personal* Gnosis, not Unverified Collective Gnosis. Take your UPG with a grain of salt (that salt is actually good for a lot of things) and be wary of anything that sounds too good to be true, or that seems to lead you into escapism or more detrimental situations.

Meditation

Meditation is a healthy source of UPG (though, again, with a grain of salt). Remember when I mentioned my frustration with people who come onto an online forum looking for definitions? In my opinion the best thing to do when confronted with a potential totem, especially of a species you're not familiar with—is to talk to the totem hirself. In *Fang and Fur, Blood and Bone* I spent some time explaining why I prefer meditation (such as the guided journey) to things like totem cards, animal sightings, etc. My stance is still the same: meditation allows you the most direct connection to the totem without the interference of another person, or the limitations of a certain number of animals in a card deck (though I attempt to solve this latter problem in chapter four of this book).

With meditation, you're able to converse with the totem and walk (swim, fly, etc.) with hir through whatever lessons s/he may want to teach. Additionally, you can find out exactly what the totem has to show you as an individual, whether it matches up with others' experiences or not. Meditations are also customizable, either by you or the totem. You can both decide on a particular meeting place that's comfortable for both of you. Additionally, unlike cards or other tools, meditation has very few limitations other than your own ability to "plug into" other realities.

That last point is a sticking point for some people. The most common meditations in the neopagan community are guided visualizations, in which a person either journeys while a companion reads a script, or uses some basic guideposts for finding hir way around a particular place.

I know numerous pagan authors and other teachers over the years have stressed that if you *just* practice visualization enough, you'll soon be up there flying along with everyone else. However, I take a somewhat different approach. While I'll agree that practice is crucial to success in anything, I have found that some people are more tuned into senses other than sight for communication. Why do I bring up communication? Meditation is a form of communication with the Otherworld, with other forms of consciousness, and/or with the self. Meditation conveys information—and the meaning of that information--to the person experiencing it.

I want you to think about the last time you talked to someone about something that required a lot of deeper communication. Maybe you were having a heart-to-heart talk with a significant other, or trying to explain the benefits of a project at work, or even in a political discussion with friends. Think about how you noticed the other person/people. What's most important? Body language? Tone of voice? How close or far away you are from the other people, and could they could ostensibly touch you?

For some people, what is heard or felt is much more important than what is seen. And this goes for meditation as well as other forms of communication. In my own case, I find that the strongest portion of a meditation is the actual conversation I have, which usually comes across as something I "hear" (not physically, of course), but also can include body language to a lesser degree. It's quite common for me to have a conversation with a spirit or other entity in meditation without ever actually "seeing" a thing. I know the "voices" of each being, as well as their general energy signature.

I have included a couple of alternative meditation techniques in chapter five, for those of you who may not be crazy about visualization, and want to experiment with other senses instead to see about getting a better result.

Natural History

One good source of information that's often overlooked is the observation of animals themselves. People often forget that many totemic and other attributes applied to animal species by humans stem from natural history: the behavior, habitat, and physiology of the physical animal. For example, some Plains Native American tribes saw Wolf as a warrior totem and emulated lupine traits for their own success. Barry Holstun Lopez says, "The Indian did not think of the wolf as a warrior in the same sense he thought of himself as a warrior, but he respected the wolf's stamina and stoicism and he encouraged these qualities in himself and others. The wolf, therefore, was incorporated into the ceremonies and symbology of war"[40]. Part of what a totem is, is the human interpretation of what an animal is and stands for (whether it has any basis in reality or not!), so while Wolf contains the behavior of a wolf pack, and the totemic lore of Native American and other cultures, s/he also is comprised of the Big Bad Wolf, and Isengrim. These more negative interpretations reflect cultures in which wolves were largely adversarial as far as humans were concerned, even though what they were doing was fundamentally no different than what the wolves near the Plains tribes did.

Studying the natural history of a totem's physical children can bring you a wealth of information, as well as help you figure out where other peoples' totemic lore for that species came from. I find that it's helpful to be able to speak the totem's "language", so to speak; I sometimes use body language in rituals with various totems. Shapeshifting dance rituals, of course, are all about moving like the animal does. However, natural history is also important simply because it's one way to figure out what makes a totem "tick", so to speak. You can't divorce the totem from hir physical counterparts, and while s/he may be able to communicate with us on our terms, we are still dealing with a nonhuman animal.

Additionally, natural history keeps us from abstracting our idea of totems too much. I've heard of people who claimed to have predatory mammal and bird totems who were horrified at the thought of a poor little bunny dying. Wolf may be the Teacher for some people, and Bear the Healer, but they aren't going to go vegetarian any time soon. It's crucial to think of totems not just in human, abstract terms, but also in grounded, non-human animal terms. This not only keeps us receptive to everything a totem can show us, but it also reminds us that there are actual wolves, hawks, and deer out there, some of whom may very well need our help in the everyday world—and, as I'll cover in chapter nine, one of the best offerings we can make to a totem is real-world aid to hir physical children. While there can be some value to anthropomorphization, if we apply our human values to living nonhuman animals too much, the result can be disastrous. Several subspecies of grey wolf, for example, have been hunted to extinction partly out of the "big

---

[40] Lopez 1978, p. 114

bad wolf" stereotype that pitted humanity against "evil, vicious beasts". Never mind that we were the ones devouring their territory and natural prey—and even their own skins—well beyond necessary limits. When we take animals for granted, they're the ones who suffer the most.

Other Pagans/Magicians/Insert Plural Esoteric Label Here

I am quite happily solitary. While I'll sometimes work with my husband and participate in the occasional group ritual at a festival, most of what I do is on my own. However, being able to trade notes and talk shop with other magical practitioners has been absolutely \invaluable, particularly since I am solitary and don't have the structure of a pre-crafted tradition to work within.

I strongly suggest talking with people of various traditions about their own work, not just with totems, but with magic and spirituality in general. Not only can this be a treasure trove of nifty ideas for your own practice, but other people may point out if you're about to walk off a cliff (especially if you go into a conversation open to commentary and constructive criticism). Even if you find you disagree with people, their perspectives are still important. You may find someone else down the line for which that information may be perfect.

As to finding a teacher or group to work with, you're on your own there. I have minimal experience with such things, as I have primarily been self-taught. However, there's nothing that says you can't work with other people and incorporate their own material into your practice. Just be aware that, as with any third-party material, it's colored by the presenters' biases.

I do want to add in an extra warning regarding people who claim to teach "shamanism" or "Native American spirituality". Remember that plastic shamanism thing I mentioned earlier? That's a common problem in this case. Granted, not all people who teach this sort of path are plastic shamans. However, if someone claims to be teaching the ways of a particular tribe, see if they'll show you credentials (such as proof of membership in the tribe). If they admit they're not attached to the tribe, just be aware that what they are teaching may not be genuine (though that doesn't mean it can't be spiritually effective). If you get someone who's dishonest about hir sources, or reluctant to give you a straight answer, be wary.

As for fees, given that I charge what I think is a reasonable fee for workshops, I don't have any personal problems with people who make money off their time to teach. However, it depends on the individual situation, particularly when it comes to one-on-one teacher-student relationships, or small private groups. I know that in the neopagan community in particular, these relationships are often formed without any money involved (except, perhaps, donations to pay for supplies). Most teachers and group leaders in this case have a day job, or are otherwise supported by someone else. On the other hand, if a person is making a living off of teaching and other services, s/he's probably going to want to be paid. *Caveat emptor.*

Incidentally, the question of charging for teaching and spiritual work in general is a relatively new controversy. In shamanism in particular, there was no opting out of paying the shaman in what served as the local currency. As an example, among the Evenk (formerly known as Tungus) in Siberia, "Shamans were treated with deference, allocated the most productive areas of clan territory, and helped with their reindeer herding by other clansmen. Paid for their services in gifts, such as a few head of reindeer, they often became as prosperous as they were mystically powerful"[41]. The more recent debate as to whether or not magical practitioners should be paid for their work seems to stem largely from a backlash against postindustrial consumerist behavior, in which consumption of resources and accrual of wealth may appear to take precedence over all else, including the health of other living beings. Often, neopagans and others who charge for services, workshops, even books are viewed as being greedy, exploiting the community, and focused on the Almighty Dollar. Additionally, pagans who have had negative experiences with Christianity may look at the practice of tithing and other donations as a negative development to be kept out of neopaganism at all costs. While there are no doubt at least some folks ready to part fools from their cash, I believe it is idealistic to the point of blindness to make that assumption about all who wish to be compensated for their time and energy.

Being Honest—Why?

One theme you'll find running through this book is the idea of being honest about your sources, particularly when it comes to material not gained from traditional cultures. It's something I feel very strongly about, because I've seen entirely too much misrepresentation.

Part of it is because I know that this misrepresentation has a negative impact on indigenous cultures. Cultural appropriation may not directly kill people, but it does affect how people may perceive the culture being appropriated from. If non-Natives are presented with an image of

---

[41] Lewis, in Harvey 2003, p. 75

Native peoples who are all healthy and happy and living in perfect harmony with the Earth, they may bury their heads in the sand when it comes to the real economic, social and political problems that plague many tribe members. Many people don't like seeing ugly things (and mainstream Americans are particularly good at imitating mythological ostriches), and so may consciously or unconsciously filter out anything that doesn't match their pretty preconceived notions. Rosemary Coombe observes, "[Native Americans] find their "culture" valued while their people and political struggles continue to be ignored. The experience of everywhere being seen, but never being heard, of constantly being represented, but never listened to, *of being treated like artifacts rather than as peoples*, is central to the issue of cultural appropriation" [italics mine][42].

Additionally, cultural appropriation takes away very real resources from the people being taken from. The traditional cultural art forms, such as certain patterns and styles, of Native American and other cultures are used on t-shirts, mouse pads, and numerous other items without any money going back to the people who originated the patterns. The debate over personal vs. cultural intellectual property rages on, and the question is raised as to who owns, say, the various geometric patterns found in "Southwestern art". Similarly, the cultural knowledge of medicinal plants that tribes in the Amazon possess is often exploited by the Western medical industry; pharmaceutical companies reap huge amounts of money on drugs that were derived from rain forest plants whose properties were revealed by the local inhabitants. Very rarely does any of the profit benefit the people who were crucial to this knowledge being disseminated[43].

However, I also do not wish to be misrepresented. For example, I was at a pagan festival where I didn't have my full wolf skin to dance in, but did have my tail. The dance moves are the same, and I spent a good part of the weekend dancing around the drum circle. At one point someone came up to me, no doubt wishing to sincerely compliment me, and said "You looked like an Indian out there!" I was rather polite at the time, but I actually felt rather offended. It's not because I think there's anything wrong with Native Americans. However, I am a neopagan, and as I've already established, I am proud to be a neopagan. I want what I do with neopagan totemism to be associated with the community I am a part of, rather than continuing the destructive meme of "Neopagan = less valid". The confusion between what is traditional in origin, and what is newly born (though both old and new practices may be living, evolving things) does a disservice to all concerned.

---

[42] Coombe, in Ziff and Rao 2003, p. 88
[43] See Ziff and Rao 2003, especially Coombe, Keeshig-Tobias, Nason, and Roht-Arriaza.

Determining the Best Sources for Your Needs

In my opinion, the best practical policy is "Whatever works best—and be honest". If your practice is entirely made up of New Agery complete with Atlantean shamans, *Bambi*-style totem animals, and crystal waving, that's fine—just be honest about the fact that you probably got your material from a variety of books at the local New Age store, not at the feet of someone who lived on the reservation hir entire life. Despite my sometimes snarky comments about the New Age and plastic shamanism, I do admit that there are some useful techniques in the material. My main gripe is the presentation of said techniques. For example, while Harner's *The Way of the Shaman* is central to many neoshamans, it misrepresents what shamanism is worldwide while focusing on stripping a few specific practices of their cultural trappings. The techniques themselves can be quite useful; however, it's not made clear that not all shamans, for example, suck illnesses out of people, or that shamanic initiation rituals and other experiences can be hazardous to your psychological, spiritual, and even physical health.

The other thing to keep in mind is what methods of learning are best for you. Granted, pagans and other magical folk tend to lean towards bibliophilia, and with the number of books out there (including pagan, anthropological, and other studies of totemism) it's easy to find plenty of written words to study. But I find that drawing from several wells is healthier. I love talking shop with other pagans and magicians about animal magic (and other topics), and I attend workshops when I can. It gives me an idea of what other people are doing, and it helps keep me from going off the deep end with my UPG. The best teacher for me, though, is experience, because all theory and no practice only make for a fine armchair magician.

So figure out which methods of learning work best for you. You may learn better through listening rather than reading, so workshops and CDs would be a stronger component for you than books. Or you may find it difficult to hit an altered state of consciousness through sitting still, but find that dancing gets you right where you need to be to talk to a particular totem. Give each form of learning a couple of tries, at least, before settling on which works best for you. Some methods of gaining information may take a little while to really understand or get used to.

Why Multiple Streams of Intellectual Income Are Important

I was thinking one day about how people who don't identify themselves as therianthropes still may identify with (but not as) their primary totems to one extent or another. There's no problem with this in and of itself, mind you. We can learn quite a bit through emulating the totems we work with, and not just our primaries. While, not surprisingly, I model Wolf quite a bit (given that I identify as a wolf therianthrope), I've also deliberately adopted traits of other totems to help balance out some of Wolf's less desirable habits.

However, one thing I am very careful of is to ask the totem what s/he can teach me before I start working with hir. As I've mentioned before, the relationship a particular totem may form with me is not necessarily the same as the relationship s/he may form with someone else. This includes the relationships formed with any totem dictionary author. It's easier to open up a book and read predigested information than to meditate or journey to get into direct contact with the totem to get more personalized information. Sure, the book might be right, but what if it isn't? Additionally, what happens if a person ignores what the totem is trying to tell them, instead looking only at what s/he's been told the totem stands for?

Let's take Coyote, for example. The first attribute most neopagans will probably come up with for Coyote is "Trickster".[44] This is based on a body of folklore from various Native American tribes (a good collection of Coyote stories can be found in Barry Holstun Lopez' *Giving Birth to Thunder, Sleeping With His Daughter*).

Additionally, this adherence to stereotypes can lead to justification of unhealthy, destructive behaviors. In keeping with the Coyote vibe, I have met several people who claimed Coyote as a totem who justified being utter and complete assholes to others simply by saying "I'm a Coyote person". And people around them sometimes turned a blind eye to this behavior with the same justification! Yet just because a person lies, plays a trick, or pulls someone's cover, does not mean that A) Coyote said to do that, or B) Coyote would appreciate this being done in his name. Some Coyote stories are pure silliness, to be true. However, in my

---

[44] It may also be pointed out that Coyote the deity is not necessarily the same as Coyote the totem. However, as these often end up blended in neopagan totemism, I will address them from that standpoint. This is another illustration of why it's not a good idea to go with just one source for your information. While I see Coyote the deity and Coyote the totem having some overlap and interrelationship, they're not necessarily one and the same. And a special thank you to Paleo for blog comments on this topic!

understanding of Coyote, there is a method to the madness, and people are often (though not always) meant to learn from his tricks. While Coyote may have done some things out of maliciousness, that doesn't justify human beings doing the same thing.

We are not gods, or totems, or other such beings. Some of us may consider ourselves to be no less and no more than them, and I won't disagree there. However, what's good for the totem isn't always good for the human. Coyote's worldview and experiences are likely to be very different from those of even his closest (or so they may claim) devotees. We can emulate totems, but that does not make us totems, or even mean we entirely understand them. Like deities, they are much larger, more complex beings than we currently are. Just because Coyote floated his penis across a river so he could have sex with some women on the far bank who didn't consent to his intrusion does not mean that he would automatically condone rape (even if it were supposedly to "teach the victim her place"). While I haven't seen that particular permutation of attempted justification, I have seen the same type of justification of harmful actions done by one person against another–and supposedly Coyote said it was okay.

Part of the problem is when people take a stereotype and run with it. The Trickster role is a lot more complex than "I'm going to do whatever I want because I feel superior to these people and I think they need to learn a lesson". The Trickster has to learn lessons, too, and Coyote may abhor a spiritually blind person as much as anyone else–in fact, he may throw tricks at his supposed devotees to help them get past their arrogance, and yet have them completely miss the point.

Additionally, "Trickster" is not all that Coyote is. As I've mentioned before, totems "include" all the traits of a given species, not just the human lore. In fact, in order to understand the human lore, it is essential to study the natural history of the physical animals, since that sort of observation is largely what formed the basis of the lore to begin with.

So who is Coyote (the totem), besides being a Trickster? Coyote is....

–A hunter, as much as Wolf or Cougar, and with the capability to be a social canid, as well as being capable of bringing down large game such as deer
–A loving parent, again similar to Wolf
–An intelligent nonhuman animal with keen problem-solving abilities, like Dolphin, Octopus and others
–Highly adaptable to human encroachment
–Capable of symbiotic relationships with badgers

There's a lot more to learn here than the sneaky one—which, honestly, could be applied to many animals that work to avoid humans at all costs, or which try to adapt to a changing environment. And these are just my thoughts on one single totem. It's just not enough to go on human lore, traditional or neopagan. We need to be paying attention to what the totems have to tell us, not just what they've told others. Otherwise we stand to miss out on a lot of important information and lessons, as well as developing a potentially incomplete or skewed picture of the totems themselves.

Journaling Exercises

1. Pick at least three of the books from appendix G (or similar books not listed there) and read them. Which did you like best? How well did you absorb the information from each? What factors may have determined your understanding of the material?

2. If possible, attend at least one workshop about animal totemism or a related topic. Again, how effective was it in conveying information to you?

3. Finally, if you can, go to a pagan or occult discussion group (in person or online, whichever works better for you visually/auditorally). How does this more informal setting work for you as opposed to a more formal workshop?

4. Try a basic visually-oriented guided meditation (such as that in appendix B). Then alter it so that it focuses more on hearing and/or touch; you may have a conversation with the animal, or feel your way through the tunnel. What sort of sensory input works best for you?

5. Pick an animal and research its natural history. Then compare the natural history to the totemic lore surrounding the animal. You should probably choose one that has a lot of easily available totemic information on it; bears are a good example as there is ample information on both traditional and neopagan/neoshamanic totemic interpretations.

Chapter Three: Some Totems You May Not Have Considered

While I still work with some of the BINABM, I've formed relationships with a number of other totems. This includes the totems of various wild animal species around the world. However, there are a couple of groups of totems in particular that you may not have thought of working with before. This includes the totems of extinct species, and domesticated animals that commonly find themselves in the American diet. Additionally, I've experimented with microscopic animals as totems, with interesting results.

I could have also included mythological totems and spirit guides, but chose not to. This is primarily because I've already discussed evoking mythological beings (as well as creating a few of your own) in *Fang and Fur*. Additionally, several books on totems include information on mythological beings, and there are at least a few that are solely dedicated to working with them. In short, it's already been done, and I want to bring forth less commonly considered ideas.

Extinct Totems

At one time I limited my personal definition of totems to animals that physically exist in the here and now. Since *Fang and Fur* came out in 2006, I've continued exploring animal magic in general, and as is normal for a person who is ever learning, I've sometimes changed my mind on things. In early 2006, my husband Taylor and I went to the Carnegie Museum of Natural History in Pittsburgh, PA. I wanted to take one more trip there before we moved to Seattle that February. The Carnegie has an impressive collection of fossil skeletons of various extinct species. Their dinosaur room includes an exceptional specimen of Camarasaurus still half-embedded in stone, a running Allosaur, and a complete Diplocodus skeleton purchased by Carnegie himself in the early 20th century. The next room over has a wide variety of later mammalian skeletons, including a couple of dire wolves, an Irish elk, and a mammoth and mastodon flanking the doorway. Ancient fish and invertebrates abound as well, with numerous trilobites and contemporary sea creatures whose imprints are forever imprinted in stone. If you've ever loved dinosaurs and other prehistoric critters, the Carnegie is a must-visit.

As I wandered through the halls of bones, I felt a familiar "ping" on my intuition. This was rather unexpected, but I opened myself up to whoever was rapping at my spirit's chamber door, figuring that maybe one of my contemporary totems wanted to talk. However, in my mind's eye I saw a number of the creatures whose skeletons I had admired standing before me in the flesh, watching with curiosity. They said nothing, but it didn't take me long to figure out that they were interested in talking to me.

I might be stubborn at times, but I didn't take much convincing this time. I loved dinosaurs since I was a kid and could rattle off dozens of Latin names and what their English translations were, as well as what each reptile ate, what sorts of special adaptations they had to their environment, and what period of time they'd lived in. Later on I'd discovered the mammals that had taken their place, from the saber-toothed cat to Eohippus, forerunner of the horse. Getting an invitation to talk to their totems was a definite treat!

I told Taylor about my discovery, and insisted that we take a detour to the gift shop so I could get a Moleskine notebook and a pen to start scribbling notes on the various animals there. He was (as always) a good sport and humored me, though I could tell he was enthusiastic to see me exploring new territory. I went home that day with pages upon pages of inspiration.

Shortly thereafter, we had an opportunity to go by a local shop that carried inexpensive fossils. I knew exactly what I wanted, and found it: a leg bone of an early Equus, the wild horse. Brown flakes of outer bone wrapped around a white core, and I knew as soon as I picked it up that this would be my steed and guide into the ancient Otherworld.

It's actually quite appropriate that I needed a horse bone, for several reasons. Horse was my first secondary totem in my teens, and I've maintained that connection to one degree or another since then. Along with helping me through the social awkwardness of my teenage years, Horse also represents the safe journey for me. Additionally, of all the animals traced in the fossil record, the species that evolved over time to become the modern horse are some of the best represented in museum specimens, and it's incredibly easy to trace the development of the horse from a tiny, five toed forest browser to the powerful plains dweller we know today. Who better to help me trace the path to older times?

The Journey to the Past

My first forays were into the Paleolithic period. I wanted to stick with a more recent time, where the animals would be at least somewhat more familiar. I wasn't sure what to expect when I went into my first meditation, holding the horse bone against my chest as I lay on the bed. Per usual, I visualized a cave in a grassy hillside, and walked on in.

The cave was well-lit thanks to the daylight shining in from the entrance. The first thing I noticed was that the floor was very smooth and well-worn, with few rocks in the way. I had to jump down into a shallow ravine, about waist-high, that cut across the path, and then climb back out. As I pulled myself onto the ledge, I saw before me a recess in the wall. Inside was a pile of bones from Equus, still white and smooth as if the animal had been alive only shortly before.

Led by intuition, I pulled out the skull and jaws and laid them on their side on the floor, then drew out the vertebrae and reconstructed the spine. In a similar manner I withdrew the rest of the bones and connected them. As soon as the last hoof was in place, the skeleton shuddered, and flesh, hide and hair flowed up from nowhere to coat the bones. Up leaped a fully alive and healthy adult Equus, looking something like a Przewalski's horse, though paler in color and with more striping on the legs and hindquarters[45].

She walked over to me and nuzzled me, then beckoned me to sit on her back, her voice a gentle touch in my mind. I've been horseback riding before, including bareback, but nothing quite prepared me for being astride the back of an extinct equine! As we turned away from the recess, I saw that to the left of the tunnel I'd come through there was a similar one, turning the cave (despite the laws of physics) into a horseshoe shape where one end started in my reality, and the other ended in the Paleolithic. We galloped out of the tunnel, to include negotiating a similar ravine as the one I'd previously crossed, and burst out onto a wide, sunny plain of high grass, with a forest to our left and mountains far off in the distance.

That scene would become very familiar to me in the journeys to come. Over time, I mapped out a landscape that was home to the totems of a number of extinct mammals from the Paleolithic era. Probably due to my being a bit unfamiliar with the smaller fauna of the time, the animals that showed themselves to me were primarily large and well-known. Additionally, since the totems themselves weren't as accustomed to being worked with in this day and age, I think it's quite possible that they may

---

[45] In retrospect, this reminded me a bit of Tanith Lee's novel, Black Unicorn, in which the main character joins together the bones of a unicorn with metal gears and other replacement "parts". While the unicorn doesn't instantly come alive, the framework at one point is hit with magic and the unicorn is reformed in the flesh. While it's been several years since I read the book, I wouldn't be surprised if this part of the meditation was partly inspired by this experience.

have sent better-known "ambassadors". Nevertheless, I learned many valuable lessons from these animals.

My experiences with Sabertoothed Cat are a good example. The first time I met her, she sniffed me, paced around me a few times, then told me to follow her into tall grass. I hesitated, but she insisted that I trust her. So off I went. She took me to her den, by which was a sandy pit. "Why are you here?" she asked. "Because I want to tell others how to work with you", I replied. "Fair enough," she said. The sandy pit turned into a pool of water[46].

The next time I visited her, Equus was very nervous. He nearly shied away as I dismounted to go to Cat. Cat told me that this was natural, that sometimes the Paleolithic totems reacted to each other as physical animals would, at least in minor ways, though there was no hunting going on. Still, the roles of predator and prey sometimes came into effect, and she warned me that it was wise to keep in mind what energies I invited into my ritual space and myself, to be wary of potential conflicts.

The next few meditations dealt with achieving balance in mind, body, heart, and sex. At the very beginning she took me back in her den to a tunnel filled with sharp rocks. "You're going to have to walk that some day, but only when you're balanced enough". As we met several times, Cat told me how sometimes I think too much, over analyzing things. For sex and body, she reminded me to remember the balance between sensuality and pain, and to not overdo either one. For my heart, she reminded me to be conscious of my reactions, especially those caused by fear[47].

Finally, the day came when Cat chased me into her den, and drove me back to the tunnel of sharp rocks. "Go in there," she snarled, "and you'll find what you seek!" She'd always been a bit uncomfortable with my motivations for writing a book, whether I was genuine in my interest or not, and I got the sense that the time had come to address that. I started walking and almost immediately ended up on my hands and knees as the razor-sharp rocks sliced into my feet. They tore away at flesh and bone until my arms and legs were only stumps. Then I crawled like a worm further down the tunnel until my body was gone and all that remained was my head. All that made it to the end of the tunnel were my eyes. They rolled up onto a stone platform bathed in light from a shaft in the ceiling. On the platform was the book I would write, the one you hold right now.

Then Mastodon, who I had worked with before, reached down into the shaft and pulled me up into his grove. Ground Sloth and

---

[46] For some reason, pools of water figure prominently in my work with the Paleolithic totems. Mastodon had one in his clearing, and Cave Bear's cavern had a clear pool as well.
[47] Incidentally, the spirit in my cougar skin taught me more about conquering fear.

Mammoth, other totems I'd worked with, were also there. They told me that Cat supported me, but that she didn't want me to forget Spirit in my endeavors, including my writing. Then she herself showed up, and apologized for putting me through that ordeal, though I needed to learn from it. I was given a new body, made from the water in Mastodon's grove. Equus came and took me away for a while, but Cat told me to return.

When I made it back, Cat took me to the pool that used to be the sandy pit by her den. She put me in the water, and I sank, then floated, then sank again. I learned that balance is circumstantial, and that what works in one situation may not work in another. It isn't a constant state that once you find it, it remains the same; rather, balance shifts as the internal and external environment change. Cat then pulled me out and sent me to meet the next totem I was to work with.

Over time I worked with Mastodon, Mammoth, Ground Sloth, Cat, Cave Bear, Dire Wolf and Irish Elk. Each one taught me unique lessons. Many of them dealt with care of the self and relationships with others. There was a strong theme of responsibility of avoiding extinction as well, and several of the totems expressed concern for humanity's current state.

Dinosaurs!

I wanted to explore with animals from earlier times, and so I bid a fond farewell (for the time being, anyway) to the ice ages and focused on talking to some dinosaurs. It was totally different experience, and my very first journey there was a good example.

I arrived back at the cave to utter confusion. I put Equus together to get some guidance, and he told me there was nothing he could do to take me to that point, then disappeared into his niche. Just then, out of a dark corner of the cave stalked a huge Allosaurus skeleton. He walked up, watched me gaping at him, then asked, "Well, aren't you going to put your hand on me and let the flesh flow again?" Then he lowered his head so I could touch his jaw. A moment later a large, coppery colored striped Allosaurus stood before me, picked me up on his back (not as comfortable as Equus) and away we went down a narrow, dark tunnel.

We came out into a hot, muggy swamp. I was rather unceremoniously dumped into the water next to a feeding Brachiosaurus. Assuming this was to be my first dinosaur totem contact, I started to try to talk to her. She lowered her head on that long neck right down to me and asked "And what do *you* want?" I tried, with no success, to explain that I wanted to convey to other people that we weren't limited to just modern totems, and that ancient ones were just as valid. She simply laughed and went on eating. Several other dinosaurs, including a circling pterodactyl[48], were similarly amused. I climbed up on a small island in the water to at least try to dry off.

I heard a voice behind me say "Hey, over here!" On the bank was a large, muddy brown Ankylosaurus. "Come with me," he said in a gruff voice, and carried me into the trees. In a clearing I sat and talked to him. He explained that dinosaurs consider humans an odd sort, and that the huge reptiles aren't really used to being worked with in a totemic manner. Treated with awe and respect, yes, but not worked with as equals. In short, they're not particularly impressed with us. Ankylosaurus, through, was more grounded, and compared himself to the modern-day tortoise (which really isn't all that far off speaking in terms of biological niches and general appearance). He told me to come back and talk to him, and he'd fill me in on more details.

Allosaurus came back and carried me back to the cave, still laughing. I ended up coming out of the meditation curious as to whether dinosaur totems were universally tricksters, or if they just had their version of the old boy's club going on.

The next evening I went back and visited Ankylosaurus twice. The first time that Allosaurus came again to carry me to the swamp, he appeared again in skeletal form, telling me that he was too big for me to put his skeleton together. I placed my hand on his jaw again, and the flesh covered him. He wasn't as sharp with me this time, though he was still disdainful.

Ankylosaurus told me that since the dinosaurs hadn't really had much contact with humans, the tunnel in the cavern was kept open primarily by human interest in dinosaurs. "Dead and gone," he said, "nothing left but dust and bones". He said that most of the dinosaurs didn't particularly have much interest in humans, though a few, including him, did keep an eye on what was going on out of curiosity.

The second time I visited that night was a bit easier. When I arrived, Ankylosaurus showed me the huge bulb on the end of his tail. "Pure bone," he said. "I could easily crush you with this. In fact, if the dinosaurs came back, we would destroy you. You're small, and weak, and insignificant".

"Yeah, but we have bombs and guns and missiles. We'd win with those," I replied.

---

[48] The dinosaur world, as with the Paleolithic world, seems to have mixed and matched species and habitats, as well as time periods. It made it a lot more convenient to find the totems I wanted to work with, having a rather homogenous place to do so, but it also made some odd juxtapositions and anachronisms.

"And *that*," he said, "is what will drive *you* to extinction. You don't adapt. Instead you meet all threats with excessive violence. You're too tied to your biological urges that have become overwrought with time and technology. If you don't adapt and learn to overcome those urges, to communicate, you'll die. We died because we couldn't adapt to difference forces, but it was still a lack of adaptation. And that is what I want you to take away with you tonight". Then he turned and went off into the jungle.

Allosaurus came and picked me up. "This isn't a good place for you to be alone," he said. "Come on, I'll take you back to your home". While the show of concern was new, I still got the distinct impression that I was an intruder.

When I made it back to visit again, Allosaurus took me down a side tunnel branching off to the right of the main one. This led into a wide grassy plain somewhat like the one where I'd met the Paleolithic mammals, but it wasn't the same place. I was dropped off with Ankylosaurus, who led me to a very specific place in this plain. Then we waited as several other dinosaurs showed up. First to arrive was Pentaceratops, followed by Brachiosaurus. The latter one surprised me, given that she'd been so snarky beforehand. She told me, "I'm simply curious about what all the fuss is about". Then came Corythosaurus, with tiny Compsognathus. A final dinosaur, a bipedal theropod resembling a velociraptor but without the huge claws on the hind feet, simply told me, "You'll know me when you find me".

One thing I found with dinosaur totems was that I had a more difficult time staying in meditation with them, compared to the Paleolithic totems. I think part of it was because of the biological distance between humanity and dinosaurs (as well as other creatures of the time period), as well as a lack of interest on the part of most of the dinosaurs. After the last visit mentioned above, I found that my connection to that particular place had degenerated enough to where I couldn't make it through even a brief journey there. After several subsequent failed attempts, I decided to shelve that particular group of totems for the time being. I'd like to try again at a later point, though; it seems that they may have had some very valuable experiences to talk about.

You may or may not experience similar problems. I have worked with two of the better-known, and relatively closer time periods. You may find that diving into Cambrian waters to speak with trilobites is exactly what you needed; or if you were one of those kids who was always fascinated by dinosaurs, you might have some incredible experiences with traveling back to meet some of your favorites. If you find that certain time periods work better for you than others, there's nothing wrong with that. Relationships, even those with extinct animals, are individual, and just because you mesh well with one group doesn't mean that you'll hit it off right away (or at all) with another.

A More Recent Extinction

One more group of extinct totems I wanted to work with were recently extinct species. I wanted to see if working with them was any different than working with totems of animals that were still alive on this plane. I also was curious as to whether I could enlist their help to keep other animals from meeting the same fate.

A good example is my work with Dodo. This relative of the pigeon was native to Mauritius, an island in the Indian ocean. Large, flightless, and completely unaccustomed to human presence, the dodo became an easy target for hunters in the 16th century, when they were discovered by Europeans. The dodo's flesh apparently wasn't particularly tasty, so overhunting wasn't the primary cause of this species' demise. Rather, the introduction of invasive species such as pigs, dogs, and cats contributed to predation and destruction of nests. The last dodo was said to have died in 1681.[49]

Because the dodo was wiped out in a relatively short time by human influences (the feral animals wouldn't have made it there without human intervention) it's become a symbol of environmental awareness; particularly that dealing with endangered species. I was curious as to how Dodo the totem felt about all this, so I went to talk to hir.

I found myself on a beach on the edge of an island. I walked along past pieces of driftwood and stones, until I got to the edge of a forest. There was a path, so I began to walk down it. Eventually I came to a clearing, sunny and bright. There, across from me, I saw Dodo. She was sitting in the clearing, and when she saw me, she gave me a decidedly hostile look. I held my ground, but didn't approach. "What do you want?" she demanded. I tried to explain that I wanted to talk to her, to find out more about her and to see if there was anything I could do to help her. I also told her I wanted to tell other people about her situation and help them to be more aware of extinction because of what happened to her children.

This made her incredibly angry. She charged me and chased me out of the clearing. Then she proceeded to chase me out of the forest altogether, biting me and cutting me with her bill as she went. "Go away! I know how you are! Get out! Don't come back! I want nothing to do with

---

you! Leave!" I tried to explain to her that I wasn't there to hurt her, but I think she just saw me as another human.

I ended up back on the beach. I sat down on a piece of driftwood, nursing my wounds and trying to figure out what to do next. Should I go back and try again? Should I just leave? As I was thinking, a feral cat spirit, white with gold eyes, walked up to me. "She's always like that," the cat said. "We just leave her alone".

The cat spirit ran for it when dodo came barreling out of the forest towards me. She drove me back further to the ocean's edge. "I know all about you! I know what's been going on! I know that you've been using my image to talk about how sad everything is, but what do you really do about it? Nothing! You just keep destroying and killing! Go! Away! Now!" Then she ran back off into the woods.

I sit here, thinking about her perched on the mound of bones of her children, and it's sobering. A lot of people talk about how sad it is that animals are being endangered, and that we're losing so many species every year, some of which may remain "undiscovered" by science. The dodo is a good example of an animal with a relatively small population that was relatively quickly exterminated. We think of animals like wolves and tigers that have several subspecies, and we don't feel so worried for them—at least not until the last subspecies is close to death.

Yet as a species we continue to engage in behavior that contributes to endangerment. Sure, there are individuals who do their best to reduce their negative impact on the environment. Yet the problem is bigger than a collection of individuals. As long as the majority of people are still engaged in harmful activities, the work of those who are more mindful in their actions will only slow the destruction.

Dodo also brought up the very important issue of image. I know people who claim Wolf as their totem who talk about how the wolf is the symbol of the wild, and how we should save the wolves. Yet the problem is a lot bigger than signing a few online petitions and yammering at our elected officials. While these things can help, if we buy new houses that chew up wild land, or drive cars when public transit and human-powered locomotion are available, and if we contribute, even unwittingly, to the attitude that there are more resources available, so why worry? Then we are contributing to the further endangerment not just of wolves, but of numerous other species. Wearing a t-shirt with a wolf on it—or a dodo, for that matter—is nowhere near as effective as changing your habits and working to convince others that it's a good idea to do the same.

My experience with Dodo emphasized the need to really question my actions with regards to the environment—and responsibility in general. Any effort is welcome, but it's imperative that we reevaluate what we're doing every now and then. Is what we're doing actually causing change? Is there more we can do? For example, recycling is all well and good, but there needs to be more demand for recycled products; otherwise, "recycled" materials may sit in glorified junk yards with nowhere to go. Along with recycling, it may be better to buy products that are made with a high content of recycled materials. This completes the cycle of recycling, and is a stronger statement than merely putting your garbage out on the curb.

It's also a good reminder of why activist magic is so important. Magic is an incredible tool with a lot of potential for making constructive change in the world. Yet when we limit it to a few spells and some blessings, we miss the opportunity to do bigger things. While magical acts should be used in tandem with mundane actions, there's a lot of untapped possibility with magic used for the purpose of not only environmental issues, but worldwide problems as a whole. I go into more detail about activist magic in chapter nine.

Further Work With Extinct Totems

My work with the extinct totems was some of my most intense and unique. If you're curious about other peoples' results, there's not a ton of material out there. However, a small selection of dictionary entries on dinosaur totems may be found at http://www.geocities.com/rainforest/4076/dinosaurlist.html. Additionally, Raven Kaldera's work with the Jotuns (giants in Norse mythology) reveals that the Paleolithic megafauna (mammoth, cave bear, etc.) are the totems (as well as the local fauna) in Jotunheim[50].

Finally, I invite you to check out appendix E, which features an essay by my friend Paleo on her own work and observations on extinct totems. Her work is quite complementary to this chapter, and I'm pleased to present it to readers of this book as an additional well of information on this topic.

Food Totems

Another group of less common totems I've been working with are what I call "food totems". These are primarily domesticated animals that in this day and age are primarily seen as sources of meat and other comestibles, as well as leather and other products. While pagans and magicians have a tendency to be more aware of the sanctity of animal life in general,

---

[50] Kaldera 2003

wildlife is often more glamorized than domesticated animals, with the exception of dogs, cats, horses, and other American non-edibles. We assume a predatory role with regards to nonhuman animals, even if it's only a result of conditioning that lies primarily within the subconscious mind. Totems are animals that we either have been taught not to eat (dogs, cats and horses) or ones that we generally don't eat on a regular basis unless we hunt for subsistence (wildlife).

This means that very few neopagans and other modern magical practitioners actually work with such totems as Pig or Cow; some do not acknowledge that domestic animals can even be totems, often stating that domestication has caused these creatures to lose their "medicine" (itself a bastardization of an indigenous concept). If an animal is unattainable for some reason, it must have some form of power, while the "dumb" animals that we slaughter by the millions every year in inhumane conditions are obviously powerless. This is another example of humans applying their values to the inherent value of a species, and thereby ignoring whatever totemic relationship could be there.

However, if we take an honest look at indigenous cultures around the world, some of them did eat sacred animals. Some members of the tribe may have abstained from eating the animal that represented their clan totem as a part of a traditional taboo. However, if we look at the case of the Lakhota, the bison was (and still is) one of the most sacred animals in their totemic system precisely because they killed and ate it. The bison represented life to this culture; this is part of where the stereotype of "Indians always use every part of the animal" came from.[51] Additionally, domestic animals could hold at least some power. Levi-Strauss in *Totemism* reported that the Ojibwe assigned domestic animals as clan totems to people of mixed tribal and white ancestry[52].

Pig, Cow, Chicken, and Turkey hardly have that sort of reverence attached to them in modern American culture. All of them are seen as stupid animals, and Pig is additionally stereotyped as dirty, stinky, and gluttonous. Yet the majority of Americans rely on them to survive, though not as completely as the Lakhota and Bison. Because we can live without eating meat, and because we assume that meat will always be available, drained of blood and wrapped in plastic and Styrofoam, we often take these animals for granted. There is an overabundance of domestic livestock; we even impact far-away places like Brazil in our hunger for beef, with thousands of acres of rain forest being slashed and burned to create pastureland for cattle.

---

[51] Brown 1997
[52] Levi-Strauss 1963

This is an unhealthy relationship on all levels. Factory farming demonstrates just how low our consideration for our fellow animals has sunk. At least deer and other wild animals are glamorized by the "thrill of the hunt" (no matter how macho and canned it may have become). Domestic animals live their brief, horrible lives in cramped, filthy quarters and die terrified and surrounded by the mechanically slaughtered carcasses of previous victims.

I realized that I shared the cultural irreverence for the animals that I was eating one night after a supper of crab legs. The entire steamed crab was brought out to me, a reminder that what I was consuming wasn't just something manufactured in a factory somewhere, but had been alive and well just a few hours before. This connection to the life of the animals is something I've worked to be mindful of not only with my food, but also the animals whose skins, bones and other remains are incorporated into my artwork. Sitting there looking at the shell of the crab, I began thinking about how I was taking this animal for granted, seeing it solely as a delicacy to be dipped in melted butter. I thought about how I would react if I saw a slab of wolf meat on my plate, and realized that my reaction would be much more respectful—not just because I would be eating an endangered species, but because I was eating my primary totem.

That night when I got home I did a meditation to contact Crab. I invited her to come talk to me, and allowed her to say whatever was on her mind, as I figured she probably didn't get too many people talking to her. The first thing she homed in on was my perception of her as different because she wasn't a vertebrate. She showed me the strength and functionality of the exoskeleton, and the delicate gills that allowed her to extract oxygen from water. Then she contrasted it with my own soft flesh wrapped around calcinous bones, and lungs that drew in air.

She explained to me that part of the reason that I saw her differently from other animals was because she was so alien in concept. Humanity in general seems to have a primarily negative view of invertebrates; crabs and lobsters are seen differently because they're "useful". But ask most people to hold an insect, spider, or other "creepy-crawly", and they'll very vehemently decline (I'll admit to being more uncomfortable with "bugs" than I was as a child). Sure, I could eat a crab, but I was less willing to see the totemic Crab as an equal with Wolf or Elk.

The conversation with Crab was a real eye-opener. She showed me that I was unconsciously buying into the cultural attitudes that led to a lot of animal abuse. I decided to open up conversations with other totems whose species I regularly consumed—this was a really amazing experience, and I could see areas of improvement that perhaps they could help me with.

Chicken was another important teacher for me. She asked me one night what was the first thing that I thought of when the word "chicken" was mentioned. I realized, rather guiltily, that the first image to pop into my mind was that of a decapitated, footless, defeathered dead bird fresh out of the oven. However, I moved beyond that thought and began visualizing chickens scratching in a barn yard, observing them as they went about their business. I admired the colorful plumage of the birds in my mind – and remembered that while they might not be as flashy the peacock or parrot, they still come in some lovely colors.

Of course, paying attention to feathers is only a single step removed from wondering how much meat you can get off the carcass, as feathers are the second greatest commodity birds provide to humans. So I tried watching the birds further as they scratched and pecked and went about their business. I realized that I really didn't know that much about them, and so Chicken asked me to do some research on her children.

The modern domestic chicken was bred from the red junglefowl of Asia, a member of the pheasant family which has been domesticated for some five millennia. Chickens are social birds, and may incubate eggs and raise chicks communally. They display more intelligence than their reputation allows, and make relatively low-maintenance pets. Unfortunately, thanks to factory farming, the majority of chickens in the United States live relatively short, horrific lives in small cages. Free range chickens may still be found, and their eggs are said to display a darker colored, heartier looking yolk[53]. Reading about this once again steeled my resolve to increase the percentage of free range meat and eggs that I buy, for the chickens' health as well as my own[54].

Not long after, when I went for a walk at a local park, I saw a feral rooster and hen, white with some colored plumage. They looked rather healthy for being forest foragers, and I was heartened to see that they ran from us, rather than expecting food like the ducks and other waterfowl in the park. It was a reminder to me that Chicken does indeed have a wild side beyond the usual "Chicken Little" stereotype. A common barnyard bird managed to look downright primal, and that evening it reaffirmed the value of this work.

I had another important experience with Crab while I was writing the rough draft of this book. Once again I was out to supper and ate crab

[53] Anonymous 2007-A
[54] Buyer beware—"free range" or "cage free" may mean a bird that was raised in a huge crowd on the floor of a barn rather than in cages. Your best bet is to buy directly from a local farmer whose facilities you're familiar with.

at a restaurant. When we first walked into the place, there was a tank of crabs right by the front door, and I figured they were on the menu. I said a silent prayer as I walked by, apologizing for my meal and praying that the death would be a quick one.

When the crab was brought out to me, I took his claws in my hand (only males are caught; females are thrown back) and asked him to forgive me, and to imbue me with his strength as I consumed his flesh. The meal became a conversation with the crab spirit, rather than Crab the totem, but it was enlightening. At first he was rather indignant at being relieved of his body before he was really ready, though he accepted my apology. Later on he reassured me that he had eaten plenty of other animals in his time, other crabs included, so what I was doing wasn't all that terrible. In fact, I had a very mild mental shift in which the experience of being a cannibal crab was superimposed over my eating my meal. It made sense, actually, and I didn't feel so bad about eating him after that. He also reminded me that even though I felt awful for his getting dropped into boiling water that it was actually a quick death compared to what a lot of water creatures went through; he himself had literally torn his food apart while still alive out of sheer necessity. This tied in nicely with my observation that Crab's bailiwick seems to be practicality.

The crab spirit also seemed surprised that I spoke to him. He said something to the effect of "All the crabs that die here every day, and I got to be the one who had the person who talked to him". He was pleased, though, that I didn't just see him as food, but also as a fellow life form, only recently deceased. I can tell a difference in how his meat has been integrating into my body; I haven't had this little trouble digesting a large meal in a long time. Maybe respect can help the essence of the animal become a part of my body easier.

A Culinary Ritual for Chicken

The first whole free-range chicken I bought after Chicken's request ended up being the center of what amounted to a week and a half long ritual. I brought home the chicken, and then proceeded to thoroughly clean the entire kitchen in preparation. When it was time for the ritual, I brought her out of the refrigerator. I laid her on the countertop, and I went into the light trance I use when talking to skin spirits. The spirit of this particular chicken had already vacated the body, but was hovering nearby. I thanked her for her flesh, and I apologized for her death. Then I asked her to show me her life; for a moment I saw her with other chickens in a field outdoors on a sunny day, next to a large barn. The chickens were scratching at the dirt, eating, and doing the various other things chickens do when not cooped up. I'd already hoped her life wasn't bad, comparatively speaking, since she was free range, but it was nice to get that confirmation.

I went through the process of preparing the chicken as though I were working with the remains of a sacrificial being. While the spices and seasonings were the usual mundane herbs and salts, in that moment they became sacred magical components to help transform the flesh into a sacrament itself. With a reverence normally reserved for holy items, I carefully placed the chicken in the pan and into the oven, closing the door to allow the transformation to occur.

I created the various side dishes with similar intent; they were to accent the center of this ritual, the chicken herself. I tried a bit of experimentation; I had been told not to waste any of the meat if I could help it. However, I had a little package of giblets sitting there on the countertop. I'm generally not an organ meat fan, so normally they end up in the garbage. This time, though, I decided to try giblet gravy. Truth be told, that was the most involved part of the actual act of cooking, and it asked a lot of my concentration to get it right.

Finally, though, the chicken was ready, and the side dishes prepared and set out as offerings to the chicken's spirit. At the beginning of our meal, along with our usual thanks to the various beings who gave of themselves to feed us, we gave a special blessing of gratitude to the spirit of the chicken, as well as the totem Chicken. The blessings were appreciated, and we tucked into our meals.

In turning the preparation of food into a ritual, I did my best to approximate the idea of rituals done to appease the spirits of food animals as well as honor the totem. Since the animal whose flesh I consumed was the chicken, I honored that spirit and corresponding totem. Perhaps chickens aren't the coolest of animals in this culture, but they are exceptionally important, and if any animal deserves honor, it's the one that feeds us.

I did notice positive effects from the meal, as did my husband. I've worked with the spirits of the animals I eat during meals before as a way to acknowledge that the energy of that animal was becoming a part of me through the process of digestion. However, I had never felt the energy melding with my own so profoundly as I did that night. For a couple of hours after the meal I could feel this transformation. If I closed my eyes I could see, in my mind, feathers on my arms, and claws on my feet; not a very strong shapeshift, but definitely an experience. My husband also noted that he could feel the energy of the chicken dissolving into his own energy, though he didn't report the shapeshift (that is a common part of my magic in general, by the way).

After we had eaten the chicken over the course of several days, I made broth from the carcass, to maximize the gift that we had been given. It was the first time I'd ever done this, and a few days later I was able to make a wonderful soup from it. When the soup was done, and the last bit of nutrition from the chicken's body was absorbed, I took a leg bone that I'd saved from the carcass and dried to my ritual room. I wrapped it in green yarn and hung it on the wall, to show the chicken spirit that she was welcome to stay.

The totem Chicken was quite pleased by the ritual. I felt by that point that I'd made a decent amount of progress in working with her, and the ceremony contributed to that. I don't have the time to go through the full ritual each time I make a meal, but I repeat this periodically to help me be more mindful on a regular basis of where my food comes from.

Other Domestic Totems

I mentioned a while back that cats, dogs and horses aren't on the American menu. However, they're considered to be quite edible in other parts of the world; horsemeat is a delicacy in many parts of Europe, and some Asian countries have a thriving trade in meat from domestic dogs and cats. My editor had brought up this point during the first round of editing, and I thought it would be worth it to speak with the totems of these three animals to get their perspectives on their roles as food totems.

Right now, my life is blessed with two wonderful housecats, Sun Ce and Ember. They're both adorable blue-grey and white tabbies whose markings are quite similar. However, Sun Ce is about twice the size of Ember, which has led to my nicknaming them "Pint Size" and "Quart Size"! While they both love me and Taylor, Ember has become "my" cat, just as Sun Ce is his.

I am acquainted with people who keep chickens as pets, and to all appearances they love those birds every bit as much as we love our cats. However, I'm also well aware of the fact that if Sun Ce and Ember lived in certain places, they'd be less pet and more food. While I have no compunction with eating a dead chicken, I'll admit that I've no plans to kill and eat our feline companions.

Still, this is largely a cultural bias. I decided that I'd talk to the totem Cat to see what s/he thought about the whole situation with cats-as-food. So I sat in a chair with Ember in my lap and meditated, using Ember's presence as a link to Cat. Cat appeared in my mind's eye as a gangly seal point Siamese kitten, about six weeks old, with wide blue eyes. She sat down and spoke with me. I asked her about her thoughts on her children being eaten. "Well," she said, "everybody has to eat. Granted, I'm not happy about how some of them are being treated, but at least they're becoming food. It's better than being burned in wooden cages, or used as bait to train fighting dogs—which are things I *am* angry about. I do my best to make it up to them, though," Cat continued. "There are plenty of people who give cats safe, warm, loving homes, and so when I send a cat that had a rough life or bad death back down to be born again, I try to get them into a better life with better care".

I then asked Cat if there was anything I could do to help. She acknowledged that while she didn't care for how some food cats were treated, that as a carnivore she could respect people's need to eat other animals. All she asked was that I continue to provide good homes to cats, and to promote humane treatment. This differed quite a bit from Chicken's perspective, not surprising since an enormous number of chickens, especially in the United States, are treated very poorly as a matter of course, whereas cats are only considered food in a few places, and are otherwise treated relatively well. Also, Cat seemed to feel that since she could send her own back into decent lives, that there were some ways to regain balance against the abuses heaped on some unfortunate cats around the world. And whereas Chicken wasn't all that crazy about her physical counterparts being eaten, Cat seemed rather accepting of it. I'm guessing this is at least partly due to Chicken's herbivorous nature. However, it shouldn't be assumed that all herbivorous totems are anti-predation. They are individuals, and Deer may have a more tolerant view of it since deer are rarely abused by humans, and death by gun (or by wolf pack) is quicker than death by internal parasites or starvation.

I haven't tried talking to Dog or Horse, but it's certainly an option for you, if you like. You don't have to have a physical representative with you to do the meditation; I just wanted to include Ember in on the fun since she likes my lap anyway, and I wanted to experiment with having a live animal involved (She didn't seem to mind one bit since her part consisted entirely of purring and exuding feline energy. Not a bad deal at all, I think.). However, if you have any interest in working with Cat, Dog or Horse, it may be worth exploring the food totem angle, if for no other reason than to get a broader view of what the totem's experience includes.

Microscopic Totems[55]

I had to ask myself when I first came up with this idea—"Is it possible?" After all, if there was ever a form of consciousness that was totally alien to the human mind, it would be unicellular and similarly tiny animals. I knew that, theoretically, any animal could be a totem, including those not visible to the naked eye. But Amoeba and Paramecium as totems? Would it work? The idea seemed far-fetched, even to me.

Of course, I just had to try it.

The concept wasn't entirely unfamiliar. Taylor Ellwood, in his book *Inner Alchemy*, talked about how he communicated with the bacteria in his body while doing a tour of his various systems and the components thereof:

I also worked with the bacteria of the body, which appeared as a young woman and told me to summon her by thinking of sunlight on golden hair. She mainly discussed the importance of interconnection in the body, showing me how every organism in the body works together for the mutual benefit of all. Her discussion can be applied microcosmically...but also macrocosmically...Everything connects together by the functions that are performed as a process that enables life to continue, but when that process is disrupted life cannot be maintained...This working is particularly intriguing given that bacteria are mostly recognized as separate beings that live in symbiosis, or occasionally parasitically, in our bodies[56].

While unicellular beings are technically protists, rather than "true" animals, I decided to give communicating with them a shot, just to see what would happen.

The first one I tried talking to was Euglena. Rather than my usual trip into a cave, I felt myself absorbed into a body of water. I became a euglena, my body water-filled, loving the touch of the sun. I fed on tiny bits of food matter, and other living beings, absorbing them into myself. I felt the sunlight on the chloroplasts in my body, remnants of plant-like protists that euglenas long ago had absorbed, and felt the flood of nutrition issue forth from them, strengthening me. I even felt myself split into two, the process of mitosis.

Euglena told me that the lessons the various microscopic totems teach are essentially the same, since their physical existences revolve

---

[55] I'm aware that by many peoples' standards, unicellular critters aren't actually critters. However, for the purposes of experimentation, I chose to work with some of the more animal-like unicellular beings. Yes, it's stretching the concept of "animal", but as you'll read, I did get results.

[56] Ellwood 2007, p. 93

around consuming, digesting, expelling, moving around, and dividing. There's some specialization, though not to the extent in more complex animals. Their strength is in numbers, where numerous amoebas can cause an illness in a human body, and clouds of protists can thrive in polluted waters.

Despite what Euglena said about the similarity of lessons, I decided to talk to Paramecium and Amoeba about totemic issues. I searched for Paramecium first. It appeared enormous, floating above me in the water like a huge whale, cilia propelling it along. When it noticed me, its first reaction was to try to eat me. Not wanting any part of that, and failing to get past its aggressive advances, I went elsewhere in search of Amoeba.

Amoeba was a bit more receptive. The initial message I got was "Hungry, must eat NOW". And this time I ended up as lunch, wrapped in a pseudopod and absorbed. I felt my body dissolve, and my consciousness melded with Amoeba while my remains were expelled. I got to feel what it was like to be this seemingly massive, amorphous being made of organic gel, a large, brain-like nucleus and other organelles, and clear membranes wrapping around the whole. I even got to experience a split, though I did so as an observer only, watching the nucleus crack in two, then the splitting membrane tightening the link between the two new Amoebae until they popped apart.

Afterwards, I headed back towards Paramecium. This time it didn't try to eat me, but the definite energy I got was "I am the top of the food chain here. I eat what I want". While microscopic organisms seem to end up as mutual predators and prey, Paramecium seemed particularly interested in eating rather than being eaten. My theory on why Euglena was so passive in comparison is because to an extent it could produce its own food through the chloroplasts in its body, and so the hunt for other beings wasn't quite as urgent.

The microscopic totems seemed primarily interested in showing me their experiences and needs, rather than anything more esoteric. There really isn't any body of lore surrounding them since they're so recently discovered, and few people would ever consider them in a magical sense. However, continuing in the tradition of creating totemic lore based on natural history, I have a few ideas for the three animals I interacted with.

Euglena speaks particularly of adaptability through observing the solutions of others. The chloroplasts are remnants of plant protists that had been eaten, but have been adopted by the euglena as an extra food source through photosynthesis[57]. Amoeba is also adaptability, though of a

---

[57] http://en.wikipedia.org/wiki/Euglena

different sort; an amoeba, when in a harsh environment, will form a cyst around itself for protection until conditions are better. It can also regulate the salinity of the fluids in its body to avoid overbalance one way or the other[58]. Finally, Paramecium seems to be quite the predator in the microscopic world. Paradoxically, this particular animal displays a symbiotic relationship with certain bacteria in its body[59].

While microscopic animals aren't as popular or as complex to deal with as others, there's still a potential for more work in this direction. We often forget that there are ecosystems that don't involve us and other large animals; if we routinely ignore the ecosystems of insects and other small creatures, then it's not surprising that we generally don't give a thought to the unseen world.

Working With Unconventional Totems

There's still a lot of territory to be covered. As you'll notice, most of the animals above are relatively well-known. I didn't work with any small mammals or non-mammals from prehistoric times, nor did I contact any of the smaller reptiles of the age of the dinosaurs, for example, and both of those groups leave a lot of exploration to be done. There are, of course, much older time periods I didn't touch on, either. Feel free to experiment with your own explorations of different types of unusual totems; many of them are eager to work with people, having rare opportunity to do so. However, also be aware that some may not be all that enthusiastic, especially if humanity mistreats their physical representatives. Still, this is a good opportunity to improve those relationships, especially if we can convey their importance to other people[60].

Finally, keep in mind that even if you aren't interested in working with something as exotic as a trilobite, that there are numerous totems of animals in the physical world today who may not get as much attention as the BINABM. The totem of the Maud Island frog may not be as well known among neopagans as, say, Bullfrog. And amphibians may not be as popular as mammals and birds. However, there are numerous less popular totems who are eager for a chance to work with people and teach them new ways to look at the world. In the next chapter I'll discuss a totem

---

[58] http://en.wikipedia.org/wiki/Amoeba
[59] http://en.wikipedia.org/wiki/Paramecium
[60] Ravenari has an awesome selection of her interpretations of a decent number of not-so-common totems at http://www.wildspeak.com/vilturj/totems.html (the rest of the site is of interest as well, particularly for those interested in and/or practicing shamanism).

card deck that can be a huge help in contacting some of these lesser-known totems.

Journaling Exercises

1. Try working with one of each of these types of totem: extinct (maybe even several from different time periods), food and microscopic. Start out with a meditation or other exercise to make the initial contact with each, then once you've established a relationship with the totem try doing a more practical ritual for a purpose for which the totem is suited.

2. Can you think of another type of totem that isn't worked with as much as the BINABM? Try working with a couple of representatives of that group and see what results you get.

When recording your results, here is a suggested format for your journal entry:

Date:
Category of totem: (*extinct, food, microscopic, etc.*)
Method of initial contact: (*meditative journey, totem cards, etc.*)
Natural history: (*a summary of the biology and behavior of the physical animal*)
Lessons: (*things the totem has taught you*)
Rituals: (*record notes from any rituals worked with this totem*)
Other Notes: (*anything else you feel it's important to mention*)

Chapter Four: The Last Totem Card Deck You'll Ever Need

I've been thinking about the concept of totem cards, decks that supposedly help you find your totem animal(s) with just one reading. In *Fang and Fur*, I explained some of the downfalls of a number of methods used to determine one's totem. One of the shortcomings of cards is that they necessarily have to limit the number of animals you have as your choices, and even the creators that add a few blank cards for "animals not pictured here" still put the odds in favor of BINABM and whatever other critters they chose to include in their decks. Additionally, unless you read for other people, once you've read your cards what do you do with them? Some sets advocate using the cards for divination, but others seem to primarily want to use them for determining your life totem(s).

Years ago, when I was still in college, I had someone give me a reading with the *Medicine Cards*. According to this particular set, everyone has nine totems (or so it said on page 18 of the accompanying book[61]). Now, I've been a Wolf's child since I was about two years old, so I assumed that Wolf would be one of the cards that came up. I don't remember all the cards that I got—the only one I remember was Hummingbird—but none of them were animals that I had any particular connection with. And Wolf wasn't among them.

This isn't to say it was an entirely ineffective reading. After all, Hummingbird did describe part of my life at the time, and could still have applications today. However, so could any totem, really—they all have relevant teachings for me, if I choose to listen and if they're willing to talk. Hummingbird didn't really strike me as one of "my" totems. The problem with that particular reading was twofold. One, it went against one of the few parts of my spiritual life that has remained constant amid the many changes. Two, the problem with having someone else read my cards is that it was filtered through her bias. That leaves a larger chance for error and misinterpretation than doing the reading (or other method) myself. Granted, that error may not be incredibly great if the reader is experienced and can interpret other people's energy/the messages from the totems with relative accuracy. But there's still no substitute for doing it yourself.

I do use Ted Andrews' *Animal-Wise Tarot* deck to do readings to find tertiary totems (totems that we evoke for help with specific problems or magical workings) for myself and others. Rather than a traditional

---

[61] Carson and Sams 1999

layout, such as the Celtic Cross, I have a directional/elemental layout that the deck and I developed together[62]. However, I have also used a second deck for magical work, the *Wolf Song* cards created by Lew Hartman. I've primarily evoked tertiary totems with them; my usual practice is to have the totem bless a candle for me for a specific purpose, then place the candle holder on top of the animal's card while the candle burned. Unfortunately, this deck is more limited than many to BINABM, so it's not absolutely ideal. While I think it's neat to have a deck that has four different wolf cards, it's not one that I would use to find totems to work with. Some decks, such as Susie Green's absolutely gorgeous (and ecologically conscious) *Animal Messages* deck, do have a wider variety of animals, but once again you can only have so many cards in a deck.

Given these inherent limitations, I wanted to come up with a system of cards or other symbols that could be used both for seeking totems and magic, as well as other purposes. I saw the limitations as a challenge, and wanted to find a way to answer them. While I'm happy with Andrews' deck for my own divinatory purposes (he does include a nice mixture of animals), and the *Wolf Song* cards for evocation, I wanted to create something that was more inclusive overall. I wanted a deck that wouldn't limit me by what totems I could work with, and that I could use both for divination and for other forms of magic.

What I came up with was a set of thirty-three cards based on taxonomy (specifically phyla), habitats, and other basic categories of information about animals. Not every card would be used in every type of reading, but I managed to create a set that had fewer cards than most decks, and allowed for more animals than any other (Not that I'm bragging or anything…). I also managed to address the issues I'd had with existing decks.

Here are the basic groups of cards I created:

Continent: The first problem was dealing with the limitations of numbers of animals. Obviously, you can't have a card for every single animal in the world; there are just too many of them. The first item of information you'd probably need would be geography. I created a card each for North America, South and Central America, Europe, Asia, Africa, Australia/Oceania, and the poles. Obviously, some of these have a lot more wildlife than others, but they all deserved a chance, and I've yet to find a deck that included *Almara alpina*, a beetle found in Arctic and Alpine regions.

---

[62] Lupa 2006

Phylum: Along with the usual five divisions of the phylum Chordata (mammals, birds, reptiles, amphibians, and fish) I also wanted to allow some classifications for invertebrates. However, that's a pretty broad group of animals, and I limited my classifications to arthropods, molluscs, worms, unicellular, and other.[63] This way if I ended up drawing "other", I could at least narrow it down by type of habitat as well as global location. Other could include everything from sponges to brachiopods.

Habitat: I also wanted to get a little more habitat-specific. First I created cards for very generic environments: air, water, arboreal, surface of land, underground, and mixed (in the case of amphibious animals or aquatic flying birds). I then divided water into fresh and salt to be a little more specific, added "forest" to the arboreal card, and exchanged surface of land for desert, mountains, and plains. So I ended up with air, fresh water, salt water, arboreal/forest, desert, mountains, plains, underground, and hybrid (for habitats that include more than one of the above, such as swamps). This gave me a nice basic collection of habitats.

Wild cards: I threw in a few "wild cards" for special cases. One was for domesticated animals, while another was for extinct. I gave a card to mythological animals as well, just for those who stretch totemism in that direction. Finally, I put in a card that simply said "Try Again Later" (Magic 8-Ball ™, anyone?).

Significator: In the event I wanted to use the deck for helping people find their totems (or people wanted to use it for their own readings), I made a card each for primary, secondary and tertiary totems. This would be used similarly to the significator card in a tarot deck, except that instead of signifying the person being read, it represented the type of totem being sought.

Initially this seemed like a pretty good setup. It focused primarily on the natural history of the animals in question; something that I think often gets left behind in primarily mythology-based interpretations of totems. And it effectively solved the problem of how to deal with the massive numbers of animals out there.

But there was the problem of what to do in the case of a biological impossibility, such as an arboreal reptile on one or the other pole. I

---

[63] I realize that you can get even more specific than that, and the categories I used still slant the preferences towards vertebrates. Feel free to tweak it however you wish. For a good list of animal phyla, go to http://en.wikipedia.org/wiki/Phylum.

decided that this would mean that I needed to try drawing the cards again. After all, not every divination is going to work perfectly, and there needs to be room for errors and totems not wanting to cooperate and readers being too tired or otherwise distracted. Of course, this could also just be a matter of chance rather than a bad reading. However, rather than letting it discourage me, I just waited for the next answer that actually made some sense.

Readings

When I talk about a reading, I don't mean shuffling this deck and laying out a bunch of cards, then putting them all away. Reading these cards is not a simple matter. In addition to the layout, it's necessary to meditate on the results to help find the specific animal. Often you'll also have to do some research as to the local fauna to try to identify the animal you saw. In fact, the animal in your meditation may not even show itself very clearly; you may see a flash of fin or antler, and nothing else. Remember, though, that you're dealing with thousands upon thousands of possibilities, some of which you may never have heard of. A single reading may take days or even weeks to complete. This deck is not for those who want quick and easy answers.

The Basic Layout

You'll want to start by picking out which significator you want to use. Don't start out by trying to find your primary totem(s). The reason for this is because this is a very complex system, relatively speaking. After all, you're potentially in contact with every species on the planet. Get yourself used to using this particular system by looking for more open results before hunting for something as specific as a primary totem.

I started by using the deck to find random tertiary totems for the sole purpose of broadening my horizons as far as totemism goes. I wasn't even looking for help with any particular magical work; I simply wanted to explore the world of totems beyond the BINABM. Only later, when I'd gotten used to the system, did I narrow down my requests. Even if you just use the deck for the purpose of exploration it's quite worth it. There's a lot of potential out there beyond the BINABM, and you can literally spend a lifetime getting to know the animals. With a set of thirty-three cards, I can get information on more animals than in all the totem dictionaries I own combined.

Place the significator card at the top of the reading. This helps to prime you for the type of totem you'll be looking for. If you're just looking for unusual totems to interact with, you can use the tertiary card, with the understanding that your purpose is basically exploration. This leaves the reading open to any totem that's ready to talk to you.

Next, lay out the stacks of phylum and continent cards side by side below the significator. Get into whatever state of consciousness you generally use for divination. Shuffle each stack separately, set them down face-down, and turn over the cards on top. This will give you a continent and a phylum to work with. Obviously, it may seem easier if you end up with a more familiar phylum in an area you live in; on the other hand, this can also sabotage your efforts because you may subconsciously push yourself towards animals you know a lot about (such as the BINABM).

Now comes the first round of meditation. You can use the generic totem animal/power animal meditation that's available in most books on the subject (see appendix B) or on various relevant websites online. Rather than going into the meditation with the intent of finding your primary totem at the other end of the tunnel, go in with the phylum and continent cards you drew in mind, and let the rest happen as it will. Don't force yourself to visualize an appropriate setting; just let the totem and your subconscious do the talking.

The meditation may give you a clear look at whatever the animal is. In that case, start doing research on that animal to find out its natural history. Do further meditations for the purpose of getting to know it more on a spiritual level. You may not actually know what kind of animal it is, especially if it's not a chordate animal, or one native to your area. In that case, you may need to start with broader research on the fauna of the continent you drew to identify the species you're dealing with before looking further.

However, if no animal appears or you only catch a tiny glimpse, you may need more information. If that's the case, lay out your cards again (unless you left them as is from before). Make sure the significator, continent, and phylum cards are all the same as before your initial meditation. Then pull out the habitat group, shuffle it, and draw a card. Add that information to what you already know, and go back into meditation again.

If, at this point you're still having trouble, this is where the wild cards come into play. Say you've gone through the layout and meditation for the phylum, continent, and habitat cards and still can't get quite enough information, even with several meditations under your belt. It's possible that you may be dealing with the totem of a species that's either extinct, a part of the local mythology, domesticated in that part of the world, or that you just need to start over again. The wild cards allow for those possibilities.

Lay out the cards, if you didn't leave them out, as they were for the initial reading and meditation. Now place the stack of wild cards at the bottom of the layout. Shuffle them and turn over the card that ends up on top once you're done shuffling. That should give you an idea of what you're working with.

In the event that this yields no solid results, I would recommend waiting a week or two, then starting over from the beginning. The most likely situation is that you simply haven't gotten comfortable enough with this system to be able to home in on a particular animal and that you're still getting used to navigating an entire world of potential totems, as opposed to a few dozen hand-picked for you by an author. Each reading and meditation you do is practice, and the more practice you have, the better you'll do in later attempts. Don't see a "failed" result as a bad sign; instead, take it as part of the growing process. This system took me a while to get used to, and I designed it! Be patient, take a break, and try again. You'll get the hang of it at your own pace, and its well worth the effort.

So why not just draw all the cards at once? I chose to set up the reading in stages because I wanted to keep it as open-ended as possible. Cards are only a tool for helping you to get in touch with your intuition/the spirit world/etc. It's quite possible to contact your totem without ever using cards or any other sort of tool. However, some people do like cards as an aid for their search. The system I devised is designed to offer that tool, while minimizing reliance upon it. With the alternate reading/meditation process, you still primarily depend on your meditations to get specific answers; the cards are there to give you a few tips to start with, but not so much that you end up with too many suggestions that may interfere with getting in touch with the totem.

Say your totem is Inland Forest Bat, totem of an Australian species of bat (but you don't know it yet since you haven't tried to find your totem yet). Suppose you draw the Australia/Oceania and the Mammal card, and then decide to draw the Habitat card without meditating first. Now, let's assume that you subconsciously tell yourself that since it's an Australian mammal, it'll probably be a land animal of some sort, and this subconscious suggestion affects the reading to the point where you draw the Plains card. You may be confused when you meditate and find yourself flying in the middle of a forest. Or you may so expect to be walking across a wide expanse of plain that your expectations override the results of your meditation. Meanwhile, Bat may be having trouble getting through to you while you wander looking for Kangaroo.

While this isn't a sure result, and you may have success by drawing all cards at once, I tend to err on the side of caution when trying to avoid suggestions that may throw off my results. Therefore I try to start with a minimum of information, and allow the meditation to be as freeflowing as possible.

One final note: if you're having issues with visualization in the meditation stages of this divination set, don't fret. You're not the only one. The next chapter includes a few alternative meditation forms that you may find more useful.

Finding Specific Totems

Once you're comfortable with using the deck for finding random totems to talk to, it's time to get more specific about things. I'd start with a tertiary totem for a particular purpose. First, determine what situation or issue you'd like help with. Lay out the tertiary card with that issue in mind, then pull your continent and phylum cards. Proceed as usual, and the totem you find should be one that will be able to help you. Repeat with the appropriate significator cards for secondary or primary totem readings.

The more specific a totem you're looking for, the more difficult it may be to focus. For example, if you have a problem that you need some help with, there could be dozens or even hundreds of totems that could help you in the tertiary role. However, secondary totems aren't as numerous, primarily because rather than being in your life for a single magical working or problem, they may have an intense relationship with you for a long period of time. While you can easily work with a dozen tertiaries a week, secondaries come to you on their own schedule, and because their work is more intense you'll work with fewer of them over a lifetime. As for looking for your primary totem, it's rare for people to have more than one (though not unheard of). If a totem in any of these roles doesn't seem to be a perfect fit right away, try working with the totem a few times anyway. You should be able to figure out relatively quickly whether the animal you initially found is the one you're actually looking for, or whether you need to try again. This is especially true if the animal is one that doesn't seem particularly notable, or that you're not familiar with. You may just need time to get to know each other a little better.

Conversely, you may find that the format of this deck actually makes finding the right totem easier. Say, for example, you live in the U.S. and your primary totem is the Kakadu dunnart, a small Australian marsupial that looks very much like a mouse. With a conventional totem deck, Kakadu may try to contact you through the card that most resembles hir, the mouse (assuming the deck has such small critters in it).

You may then simply assume that Field Mouse is your totem and not do any more exploration, unless Kakadu starts raising more fuss until you pay attention to the fact that s/he is quite a different species than you originally thought.

Using this deck allows the totem to push you in hir direction, rather than settling for the closest cousin, so to speak. It also gives more room for less common totems, such as insects (besides Butterfly, Bee, Grasshopper, and Mantis), to get their word in. Regardless of how much practice it takes to use the deck, the flexibility is one of the main reasons I've enjoyed creating and working with it. I've gotten to talk to some interesting totems I never would have thought to contact before.

As with other totems, don't be discouraged if you end up with a not-so-flashy animal. There's a reason that I designed this to allow for any totem to show up, and as I demonstrated earlier, it's quite possible for domesticated and "invisible" animals to have totems that we can work with. Part of my goal with this book is to help convince people that they don't necessarily have to have the biggest, most amazing totem animal in the world. Rather, what's important is finding the totems that work best with you. I want all of them to have the chance to work with people, not just the BINABM.

My Readings

I'll admit I was a little nervous the first time I did a reading for myself. What if the cards gave me something really obscure? What if this system was entirely too complex to be practical? But I shuffled the continent cards and came up with South and Central America, followed by Chordata: Fish for my phylum.

Not surprisingly, in my meditation I found myself in a river surrounded by lush jungles. Before me, swimming in the warm green waters, I saw a small silver disk-shaped fish with big round eyes. It wasn't a piranha, though it resembled one in shape. I knew I'd seen the fish before in pet stores and home aquariums, but I couldn't for the life of me remember what the name was. I kept getting a word beginning with "c" popping into my head; my first thought was "cichlid", but that wasn't right, as the fish was the totally wrong shape to be a cichlid.

I logged onto the computer and started looking for tropical fish originating from South America. Within five minutes I found pictures of my fish—the silver dollar, a harmless relative of the piranha found in the Tapajos River in Brazil. This docile, social fish is an herbivore and is a popular aquarium fish, growing up to six inches in diameter. Silver dollars can be skittish, but tend to get along well with other aquarium fish, and in the wild are so social that they spawn in groups routinely (piscine orgy!). And they're members of the Characidae family, which may explain why I was seeking a word starting with "c".[64]

When I meditated further with Silver Dollar, he showed up as a school rather than a single fish. They curiously, though cautiously approached me as I floated in the water, and they nibbled on my hair and clothing. If I moved, they flitted away, but came back soon thereafter. The message they gave me was one of trust and caution involving others, striking a fine balance between the two. Part of their skittishness seemed to be because they weren't used to being worked with on a totemic level, but some of it was simply part of the Silver Dollar nature.

A later meditation led to a ritual in which I evoked Silver Dollar individually. He had me shift to his form and swim first alone, and then with a school. I had been working on the balance between "me" time and social time, and the ritual helped me to address some of the discomfort I had with being social at times when I'd rather be alone. I explored why I sometimes felt crowded in a group setting, and how I could alleviate those feelings without ignoring my need to have my own space. Silver Dollar then gave me a sigil that I used to help myself engage in social interactions more fully, rather than being distracted by thinking about what I could be doing on my own.

Later on, I did a ritual with Silver Dollar to further charge the sigil I'd been given. I evoked him, and asked him for his help. I found that he preferred talking to me in quiet trance, so once he had arrived I lay down and began to meditate. We talked for a while about some of the issues I'd been having with balancing my own time and time spent with others, including my husband. I explained to him that since I'd gotten married, and particularly since I'd started working jobs with long hours, that I felt stressed over the reduced amount of "me" time. However, I also knew that I'd felt this stress even when I'd been single and had fewer hours away from home, and so the answer wasn't in getting more "me" time, but in learning to not stress about quantity over quality.

He then told me to make two copies of the sigil on some paper I had that had images of water printed on it. He told me to put them in the two places where I was most prone to getting too immersed in me time— by my computer desk, and in my art studio/ritual space. The goal wasn't to take away my own space, but rather to help remind me not to get too wrapped up in my own head and to cultivate the relationships with other people in my life. The sigils would help me to be more conscious of my

---

[64] Anonymous 2007-C

choices and my reactions to events beyond my control, as well as finding a way to balance my own needs with others' requests.

Silver Dollar was a good teacher for this. While each individual fish has hir own mind, they're all able to open up to each other as a school, to be able to protect each other through numbers, but also to be aware of individual needs when feeding, mating, etc. Additionally, the relaxed manner of his communication with me worked better for dealing with an already stressful situation. Silver Dollar's calm, centered demeanor made him a good reminder of my own need to relax, rather than worrying about every single minute. I do have to say, several months after the initial sigil casting and meditations, that I have achieved a better time balance, and have learned to relax more (something that's been excellent for my health!).

My next draw resulted in a North American bird. My initial meditation showed me a songbird of medium size with a green back and a yellow belly, and a somewhat upturned tail when excited. I looked through a book of birds and narrowed my options down to two possibilities, Bachman's warbler and the common yellowthroat. Both birds, incidentally, showed up as females of the species.

Bachman's warbler is a highly endangered species found in the southeast U.S. and Cuba throughout its yearly migration. The numbers of this bird dropped dramatically in the 20th century, primarily due to habitat destruction. The yellowthroat, on the other hand, is found in marshy areas across the U.S. down into Mexico, and winters as far as South America.[65]

I spoke with Warbler first. She carried me on her back to a nest with a single egg in it. "I have one last hope," she said, showing me the one egg turning into many. "I need your help—all my energy is put towards helping the last few survive. I cannot afford anything else." The message was clear: Warbler needed my help more than I needed hers. I decided to do a ritual to help any remaining Bachman's warblers thrive. While the species has been considered extinct, a 2002 sighting of what very well may have been a warbler in Cuba reported by the Cornell Lab of Ornithology points to a glimmer of hope—that single egg.[66] I worked a series of rituals to help give that egg a boost; I elaborate on what I did in chapter nine.

In speaking with Yellowthroat, I discovered that while Warbler certainly needed to speak with me, this was the bird I'd originally been trying to connect with. I sat on Yellowthroat's back as he took me to the nest where I encountered the same totem as a female. She whispered in

[65] Perrins 1990, p. 328-329
[66] Beetham 2006

my ear, "It's not about what you say, but how you say it. Maximize the effectiveness of what you want to say". With that simple message, both birds flew away, with the assurance that they would help me if I asked. This didn't surprise me, as improving my communication, particularly with other people, had been on my mind quite a bit during the time period where I was doing this experiment.

I had previously been working with Lynx to help me watch my words. So I was rather curious as to how Yellowthroat's help would differ from Lynx's. I went back on another visit to Yellowthroat, and asked both the male and female versions for clarification. "We teach you about how to say what you do choose to say, while Lynx teaches you when to say it". Yellowthroat emphasizes what the motivation behind the words is, why they're said, and how to craft the words more carefully. This somewhat overlaps with Lynx, who teaches the appropriateness of time and place, but may also help with word choice. Yellowthroat simply asked me to continue what I was doing, and thanked me; I then returned "home".

Other People's Results

Since this was a brand new system unlike anything I had encountered, I wanted to field test it to be sure that I hadn't made it too complicated, and that it worked for people besides me. I asked for a few volunteers to take it for a spin. Here's a sampling of their results, drawn from personal communication.

Paleo

Paleo drew Amphibians and Central/South America. She admitted that her initial bias was towards frogs in the rain forest, particularly poison arrow frogs, but she kept this bias in mind while doing her meditation and research. Her initial walking meditation yielded an image of a salamander in her mind, though no specific species. She also got a distinct feeling of hydrophilia (not surprising) and the need for a hot rain forest. She experienced what she describes as "mild shapeshift into a somewhat gecko-like body. Definitely four legs (none being the specialized jumpers of frogs), a tail, and large semi-protruding eyes".

Her research revealed that although the bulk of salamanders are actually North American, that South and Central America have only one family of salamander, Plethodontidae, or lungless salamanders. This matched one very distinct trait she had noticed during her shapeshift, the feeling of breathing through her skin. Lungless salamanders do respirate through their skin and mouth tissues[67]. Other distinguishing characteristics she encountered were a tongue that extended like a frog's, and the need for specific plants for laying eggs. While she was never able to narrow down the exact species of salamander, she did learn quite a bit spiritually as well as biologically.

One important lesson was that humans need to pay more attention to detail. Being smaller than we are, salamanders naturally notice things we may overlook. Salamander also stressed relating to the elements on "a...well...elemental level. Its very body is intimately connected to and dependant on water, earth, air, and fire (as an ectotherm it needs external heat to survive). It feels that if humans took more time to acknowledge our own utter dependency on the elements we would be far more hesitant to pollute, drain, and deforest on a massive scale. Humans need to respect and take joy in exposure to the raw elements as a way to counter this deadly trend... just as the Amphibian Clan led the way to great evolution, they are in a position where they may be leading the way to great extinction. There are some frog spirits out there who are quite angry over the fact that many humans aren't noticing them disappearing all around them. They wonder if humans will even miss their songs and displays. The particular salamander I am working with is especially concerned about the clear-cutting of rainforests."

Paleo said that the actual process of researching what sort of salamander she was talking to was absolutely fascinating. She was amazed at the sizes, colors, and specialties of the various salamanders she considered. She had admitted at one point that she hadn't really considered amphibians before, and had even worked with mollusks more than them. However, being able to work with Salamander gave her an entirely new experience.

innowen windchaser

During Autumn 2007 I field tested the deck in person with a group of friends in Portland, OR. Over a period of about six weeks I guided them through finding two tertiary totems, one just for exploration's sake, and one for something specific each person wanted to improve in hir life. Innowen, one of the participants, was kind enough to allow me to write about the ritual she did with Komodo Dragon.

She had previously met with Komodo Dragon on a sandy beach in her meditations, and this was the setting for the ritual, which was meant to bind them closer to each other energetically. When they both had

---

[67] Anonymous 2007-B

arrived at the beach at nighttime, they sat under the moonlight for a while. She asked him his name, and he replied, "Wilbur".[68] She touched him and they merged their energy together; as she absorbed his energy, she got to see a bit of what it's like to be a Komodo Dragon. While she retained some of the energy, she allowed most of it to disperse into the Universe at large.

After recording her results, she bid Wilbur a fond farewell. Overall, she considered the working to be a success, and it's my hope that they continue to have a good working relationship together.

Creating Your Own Deck

Another goal I have with this deck is for people to be able to make their own totem cards. I don't intend to mass-produce sets of totem cards based on this chapter, although I've kicked around the idea of a limited edition small run just for the fun of it. However, my main purpose is for people to do things themselves, and that includes working with something a little more personal than an impersonally printed deck[69].

As for construction, you can get a deck of blank tarot cards (just type "blank tarot cards" into a search engine and you'll get links to places that sell them). Poster board is a little too flimsy for long-term use, but if you can find heavier card stock that will hold up better, you can use that. The pre-manufactured cards feature the Rider-Waite crosshatching on the back; you may want to add a similar sort of repeated pattern on the backs of cards made from other paper stock. This way you can't see the illustration or writing on the other side. http://www.plaincards.com/ features perforated sheets that you can stick in your printer, similar to business card sheets; this allows you to print your own designs a single deck at a time. Two people who field-tested this card deck used regular playing cards coated in several layers of white gesso, and then added their own words and pictures. If you're really working on a budget, you can even use index cards, though be aware that they won't be nearly as durable, especially if you're fond of shuffling your deck several dozen times before drawing the cards.

---

[68] I do want to add that, in my own paradigm, I see totems as archetypes. I do not give them special names as some people do with individual spirit guides. For me, Wolf (or, to be more specific, Timber Wolf) is just Wolf to me, not Grey Howler or Fuzzbutt. However, if Komodo Dragon told innowen to call him Wilbur, who am I to say it's wrong?

[69] I'd really prefer that this system wasn't commercially produced without my permission. If you feel you absolutely must, please contact me first to obtain permission. At the very least, some credit for the idea would be nice.

If you don't like cards, you can use stones, or slices of wood or antler, or whatever else floats your boat. What's important is that every item that has a symbol is about the same size, shape, and color, and looks relatively identical from the back. It's amazingly easy to accidentally memorize small details that tell one card/stone/etc. from another, especially if you use the set frequently.

As for the illustrating itself, make sure you use something durable. Pencil probably won't hold up too long on any surface unless you put a layer of acrylic sealer over it (spray cans are available for cheap in any artists' supply store—make sure you use it outside so you don't suffer the ill effects of fumes!). In fact, regardless of what medium you use you should probably seal the final product. For more durable materials like stone, I like using Mod Podge, a type of adhesive, as a sealer, but I only put it on the painted/etc. part because I like the natural texture of the stone.

If you have a Dremel or other electric carving tool and the right kind of bits you can engrave stone, antler, or wood which. Or you can pick up some of those smooth colored glass stones that end up in glass vases and aquariums everywhere. Get some glass etching acid, an old paintbrush with soft bristles, contact paper, and a small craft knife with a fresh blade. Cover each stone with the contact paper, and try to keep the paper on the side you want your design on as flat and smooth as possible. Then cut away the paper in the design you want to use (you can sketch it out on the paper first to use as a guide). Paint acid over the design, and let it sit however long the directions say to. Carefully clean the acid off and dispose of it properly.

Most of the materials in this section can be obtained at any well-stocked craft store. You should be able to make a deck or other divination set for well under twenty dollars, unless you're absolutely set on having semi precious stones with solid gold set into the engravings. Here's the part where every other person who recommends making your own divination set/ritual tools/etc. says that "you don't have to be a great artist—what matters is that you made them!" Now, I could be a real jerk and tell you that only the pretty cards work, but that's not true. However, for some people aesthetics are important, and if you're one of those people and you can't draw worth a whit, there's no shame in commissioning someone else to do the artwork for you. On the other hand, I am not the world's greatest artist, at least when it comes to drawing (my rendition of Africa looked something like a green t-bone steak that had been left in the back of the fridge too long). But it worked for me, and I was happy with it.

The actual symbols you use are also up to you. I primarily used words instead of pictures in the phyla cards, and very simple drawings for the continents and habitats. You may want to avoid using actual animals as symbols for any of these simply because this may increase the chances of having that animal show up in the reading due to subconscious influences.

As I have mentioned before, it's quite possible to modify the deck as needed. For example, if there are particular magical purposes that you routinely need tertiary totems' help with, you can create cards for those purposes. You can also add other parameters to help you figure out what totem you're dealing with; you might add, for example, cards marked "carnivore", "herbivore", "insectivore", "omnivore" and "other diet" to help narrow down possibilities based on what the physical animal eats. One person who tested out the deck considered moving "domestic", "mythological" and "extinct" up to the first draw, along with a "wild" card to help give more initial information. This is somewhat of an open-source system, so feel free to mess around with it as you will.

On Reading For Other People

This is a highly personal divination system. Because of its complexity, and the amount of meditation that is necessary to get a thorough answer, it's not the easiest system to read for someone else. Even I don't use this deck for other people; I only read for others using my *Animal-Wise* deck, and then only for tertiary totems.

That being said, if you feel the need to read for someone else, it is crucial that you don't just give them a reading and then send them home with no follow-up. Make it very clear that this is not a quick-fix system, and that it requires a lot of commitment over weeks or even months. This commitment isn't just limited to having the person come back for several subsequent readings, but also making sure that s/he realizes s/he'll have some "homework" to do with the meditations and research.

I would suggest that your first session with the person consist of the first reading and guiding hir through the first meditation. You can determine how many follow-up sessions are necessary depending on the results. Even if s/he find hir totem in the first session, a follow-up is strongly recommend to monitor how well the relationship is progressing. There's always the possibility that the wrong connection got made, but only time will tell.

Non-Divinatory Uses

Just as the tarot or runes aren't limited to divination, neither are totem cards. There are a number of magical rites that they may be incorporated into. I'll discuss a few suggestions, but as always you are limited only by your imagination.

I mentioned earlier that I had a deck that I used specifically for evocation. You can use the cards I've described for the same purpose. If you want to work with a specific totem, draw out the relevant continent, phylum, and habitat deck (and any other appropriate cards). Lay them on your altar and use them as a focus when calling the totem to come and join you. The totem may also use them as a focus; for example, if you evoke multiple totems, and offer each one a candle, sigil, or other object to charge individually, you can place the items on the appropriate totem's cards for the duration of the ritual. If you have more than one totem that you're working with that are in the same phylum, for example, you may arrange the cards so that they're "sharing" the candle/etc. Or, if they happen to share all cards, simply place all items on the cards.

If you're not sure which totem to work with, but you have a specific issue in mind that you'd like to deal with, figure out which type of habitat best represents that issue to you. For example, if you're in a financial dry spot, you might feel as if you're stuck in a desert, in a way, and need help utilizing the limited resources you have. Journey using a guided meditation to find an appropriate totem, and go from there.

Paper cards aren't quite as impressive as skins and bones, but they can still be useful in invocation, especially if you don't have much money or are opposed to working with animal parts. Again, you can lay the cards out on your altar, or you may even carry them with you in a shapeshifting dance. One ritual I did involved giving Badger an offering of sushi as thanks for helping me to gain employment, allowing him to "eat" the sushi through invocation into me.

Whenever I need help finding a new job, I ask Badger for help. He's resourceful, Earthy, and persistent—and he seems to like helping me with such things. When my husband and I first moved to Portland, he had a job, but I didn't. So I asked him to help on the magical end while I continued talking to headhunters and sending out resumes. Sure enough, less than a month after we arrived, I had a job that paid well and utilized my skills, just as I had wanted. In return, I gave Badger sushi, which is an offering he seems to enjoy quite a bit.

I went to a sushi restaurant near my home by myself; I wanted to dedicate the meal to Badger rather than socializing with Taylor or some of our friends. When I got to my table, I laid out a specific selection of cards:

Tertiary, since that was the role Badger took; Mammal; North America; and Plains, Underground, and Mixed, to signify his favored habitats. As I laid out each card I felt the energy of what it meant. Tertiary reminded me of the initial job ritual; Mammal made me think of warm fur; North America sent a tendril of energy down into the Earth beneath me; and with the habitat cards, I saw myself briefly hurrying through a tunnel and out onto a grassy plain.

When the plate of sushi arrived, I invited Badger to experience eating it with me. I could feel him in my head, so to speak, in a very light invocation. He seemed to take great joy in temporarily experiencing a different body. He/I noticed little things that I normally don't pay attention to, like the way my tongue feels against the sides of my teeth, and the way that good miso soup tastes just *so*. He liked the fish portion a lot better than the rice, didn't particularly like soy sauce, and was puzzled by the wasabi. He declared himself satisfied after he got the piece of shrimp off the nigiri-ebi all to himself. (Considering that's my favorite kind of sushi, I do consider it a sacrifice!)

Because of the continent and habitat cards, you can use the deck to help you find totems for the purpose of learning more about a particular regional magical tradition or other cultural components. Say you wanted to learn more about Australian aboriginal traditions. In addition to reading about them, and maybe trying to find someone trained in them (or who has at least studied them), you might talk to Kangaroo or Bandicoot or any of a number of other Australian animals as a way of getting an additional perspective on the traditions in question. Just understand that anything you learn from the totem that doesn't match up with traditional practices is UPG, and may not necessarily be agreed with by other practitioners of that system. It doesn't, of course, make it invalid for you; however, if Wombat happens to tell you that you need to buy him a crystal skull and paint some Celtic knotwork on it, you need to also understand that this goes way outside the normal boundaries of traditional aboriginal practices, and so is probably limited only to you in this context.

You may be wondering why go to all this trouble when the reading alone won't give you a quick-and-easy answer. I still maintain that the guided journey is the best method of seeking primary and secondary totems. But for those of you who want to have the tangible tools in your hands, feel free to make use of what I've described here. Yes, it's a little more complicated than one card = one animal, but the global ecosystem is a lot more complicated than the average totem deck. This opens up the odds a bit more for animals besides the BINABM who, due to cultural and geographic conditioning, will probably still have greater presence in the subconscious minds of most animal magicians.

Totem card decks can be an incredibly versatile tool if used creatively instead of within the usual limitations. By allowing yourself the possibility of working with any species on the planet, instead of a few dozen BINABM, you expand your potential experiences quite a bit!

Journaling Exercises

Create your own totemism deck. As you work with it, make sure you record your results as you go along. You're going to be drawing on a lot of information, and you may as well add it to your own totem animal dictionary along the way. It's guaranteed to be more accurate for you as an individual than anything anyone else could write for you.

What you and the various totems discuss is entirely personal. However, here are some ideas for a journal entry:

Significator:
Continent:
Habitat:
Phylum:
Species:
Purpose: (i.e., *if there is a specific purpose for the reading*)
Date of first layout/meditation (*you can add the dates of subsequent layouts and meditations if you wish*):
Rituals: (*record details and results of any rituals you may have performed with the totem, to include evocations using the cards*)
Notes (*use this to compile information on the messages the totem has for you, as well as any other qualities it discusses, and any other pertinent information, including natural history which often is the basis for totemic qualities*):

Chapter Five: Everyday Totemic Work

Continued Meditation and Communication

While I offered a selection of potential wells of source material in chapter two that I think you should consider, I'm a fan of regularly "touching base" with the totems. As a part of my personal spiritual work, I have been meditating with the totems on a daily basis. For me, this often involves talking to Wolf, my primary totem, who acts as a sort of envoy for the rest of them when working with me. If another one has something specific to convey, though, s/he'll show up and chat.

I find that having that regular connection does make me feel more content in my relationships with the totems. It also lets them know that I'm listening—it's not just a time for me to talk their ears off. If they have a request to make of me, meditation gives them a chance to get through to me with less effort. It's also a good way to ask a totem whether s/he wants to help me with a particular practice before I go through with it. And if I think a totem may be trying to get a hold of me, meditation is the perfect way to contact hir and ask whether s/he is indeed tapping my shoulder, or if I was mistaken.

The other nice thing about the daily meditation is that it's a break from all the crazy goings-on of everyday mundane life. My job isn't exactly the most relaxing thing in the world, and on top of it there are always concerns with writing, editing and other such freelance pursuits. In short—I'm a busy person! While I don't support spirituality as escapism, daily meditation gives me a chance to breathe, and acts as a reminder that there's more to life than just the rat race (no offense to Rat, of course).

For the purposes of creating your totem dictionary, meditation is a chance to get to learn more about the totems you're building relationships with. You can ask what various lessons the totem has for you, what offerings s/he likes, and anything else s/he deems important. If you have a vision, dream or sighting involving an animal that seems important, or out of place, or otherwise notable, this is a good time for you to contact the corresponding totem to see if there was a message involved. If you're going to contact a totem for the first time, especially for the purposes of magical work, it's better to do so in meditation than through a full evocation ritual. Otherwise it's like walking up to a complete stranger and saying "Hi, will you help me find a job?" The totem in question may not even be able to help you with that particular situation. For example, I used to ask Beaver and Otter for help with finding a job. I did so because I thought Beaver was a hard worker, and Otter could remind me to not push myself too hard in my workaholic tendencies. While they did what they could, when I later did a meditation to allow whatever totem was best suited for job hunting to appear, I ended up with Badger, and subsequently we got great results.

Finally, meditation is a great way to imprint and work with some of the lessons that a totem has to teach us. A good example is my relationship with Bear. She is my healing totem, and part of her work with me involves helping me get over a bad tendency towards workaholicism, which can have a lot of negative effects psychologically and physically. One thing she'll do during meditation is talk me through the reasons why I may be pushing myself too hard. She'll ask me questions about what's motivating me and how it's affecting me. Then we may come up with some better solutions and behaviors. What I learn from these meditations later translates into changed decisions on my part on a daily basis. The meditation gives me the time and space to really focus on the issues at hand without being distracted by everyday life.

Alternative Forms of Meditation

I'm not going to rehash introductory meditation for the billionth time here; there are numerous 101 texts that have already covered that admirably. However, I'd like to offer a few alternatives for people who may have trouble with visualization, no matter how hard they may try. Granted, sight is an incredibly important sense, as is hearing; however, touch is downplayed quite a bit (particularly in regards to one's environment), and smell and taste are almost ignored except at mealtimes. But this doesn't mean that everyone is equally sight-oriented, especially when it comes to communication. Meditation is a form of communication, and so I'm offering some alternatives for folks who may work with other senses more strongly in meditative communication.

Conversation

Conversation is my favorite form of meditation. It's as simple as it sounds—get into a light trance, and have a chat with the totem or other entity I'm working with. I generally don't need to actually see who I'm talking to, though I usually do concentrate on visuals if it's the first time working with an entity, or if there's a specific reason for doing so otherwise. When it comes to communication I'm very hearing-oriented, which means that the things that stick with me the most from meditation (and which are easiest for me to pick up on) are the ones I "hear". However, conversation may involve several senses:

Hearing: This is the obvious one. It's not your physical hearing, of course, but the ability to pick up "sounds" on nonphysical planes of reality. I recognize the different "voices" of each deity, totem and other spirits I work with, and I know when I run into someone new.

Touch: Again, this isn't physical touch. I "feel" when an entity "touches" me in meditation; while the visual, for example, of Equus carrying me through the cave and into the world of the Paleolithic totems, was sometimes spotty, the (nonphysical) sensation of riding the horse (as well as the sound of the hoofbeats and Equus' voice, incidentally) was much stronger for me.

Sight: This is actually not necessary for conversation. Just as a physically blind person can quickly tell the difference between people through sound and touch (and in some cases, smell), a person meditating without good visuals can still determine who they're working with relatively quickly. Still, if you can see what you're doing, even sporadically, it can help with quicker identification, especially if the totem you're working with doesn't tell you hir exact species (for example, working with Gazelle but only getting the general sense of "antelope", via touch, because of the way the legs and horns are formed).

Shapeshifting[70]

Some people may be utterly and completely shocked that I'm advocating using shapeshifting ritual as a way of making first contact with a totem. Shapeshifting is generally considered to be an advanced technique, not to be taken on by beginners. However, shapeshifting in quiet, sit- or lie-down meditation is (generally speaking, in my experience) much less intense than doing shapeshifting through dance. This also doesn't involve full-on invocation or trance possession; rather, it's a method of mirroring the energy of the totem encountered without merging with the entity hirself. It's good for use in determining your totem, though it can also be used to solidify a bond with a totem, and may even be used in conjunction with the conversation method above.

The process isn't too difficult. Get into a light trance, and journey into the Otherworld however you see fit, whether you feel yourself diving into a tunnel, or actually see your surrounding as you travel (depending on how good you are at visualization). Then invite your totem to come join

---

[70] Chapter seven has more information on magical shapeshifting; I included this here since it makes a convenient alternative to visual-only meditation.

you. If you sense that the totem has arrived and cannot see hir, ask hir to give you a bit of hir energy. Take that energy and absorb it into yourself; wrap it around you like a blanket.

Once you have a good hold on that energy, allow it to meld with your (nonphysical) body. Let it change your form into that of the animal. Here's how you might try using your various senses to figure out the identity of your totem (if s/he's not willing to tell you directly, or if you're having trouble maintaining a good conversation for some reason):

Hearing: Try making a noise as the animal. What sound comes out? Move around; do your footsteps (or other form of locomotion) make any particular sound?

Touch: How does your body feel? Is it quadrepedal, bipedal, or have more than four limbs? Does it feel heavier than your physical body, or lighter? Do you have antlers, wings, fins, or other such parts? Do you have fur, feathers, scales, or smooth skin? How do you move around?

Smell/Taste: As humans, we have pretty crappy senses of smell, compared to most animals (I think we're really missing out, honestly.). However, I've found that, to me, energy translates over as "taste", which is connected to "smell" (Energy, in this case, is the energy that surrounds each individual being and has a distinctive resonance; it has been tied to the biophotonic energy in DNA[71].). See if you can taste/smell the animal's energy, and if it gives you any impressions; I usually get either a brief mental picture or a name. Another thing you might try is accessing the sense-memory of what the totem's species typically eats. Some animals, such as deer, have pretty broad tastes, though others, like koala bears, are very specific in diet. It may not be the only thing that informs you, but it can be helpful in some cases.

If you're concerned about getting stuck or losing control, one thing I work into every meditation is an "escape hatch"—if I need to get out of a situation quickly and back into my body, I simply look down at the ground beneath my (nonphysical) feet. There will be the hole leading back into the tunnel I came through (I like the cave/tunnel method of meditation/journeying) and all I have to do is drop down (Sort of like the magical version of the ACME portable hole!). I've never had a totem try to forcefully possess me, and since all you're doing is carrying a piece of

---

[71] Ellwood 2007

the totem's energy, a simple banishing ritual once you're done will help break the connection.

The only thing to keep in mind is the exchange of energy, where you and the totem give each other a piece of your own energy during the first invocation. While I've found totems to be generally respectful of boundaries and our personal territories, there's always the possibility that you or the totem may find the relationship to no longer be healthy. In this case, it's best to do a formal ritual in which you return the energy to each other. If for whatever reason the totem doesn't show up, send the energy back to hir, wherever s/he may be.

Walking Meditation

I get bored sitting around quietly. I've always been that way; I was that kid in school who was always fidgeting in my seat, waiting for recess and glancing at the clock every thirty seconds. I've gotten better at it as I've gotten older, but I still am a big fan of meditation involving movement. One of the easiest forms of this is walking meditation.

I walk a lot. I usually get at least two to three miles in a day just as a matter of course. It's very easy for me to go into a light trance while walking; the rhythm is just right for lulling me into trance. Granted, I don't go too deeply in, especially if I'm walking near or across busy roads. But I find that I can flow in and out of trance easily as needed.

The easiest way to start with this is to go to a place you're already familiar with that has low traffic and is generally free of other major distractions. Get into a fairly quick pace; two to three miles an hour is a good speed, though be aware of your own physical limitations. Then let your thoughts flow freely.

I find that after a few minutes I start to relax and "zone out". I don't really concentrate too much on one train of thought, instead letting myself daydream idly while my mind relaxes. I make sure that I breathe deeply and evenly, breathing from the diaphragm instead of high in my chest. My goal is to let my mind clear out the idle thoughts, letting them go as I walk along.

Once I hit that point, I start meditating. This usually takes the form of verbal conversation in my mind, as visualization would quickly become dangerous, and speaking out loud with the totem might get me some really strange reactions from passerby. It usually works better with totems that I have a stronger relationship with, since I can't concentrate as deeply as I would sitting at home with no cars speeding by and people making noise all around me. The walking meditations also seem to have a bit of a stream of consciousness quality to them; my focus is more free-flowing than in other types of meditation, and we can jump from topic to topic more easily. And I find that it's easier for me to "come down" from the meditation while walking; if I slow my pace, it helps to bring me back to my everyday state of consciousness.

These are just a couple of suggestions of non-visually-centered meditations. Feel free to experiment with them, or come up with other alternatives. Additionally, I would like to recommend (again) *The Personal Totem Pole* by Eligio Stephen Gallegos, which I mentioned in chapter one. I love the useful combination of psychotherapy, chakras, and totemism wrapped in meditation. While it doesn't have exercises laid out (it's meant to be a case study for therapists) it's very easy to figure out exactly what the author did in each case. You can use the basic meditation format in appendix A of *Fang and Fur*, or appendix B of this book, to find the totem of each chakra, as well as talk to the totems in subsequent work.

A Few Basic Totemic Rituals

While the rest of this book deals largely with a variety of ritual forms that may be used with totems, I'd like to offer a few introductory ideas to get you started. One of the simplest rituals I like to do involves taking a walk in a park or, if I have the time and the weather permits, going for a hike further out in the wilderness. Rituals don't necessarily have to be particularly formal. To me, the natural world is the most sacred place I could possibly be, so taking time to connect with it in any way is always a special occasion. Small things in my everyday life, such as taking kitchen scraps out to the compost bin, or working in a garden, are sacred rituals in small ways. However, for special occasions, I like to be a bit more formal about my walks and hikes.

As I walk/hike, I take particular notice of the environment around me. What plants and animals do I see? What is the weather doing? How do I feel, and how does my body respond to the stimuli? I invite the totems and other spirits to accompany me in this sacred procession through a natural cathedral. Then, when I stop to rest, I ask them to join me in meditation. I've also been known to invoke one or more totems while walking or hiking and allowing them to "wear my body" as I go along. I tend to keep this to a more mild form of shapeshifting, one in which the totem is more tagging along rather than taking control of my body. I allow hir to sense the wilderness through my senses, which also allows me to get a bit of hir perception temporarily. It's not so much a matter of my physical senses changing, as it is being more aware of them, particularly those that the totem hirself may find more important.

Depending on where I am and how private the area is, I may do a more formal ritual, with or without magic involved.

Speaking of magic, formal rituals are a great time to work magic, either for yourself or on the behalf of others (including totems and their physical counterparts). The type of magic can vary according to your preferences. I've used everything from candle magic to sigil casting with totems. First I prepare the ritual area, get the various implements I need (a candle and something to carve it with, a piece of paper and pen or colored pencils, etc.), and purify the area if I feel it's necessary (I like sage smudges). Then I will call on whatever totems I would like to help me with the magic, including the directional/elemental totems (who I'll talk more about in a bit). Once they've arrived, I ask them for help with the magic. If I'm creating something, such as a charged, carved candle or a sigil, I'll hold the finished product up once I'm done and ask the totems to add whatever energy they're willing to contribute to it. Sometimes I may dance or otherwise build up some of my own energy to add in along with the energy I put in through the creation process. Then I'll complete the spell or sigil, confident that it's packed with combined energy from me and the totems. After that, I'll make whatever offerings are appropriate (see chapter nine for more information on offerings, including protocol on food offerings) and send the totems off with my thanks.

Another fun ritual activity involves essentially throwing a party in honor of the totems. Cook up a big feast with food the totems like, drum for them if you like, and otherwise create a celebratory atmosphere. Invite them to join you, and tell them why you appreciate them. You can eat the food yourself, though let them know that the energy that went into it is dedicated to them. You might even put out plates for them with food on it, and then put each one away as leftovers. When you eat the food later, think of the totem that each plate is dedicated to. You can even evoke that particular totem during that meal for a more personal rite. Be particularly aware of the food totems involved if you're not having a purely vegan meal. It would be rude to serve roasted chicken in honor of Fox, but ignore Chicken herself.

If you have a group of people that you like to work with, you can hold a communal celebration on honor of all the totems you work with. You can hike together, hold a feast, and even work magic for a common cause. Just be sure to come to an agreement on what the purpose of the ritual will be, and how things will proceed beforehand. Also, I have heard people show some concern about inviting totems of various species into the same place at the same time, worried that perhaps Wolf will chase after Rabbit. In my experience, there's no danger here. Totems may be archetypal animals, but they don't need to eat each other to survive.

Hunting is triggered by hunger; a wolf pack that is not hungry can walk right past a herd of elk or deer without causing any alarm among the prey animals. It is only when certain behaviors and signals are exhibited that the deer will take notice and prepare to run.

Totemic Dreams

I'm not a big fan of trying to determine what your totem is using your dreams. This is because I see dreams as more symbolic, abstract experiences that largely deal with your own subconscious mind. Therefore, if I find myself dreaming of anteaters repeatedly, I'm not going to assume Anteater is my new totem. Instead, I'm going to look at the anteaters in the context of the dreams I had. Here are a few contextual points to keep in mind:

--What was the emotional theme of the dream? Fear? Joy? Anger?
--How much interaction did you have with the animal? Did s/he make contact with you, or avoid you? Was s/he hostile, friendly or neutral?
--Did the animal communicate with you at all?
--How did encountering the animal make you feel?

Now, take the answers from the above questions and meditate on them as they relate to your everyday life. Is there a situation that gives you similar feelings and experiences in your waking life? If so, what could the animal symbolize? For example, while I think snakes are wonderful beings, when I'm stressed and feeling like I don't have any way out of a situation, I dream about being cornered in a room of poisonous snakes. I try to jump over them, but they bite me as I pass by them. This has less to do with Snake, and more to do with what the snake symbolize in the specific context of my dream.

I have, on occasion, had what I call Big Dreams, ones that I know are more than just my own subconscious mind communicating and processing. In these dreams, there's not a single doubt in my mind that a totem (or other spiritual entity) came and visited me in my dream. In that case I will do a meditation when I'm awake to verify the encounter and clarify anything that needs to be discussed. I can't really put my finger on any single quality that determines whether a dream is a Big Dream or not; the best I can tell you is that I know it when I experience it.

It is useful to keep a dream journal. Record any dream you remember, even if it seems nonsensical. Even if you don't end up with any Big Dreams, you may find psychological patterns and issues that you can ask various totems for help with. Additionally, some people are really good at dreamwalking, being able to journey while dreaming. Journaling can help build your focus while dreaming enough to where you may eventually may be able to dreamwalk, and therefore go to visit totems and other entities in your dreams.

I am, however, even less of a fan of dream dictionaries than I am of totem dictionaries (which should come as no surprise). Dreams are highly dependent on context—not just the culture you're a part of, but your own thoughts, feelings and experiences. A cut and paste dictionary that lists routine symbolism for various things you may see or encounter in your dreams will only give you a pale shade of the truth—and may actually mislead you. Say, for example, you dream of a cat. You read in a dream dictionary that cats mean home, so you start looking down that path. After trying hard to find connections between your dream and your home, you may either get an incomplete idea of what the meaning was, an inaccurate one, or none at all. However, if you consider what cats mean to you, personally, you have a much better idea of understanding what your subconscious mind (and the spirit world) may be trying to tell you. Yes, I am a big fan of Jung. However, dream dictionaries are nowhere near being a substitute for years of studying psychology, dream analysis, and other such pursuits.

Cyclical Work

One thing you'll want to keep in mind is how often you want to interact with the totems. Daily meditation is one form of cyclical spiritual/magical work. It's far from the only one, though.

Most neopagan religions have a series of holidays throughout the year. For Wiccans and some other neopagans, the eight Sabbats and thirteen Esbats are a good way of keeping tabs on the solar and lunar cycles of the year. I personally never really felt all that connected to the mythology surrounding these cycles, but that's just me personally.

However, I do find that the solstices, equinoxes, and full and dark moon phases are good times for me to review different aspects of my spirituality. The solstices and equinoxes are times for me to check in with the natural environment to see what has changed in the past three months, and be more aware of what's going on with the animal life there. I have dedicated the new moon to working with the spirits of the skins and bones in my ritual room, and the full moon to working with the totems. This means that at least twice a month I set aside time for ritual work, journeying, and other practices besides my daily meditation. It's often enough to keep me in touch with the Powers That Be, but not so often that I feel overwhelmed.

In my experience, having a regular schedule of magical and spiritual work helps to keep me more focused on my path. It's all too easy to let the mundane worries in life overtake our spiritual work, to the point where we may realize one day that it's been months since we really did anything. Take the time to find a schedule that works best for you, and you may very well find that you begin to look forward to those special days throughout the year. Granted, this doesn't mean that you can't do other rituals and meditations and such on other days; however, if you're like me and have a busy life, having a schedule in place helps to keep me from getting eaten by mundane concerns.

First, you need to honestly assess how much time you have. If you're too busy to do a full three-hour ritual every single day, as well as meditating before every meal, and at least one shapeshift before bedtime, then don't feel guilty. A successful magician is one who can blend magic into everyday life, and function in both the mundane and spiritual spheres. Look at your normal schedule. Where do you have the most free time? Do you have an hour to yourself at lunch, where you can go find a quiet place to sit and meditate? Can you set aside thirty to sixty minutes in the evening a few nights a week? What about weekends?

Now, look at the times that may be particularly special to you. The solar and lunar cycles are important to me because they offer a natural calendar for me to work by, and their timing works well with my own schedule. I use the solstices and equinoxes as times to check in with them about my spiritual progress, as well as make goals for the coming quarter-year. Are there specific days throughout the year that are special to you, such as the anniversary of successfully meeting a particular totem? Additionally, is there a specific time of day that you find more appropriate?

Ask the totems, too. They may have their own input on when would be a good time to work with them. I came about my current schedule through discussing with my totems what would work best for all of us. They're somewhat flexible; if the full moon falls on a Wednesday, for example, I may be too tired that night to really do much in the way of magic. However, the following Saturday when I'm better-rested and have more time to work with may be better for me, and the totems tend to be perfectly fine with that.

Don't overwhelm yourself. Try adding in one set of rituals/practices at a time. You might start with doing things on the equinoxes and solstices, and maybe the full and/or new moon. Once you're comfortable with that, then perhaps add in something more frequent, like meditating three times a week for at least fifteen to twenty minutes at a time. If you find something you've been trying for a while just isn't working out, don' feel bad about changing things around. However, if you've only given it a week, chances are you haven't really taken enough time to give it a fair chance.

You may also find that a particular totem asks for a ritual on a specific day each month or year, or otherwise set aside special time just for hir. Do your best to accommodate hir, but again, don't take on more than you can reasonably handle.

Is Daily Practice Necessary?

While some people are very much "When and as I need it" about magic, others prefer more of a routine. I spent the first decade and change of my practice being primarily the former. However, as I've gotten older and more settled (though never domesticated or tamed) I've felt more of a draw towards the concept of standardizing and formalizing my practice. I don't want an organized religion, but now that I've had some time to explore the world of magic, I'm ready to set my roots down deeper in the practices and beliefs that have the most meaning for me.

For some people, daily practice is a must. Routine can be quite comforting to some people, and adds a certain amount of stability to their lives. To be quite honest, I've never been very good at doing things consistently on a daily basis beyond sleeping, eating, bathing, and checking my email (and even that last one has become less important as I've gotten sick of the internet). I've tried Yoga, Taoist breathing, and all sorts of other such things. About the only practice that's stuck (until recently) are the daily prayers I do, usually in the evening as I'm relaxing in bed, and again in the morning. There's no problem with the systems I've tried; I'm simply not the kind of person who focuses well on doing the same exact thing day after day.

That doesn't mean, of course, that I'm condemned to flightiness forever more. I may not always be inspired to sit down and breathe in a particular way for half an hour a day, though I can appreciate the reasons for doing so. But I can find other ways to work my spirituality into my everyday life. Sometimes it's the small things that matter most. I frequently, in the warmer months, will pick up worms that are in danger of baking on the sidewalk once the sun comes out after rain, and deposit them in a nice patch of cool mud. I do the same for helping turtles across the road. And I suppose you could say I'm rather "religious" about recycling and using canvas bags for groceries, among other small favors to the environment. When I get frustrated with my commute by bus and train, which may take a bit longer than driving in the car (some days, depending on traffic, the commute is actually faster) I remind myself that not only am I reducing the amount of pollution I create, but that I'm also saving myself serious gas money (I'm allowed to be a little self-serving, aren't I? Though now all the gas stations in Oregon require attendants to pump your gas, so that sort of limits how self-serving I can be…)!

These seemingly small acts do connect me more to my spirituality. They may not always directly affect animals and other denizens of the wild, but the effect is there nonetheless. My awareness of my impact is similar to my awareness of how magic is a constant reality, and rituals serve to help tap into it as needed. Even the most seemingly mundane act can be sacred and magical with the right intent behind it.

However, small everyday acts aside, you may feel (as I do) the need to also have more formalized expressions of belief/magic. What you do, how you do it, and when, is all entirely up to you. One of the reasons I liked being introduced to totemism way back when via Ted Andrews' *Animal-Speak* was that the author included a number of ritual practices that were quite effective for strengthening the bond between the reader and hir totem(s). While I don't use those rituals myself, they were good inspiration early on.

These days, I'm in the process of constructing my own (neo)shamanic practice, therioshamanism[72]. Through it I've begun to construct a personalized cosmology, along with a set of regular rituals and practices that have meaning for me, as well as for the totems and other entities I work with. Not only has it been spiritually fulfilling, but it has added a certain amount of discipline to my practice that I've never had before. It's still largely based on my experiences and teachings from the spirits, but I also supplement with a lot of reading on shamanism in general, as well as talking shop with other folks on similar paths. It works a lot better for me than trying to stuff myself into someone else's spiritual parameters—but this is what works for me.

What you choose to practice on a regular basis is entirely up to you. You may find that meditating with a different totem each day, perhaps using the totem deck described earlier, is a good exercise for you. Or perhaps you'd like to make regular offerings to choice totems on an altar, or periodically send money to a nonprofit organization that helps animals in honor of a totem. There's also the option of setting aside time each day, week, or other time period that works for you, and allowing yourself to use that time with whatever ritual seems appropriate.

One thing I find useful is looking at my life on a regular basis and seeing what areas need work, then working magic (along with mundane efforts) to improve my situation. There's almost always something that

---

[72] See Appendix E for more information.

could be better, and since I tend to do most of my ritual magic on the weekends when I have more time to work with, there's enough time during the week for things to happen that need attention. Additionally, it's always a good practice to ask your totems what they need help with; after all, it's not all about you (much as you may think so!).

Don't feel horribly guilty, though, if you just can't bring yourself to work ritual magic on a daily basis. Each person is different, and while it's quite possible to reprogram yourself, if your attempts are making you decidedly unhappy and it's not hurting you to be sporadic, then don't worry about it. Proceed at your own pace, and if later on down the line you feel a desire to be more formal about things, then is the time to start making changes in that direction. Otherwise you're just wasting your time and making yourself miserable in the process. There may come a time, later on, when you're more focused, and you'll probably discover that your growth and experience increase accordingly; daily practice does lead to accelerated development, and the person who practices daily almost always advances quicker than the one who does a ritual ever now and then. Just remember to work from where you are, not from where you wish you could be.

Long-Term Commitments

If you find you have totems that you'll be working with on a long-term or even permanent basis, there are things you can do to honor those relationships and give them a particularly special place in your life.

Your primary totem(s) is/are generally with you for life. Secondary totems, the ones who come to you to teach you something specific, may or may not be there for a while, depending on what they have to teach you. However, one particular set of long-term totems I'm fond of are my directional/elemental totems. These are the totems who embody the four cardinal directions and the qualities I associate with them. Wolf is North, Hawk is East, and Bear is West. South has been occupied by various animals over the years (not surprising, since South is Fire, and therefore change) but currently Fox is the animal of that direction.

Most pagans have a collection of shiny objects related to their beliefs. This may be anything from a collection of knives and swords, to pictures of deities and spirits, to a variety of sacred jewelry. These objects can easily be turned into altars and shrines, physical havens for various beings in the home and elsewhere. The altar serves as a focal point for your work with whoever it's dedicated to, as well as offers a sacred space set aside just for hir/them. This actually makes it easier for the totem to interact with this reality, a specific place for hir to inhabit.

I won't go into detail about how you should or shouldn't set up your altar. Altars are as personal as the people who create them. If you would like a good resource on ideas for altar setup, including layout and sacred objects, I highly recommend *Your Altar: Creating a Sacred Space for Prayer & Meditation* by Sandra Kynes (Llewellyn, 2007).

My personal altar has always been arranged by the four cardinal directions. Each of the directional/elemental totems has a statue of hir species on the altar in the appropriate corner. Other statues representing various other totems and spirits in my personal microcosm adorn the rest of the altar. It is essentially a map of my personal cosmology, and it's where I do the bulk of my ritual work and meditations. On the walls surrounding the altar, I have a variety of animal skulls, each inhabited by an animal spirit. There are also the skins I dance in nearby, and a box with my ritual tools in it. While I don't actually put much on the altar during rituals, other than perhaps a burning candle or an offering, it does serve as a concrete reminder of how I understand the world to be. I have changed it around over the years as my understanding has evolved, but the four directional totems have always been there.

Having an altar offers both you and the totems a central meeting place. The more you do with it, the more the power accumulates around it. If you can keep it up on at least a semi-permanent basis, so much the better; I find that constantly disassembling and reassembling my altar disrupts the energy around it if done too often.

You may also find that individual totems ask for their own private shrines. Shrines may be small altars on shelves or windowsills. They can also be as simple as a drawing or other piece of artwork depicting the totem. These may be scattered around your home; the totems may or may not ask for specific places for their shrines. They generally prefer that if you're working with them alone, that you use their shrines as a focal point rather than the main altar. You can also leave offerings for them at their respective shrines.

There's nothing wrong with portable shrines. Obviously you'll have to keep it simple; however, something as simple as a piece of jewelry dedicated to a particular totem will work. Some people like to carry around a small stone fetish of their totem. Others like something a little more elaborate. The Pocket Shrine community at Livejournal features individual artists who create small shrines out of Altoid tins and other such things[73].

I'll go more into totemic artwork in chapter nine. However, one form of artwork that may be overlooked for devotional purposes is the

---

[73] Located at http://community.livejournal.com/pocketshrines/.

tattoo. These pieces of permanent skin art have a lot of personal energy invested into them, and may even be applied in a ritual setting. It's not at all uncommon for people to get tattoos of things that they consider spiritual, though oftentimes this is done for aesthetic rather than deliberate magical purposes. Your tattoo, though, can be a shrine in and of itself.

If you haven't gotten the tattoo yet, the process of making it into a shrine is a lot easier. You can work that intent into the design, and meditate on it while getting inked. When you're done, you can then invite the totem to make hir home in the ink, a sacred sharing of your body with your permission. Even if the tattoo is already in place, you can still do a ceremony to dedicate it and open it up to the totem as a dwelling-place. I'll leave the details up to you; however, I do want to warn you that you need to be very sure that this is a totem that you will be working with for the long run, since the tattoo is permanent. In my own case, while not every tattoo I have is a shrine, each one has marked a rite of passage. Even if the period of life that a specific tattoo may come to an end, I still keep the artwork as a reminder of where I've been.

It's a good idea to do some regular work with more long-term totems. This includes not just meditations and magic and other formalities, but sometimes just a "social visit". The aforementioned parties, hikes and other fun activities are good ideas. Additionally, I'm fond of shapeshifting through invocation as a way of allowing Wolf and other totems some more one-on-one time with me. Not all acts of magic have to have a practical purpose beyond making connections.

Journaling Exercises:

1. If you haven't meditated much, try several different methods of meditation and see which ones work best for you and the totems. If you are experienced, compare your usual method(s) with something you may have not considered before. What works best? Are there better types of meditation depending on what you're meditating on, or who you're communicating with?

2. Try a couple of the basic ritual formats I suggested. Then create a few of your own. Keep track of what types of ritual work best for you, and which ones each totem you work with prefers.

3. Start keeping a dream journal. Look for consistent patterns in your dreams, not necessarily just the ones that involve animals. Then seek a totem to help you with these patterns.

4. Work out a schedule for working with your totems. What can you do daily, weekly, monthly and yearly? What is feasible for

you now, and what could you work in later? What days are important to you, and which ones are important to your totems?
5. Talk with your totems about altar and shrine setups. Do they have any special requests? Is there anything, aesthetic or otherwise, that you may want to change about your current setup?

Sample Journal Entries:

For meditation:

Date:
Type of meditation: (sitting quietly, guided visualization, walking meditation, etc.)
Totem(s) communicated with:
Messages received and other notes:

For rituals:

Date:
Type of ritual:
Totem(s) communicated with:
Purpose of ritual:
Outcome:

For dreams:

Date:
Approximate time of dream: (nighttime, daytime nap, etc.)
Detailed recounting of dream: (include observations on recurring themes)
Animals in dream (if any):
How the dream made you feel:
Relationship of dream to waking life:
Other impressions:

Chapter Six: Animal Totems
and Chemognosis

DISCLAIMER: This chapter describes the theoretical human ingestion of substances which may be deemed illegal in certain parts of the world. Neither the author nor the publishers of this book are responsible for any actions taken by readers of this chapter. It is the readers' responsibility to know local legalities as well as the potential health risks associated with ingesting any mind-altering substance, to include supposedly "safe" legal drugs such as caffeine, alcohol and nicotine.

Altered states of consciousness are central to magical practice. Magic occurs most successfully when our focus is brought to a fine point aimed at making the magic happen, while completely ignoring distractions. This focus may be achieved through any number of methods ranging from hours of dancing, to complete sensory deprivation. In that moment, nothing else matters except for the magic, and it is this single-pointed focus that is so crucial to magic working.

When it comes to totemism and related forms of animal magic, certain methods are more common than others. Shapeshifting dance is probably one of the better-known ones, and it often finds its way into books on neopagan totemism. Guided meditations and shamanic journeys, too, are quite popular among modern totemists and animal magicians, and are exceptionally versatile as they may completely transcend physical limitations.

However, as these have been covered quite thoroughly, both in my writings and in others', I wanted to explore something a bit different: the use of entheogens (drugs used in a ritual context) in connection with animal totems. Drugs in shamanism and other forms of magical practice are quite controversial these days, but in many (though not all) indigenous magical systems they've played a part. Most of the negative attitudes towards drugs in magic, at least in the U.S., stem from the "War on Drugs" that political figures have been waging for years in the hopes of gaining a few extra votes around election time. While it's true that certain substances such as heroin and crystal meth can be exceptionally addictive and destructive, it's exceptionally short-sighted to throw hallucinogens such as LSD and psilocybin into the same boat—never mind legal drugs such as alcohol, caffeine and nicotine.

So I present this chapter in the spirit of balance. The ideas may be used with any substance that you choose to partake in, though the effectiveness of the magic will vary according to the effects the drug has on your system, and the dosage you use. You are not at all required to utilize the material in this chapter; as with anything, your personal boundaries take precedence. However, since there are people who are interested in chemognosis (magic through drugs, legal and/or not), and since I have found certain substances useful in totemic work, I decided to add this chapter in as an additional set of resources in working with totems. As I mentioned, shapeshifting dance and guided meditations have been thoroughly explored elsewhere; here, I present something a bit different for you to utilize if you wish.

Entheogens and Magic

People have been getting high, stoned, buzzed, and drunk on various substances for millennia. However, this hasn't always been for recreational purposes. Prehistoric burials included offerings of marijuana, and two-thousand-plus-year-old art from Mexico depicts psilocybin mushrooms with deities emerging from them. Cults surrounding dying/rising gods in Imperial Rome involved the use of henbane, mandrake, and thorn apple, all of which were apparently used for hallucinogenic as well as aphrodisiac purposes[74].

Just as with any altered state of consciousness, those caused by entheogens are useful to the magician who takes the time to learn to use them properly, instead of jumping in with the intent of getting "fucked up". It may take a little practice to learn how to be in a state where you may not have 100% control in a situation (such as drinking too much alcohol and losing motor functions), but it is possible to control doses and environments (external and internal) to minimize bad trips.

I'm not going to tell you how to do entheogens. Mostly it's because my experience is incredibly limited. I have chosen to stick to legal drugs in this book for personal reasons, and also to allow options to readers who may be wary of illegal substances for whatever reason. This doesn't mean that you have to stick to what's legal if you choose otherwise. However, *you are responsible for your decisions*, not me.

I would recommend that you do your research before doing any experimentation if you haven't used a particular substance before. An excellent free resource is http://www.erowid.org which has an enormous amount of information on various controlled substances. This site has come highly recommended to me by pretty much everyone I've talked to who has experience with drug shamanism and chemognosis. It's a starting point, though, and you should further your research to other sources. This

---

[74] Wilson 2004

should include people who have responsibly used the substances—if they've used them for magical purposes, so much the better.

As you're researching, you'll want to find out what both the positive and negative effects of the drug are. What is the potential health hazards associated with it? Do you have any health issues that may be compounded by a particular substance? What is a safe dose for someone of your weight? What's the best way to dose yourself (smoking, ingestion, etc.)? Is the substance physically addictive (Anything can be psychologically addictive, even television.)? How about legalities? If it's illegal, what are the penalties for possession in case you get caught? Are there any safer alternatives that might be better for you?

Be aware that I am not a regular drug user, and so I have deliberately chosen things that are (for the most part) relatively mild, and also in small enough doses that I was not overwhelmed. Those of you who are more experienced with drug trips in general and have more control with more intense experiences may choose to work with substances that will give you more of an effect. However, even a small amount of a substance, not even enough to cause a significant shift in consciousness, may be sufficient for at least contacting the totem (or the spirit of the plant, if it's a plant-based drug). I chose to balance my doses to get some effect, but not so much as to lose all control.

Chemognosis in Animals

My interest in this topic was sparked by *Animals and Psychedelics: The Natural World and the Instinct to Alter Consciousness* by Giorgio Samorini, and it inspired some thoughts. The basic premise of the book (which is more of a long academic paper in bound and printed paperback format) is that non-human animals are known to consciously seek out plants that cause altered states of consciousness. A large portion is dedicated to specific examples of animals drugging themselves, to include elephants eating fermented fruit[75], lambs, rats, and other creatures feeding on cannabis seeds[76] and a short chapter dedicated to animals that intentionally ingest *Amanita muscaria* and other "special" mushrooms[77].

The conclusion that Samorini comes to is that drug use may very well be an aid to evolution. This is because the altered states of consciousness help to break up the ingrained psychological behavior patterns of the animals (including humans) who take them, which then

---

[75] Samorini 2002, p. 27-30
[76] Samorini 2002, p. 59-60
[77] Samorini 2002, p. 38-42

allows for a greater chance of adaptation in light of the more flexible worldview. The evidence to support this in nonhuman animals is scant, as most of what was presented was a collection of examples of animals purposely seeking out drugs.[78] However, because this is a rarely-studied field of interest, it may take time for the few researchers who do concentrate on this area to find a direct link between the ingestion of a particular plant, and a subsequent advance in behavior.

Still, the primary value of the book is that it demonstrates that the ingestion of drugs is a natural activity, and not limited to humans alone. The lack of control that is shown in addicted animals in numerous cases, however, mirrors the irresponsible use of drugs by some—not all—humans. This has led to legalities and prohibitionist attitudes that hamper the efforts of some modern shamans who wish to utilize the aid of mind-altering substances directly. But the attempts to completely destroy the practice of chemognosis—attaining altered states of consciousness through external substances for magical purposes—have been unsuccessful. Magicians of all types still use drugs, legal and illegal, natural and synthetic, for a variety of magical workings, experiments and journeys.

At least to a limited extent, drugs may be used even while taking legal and health issues into consideration. The idea of spirits within the plants themselves is fairly widespread among traditional cultures, and may still be encountered, though more rarely, in postindustrial societies today. In their book, *Plant Spirit Shamanism*, Ross Heaven and Howard G. Charing offer the reader a guided journey to be used for contacting the spirit of a particular plant[79]. And while certain drugs, such as marijuana, peyote, and psilocybin, are illegal in many areas where magic is commonly practiced, others like *salvia divinorum* may still be relatively easy—and legal—to obtain, depending on where you live.

Let me make something clear before I go on. I am not a drug shaman. I have very limited use with ingested drugs beyond those prescribed to me by health care professionals, and a very small amount of experimentation earlier in life. I do not even indulge in "legal" drugs such as alcohol and tobacco. These are personal choices, not moral standards that I expect my readers to adhere to. My experimentation was limited solely to what I needed to explore this topic, test my hypothesis, and complete this chapter. Your choices, however, are your own.

As I was reading Samorini's research, I began to consider the animals themselves that seemed to gravitate towards certain drugs. There

[78] Samorini 2002, p. 84-88
[79] Heaven and Charing 2006

are spirits associated with each plant, but what about the totemic versions of the animals that habitually indulge in them? Obviously, the reason that animals use certain drugs is accessibility—a goat can't log onto the internet and order a nice bag of Morning Glory seeds. Therefore reindeer intoxicate themselves on the fly agaric they have access to; Robins in California stuff themselves silly (literally) on holly berries[80].

One thing that I have learned through personal experience with totems as archetypal beings is that they absorb all the experience of their species, from human lore to the natural history of the physical animals themselves. Therefore, it stands to reason that the habits of intoxication found within certain species will be reflected in the corresponding totem.

As to accessing that knowledge, there are a couple of options. The first involves contacting the totem under the influence of the drug itself. Obviously this rather limits the possibilities for those who wish to remain within the realms of the law. Additionally, some of the plants mentioned, including holly berries, are quite toxic to human beings beyond the point of safe experimentation. Still, those who wish to try this method may employ several possibilities.

Elephant, Butterfly and Alcohol

Elephants are known to seek out not only fermented fruit, but manmade alcohol as well. This is quite possibly the reason for the rather strange drunken interlude in Disney's *Dumbo*, complete with dancing pink elephants[81]. Therefore, alcohol may be employed in contacting the totem Elephant—which is exactly what I did. I specifically chose to work with African Elephant, who is more connected with alcohol.

I drank some wine; given that I don't drink more than a tiny amount once every few years, the alcohol hit pretty quickly. Elephant seemed to descend from the sky and stand before me, then leading me off into a number of scenarios. The scenes I saw switched back and forth between an angry elephant chasing a man carrying a barrel of beer (something that is known to happen), and a herd of placid elephants eating fermented fruit from trees.

Elephant emphasized to me the need for responsibility when seeking to let go of control. He contrasted the raging thief with the gentle sharer, and explained how greed and desperation could affect our perceived need for control. With the raging elephant, the need for alcohol transcended its natural availability through the fruit, and more violent

---

80 Samorini 2002
81 Samorini 2002

means were used to try to gain the prize. Additionally, while not all alcoholics are solitary in their drinking all the time, he emphasized drinking for the purpose of an intentional altered state of consciousness (ASC) as a communal event, relying on others to share in the experience but also keep an eye out for each other.

One other thing Elephant told me was that with ASCs in general, it's easy sometimes to use them as escapism (hence alcoholism and other abuse, as well as addictions in general). If we feel we absolutely need to have a drug in order to function, then we may take actions that cause trouble for others. An extreme, though sadly too common, example is that of a meth or other addict who resorts to theft and other crime in order to get enough money to pay for the next fix. However, some people feel they can't even function without their daily caffeine and nicotine fixes.

This means that although you don't necessarily have to quit smoking or your morning coffee cold turkey, it is a bit of a wake-up call to really question why we depend on the things we do. This can be extended not only to drugs, but to anything we may be addicted to, or at least dependent upon. What happens if we try functioning without these things for a few days, a few weeks?

Elephant told me that I needn't use alcohol again to contact him, that regular meditation would be just fine. I generally don't like its effects on me, and since I don't have to have it to contact him, it's not necessary. He did tell me that should I ever find myself drunk or otherwise in an ASC, and in need of stabilization, that he'd be more than willing to help. Indeed, Elephant's wisdom does extend to knowing one's limits, and learning to surf the ASCs without being overwhelmed.

I did decide to work with two different totems to see if the effects would be different with each for the same drug. The other totem I chose to try to contact was the totem of Two-Tailed Pasha, a large butterfly native to the Mediterranean. *Charaxes jasius*, which Samorini refers to as the jasio, and which is commonly known as the two-tailed pasha, is known for being easy to bait with alcohol. Once the butterfly has been satisfied, the subsequent sluggish flight attests to the alcohol's effect on the insect.[82]

The effect with Pasha was less intense and more scattered than with Elephant. She seemed less in control of herself. She told me that because her children spent so much of their short lives focused on specific things—food, mating, avoiding prey—that it was a rare opportunity to get a chance to let go and unwind. In this I saw people

---

[82] Samorini 2002

who can't seem to relax or be social without the aid of alcohol. She also struck me as being more confident in her awareness and ability to hold her drink than she actually was, again reminding me of certain people under the influence. I didn't feel that there was anything bad or wrong with her; Pasha simply doesn't seem to have as good a handle on alcohol as Elephant does. On the other hand, she may just be more willing to lose herself in the experience. After all, if your lifespan is in months rather than years, you may relish any chance to take a break. I did feel there was a good lesson in remembering to take a break now and then, but not to fall prey to escapism, losing yourself in a bottle as it were. Granted, if I knew I only had a few months to live I might be more reckless. But for the time being, I took this as a reminder to relax without having to depend on any specific stimulus.

Goat and Caffeine

Other than occasional chocolate, I don't use caffeine. I don't drink coffee or tea in the morning, mostly because I dislike the taste of both. Therefore, I don't rely on caffeine to wake me up in the morning, and I figured that chocolate covered espresso beans would be sufficient to give me the necessary buzz.

I decided that since goats are credited with discovering coffee by eating the beans and then prancing around like crazy beings while the goatherders put two and two together[83], that I would use caffeine to contact Goat the totem. I started by meditating prior to eating the espresso beans and making initial contact with Goat. I entered through a wooden door with a brass handle in the trunk of an enormous old tree and went down through a tunnel under the tree's roots. The other end of the tunnel was too small for me to exit, so I turned into a four month old wolf pup and climbed on out.

I found myself in a farmer's field on the other side of the huge tree, accessible not by going around the tree, but underneath it—same tree, different reality. In the field I found Goat browsing in the hedges on the edge of the field. He was a bit irritable and cranky, but didn't chase me off. I explained to him my experiment, that I wanted to not only test my theories with chemognosis and totems, but also to help him gain a better reputation among people, similar to my work with food totems. After all, most people think of goats as being rather smelly, and overly lustful (at least in a mainstream moralizing sense), as well as being a common

[83] Samorini 2002, p. 44

sacrifice to banish evil. Like so many other domesticated totems, Goat has a bit of a bad reputation.

At first he balked, thinking my idea was rather silly, and not liable to work. However, I eventually convinced him to let me try. His response: "Sex, death, and drugs, the holy trifecta! Fine, give it a try, but don't be surprised if people still say I stink". So I came back up from the meditation and chowed down an ounce and a half of the coffee beans on an almost empty stomach in the space of about three minutes.

It only took about fifteen minutes for me to really start feeling the effects of the caffeine. I noticed that I was much more awake than I usually am an hour after I wake up; I had decided to do the experiment in the morning where I would be more likely to notice the difference. I paid closer attention to details in what was going on around me, things that I heard and saw. I also noticed much more clarity of thought.

I wanted to see if I could duplicate the results without the actual drug. I found it a lot easier than I'd expected to get back into meditative trance and head back to Goat's realm; I hadn't realized how much my long term sleep deprivation had hindered my ability to concentrate on such things. When I arrived in the field, some rather out of place coffee bushes had sprouted, and Goat was quite happily eating the beans fright off the plants. While he was still cranky, it was in a more joking manner, and he was much more communicative.

He explained that since the coffee beans had made it easier for me to concentrate on the journey to him, that they would be a good tool for getting into contact with him. I didn't necessarily have to limit my workings with him to working with heightening my awareness, but that I could simply use caffeine as an easier way to contact him if I wanted to work with him on other areas of his influence. These areas included the classic associations of lust, as well as sacrifice and the scapegoat, as well as survival since goats are known for their tenacity and ability to eat just about anything. He also stated that coffee beans or liquid coffee would make a great offering to him, and he would always appreciate the gift, whether given to him as a trance, or simply placed on an altar.

Incidentally, the night after I did the caffeine working I had a massive amount of trouble getting to sleep. Some of this was doubtless due to the fact that we'd just had a brand new bed delivered that day, and I wasn't used to the mattress. However, it gave me a valuable reminder to banish after the work is done, just in case of residual effects. On the bright side, the next day I was able to work with Goat to invoke the effects of caffeine to get through my day on three hours of sleep without actually having to ingest coffee or tea. While the altered state wasn't as strong as it was after eating chocolate covered espresso beans, I felt much more awake (relatively speaking) throughout the day than I normally do at that level of sleep deprivation, a good thing since I had to go to work that day!

This was achieved simply by sitting on the bus on the way to work and silently calling Goat, requesting his presence to help me with the invocation of the caffeine energy. Once he had arrived, I remembered the sensations and the headspace of being on the drug as much as I could and absorbed it into my mind and body. I had been inspired by my husband's work in *Inner Alchemy* working along similar lines[84]. My results weren't as good as his were, as I'm not that great at inhibitory trance. But I'm still glad I was able to utilize the basic concept.

Cat and Catnip

Cats are probably the best known animals who enjoy a little recreational drug use, in the form of the appropriately named catnip. I decided that as I already share my home with two feline friends who are quite fond of the mint, I should see what all the fuss was about and talk with Cat as well.

I had heard that catnip tea was effective, though I double checked on Erowid to see what experiences others had had. Both smoking and tea seemed to get results from people, and being a nonsmoker, I decided to brew up a little feline-friendly goodness. So I put three heaping spoonfuls of catnip in a mug, sprinkled more of the herb liberally around the living room for Sun Ce and Ember's enjoyment, and waited for the water to boil. Since catnip tea was said to have sleep-inducing properties, I waited until later in the evening and prepared for bed, just in case it hit me hard enough that I decided to simply drop off into dreamland.

After filtering out the leaves, I had about half a mug of potable liquid left. I drank it relatively quickly (sweetened with a bit of raw sugar), drinking most in about five minutes. The effect was almost instantaneous, at least as far as the relaxation went. The warmth spread throughout my entire body, and my muscles relaxed considerably as I slumped back against the wall. I had chosen to curl up on the floor in the cats' favorite spot, right under the window where they bird watch and between their two perches. I was buzzed shortly thereafter—not a really heavy buzz, but enough to feel it. At that point I finished as much of the tea as I could and put the cup out of cats' reach. I then settled in for meditation.

The very first thing I noticed was feeling as though I was shrinking into the body of a small female calico, mostly white but with red and black ears and a black striped tail, and a couple of small patches of color

---

[84] Ellwood 2007

on one side. I saw Cat as a white feline with huge pupils, and while our conversation was stilted at first, we slowly settled into a more casual chat. Cat extolled the virtues of her children, telling me how they really were different beings from most, and that humans had every right to sometimes be unsettled by them. Not that they're truly alien in the literal, physical sense, but they're rather unique among mammals, particularly domestic or quasi-domestic ones.

She also told me that there was some truth to cats being more sensitive to spirits, but that it was less about them being physically different, and more about them being simply more aware in general. The quick reflexes of cats mean they are more tuned into what is going on around them, and that includes on the nonphysical end of things. Just because they don't have the types of brains to process their experiences in the same way humans do didn't mean they don't notice at all.

Cat then told me to go outside and see how I felt. By this point I was exceptionally relaxed, to the point where I felt like I do when just waking up, or after a really good massage or stint in a hot tub. But I got up smoothly, and while I was a little woozy I made it outside with no major effects on my motor skills. And she was right—I was still relaxed, but I was more aware of what was going on around me. I was alert, but not tense. Oddly enough, while I was back in my own body, I could feel my little calico cat body walking down at my feet. I tried shifting my awareness down there, but Cat told me to focus on my own body so I wouldn't hurt myself. The cat-body was fine for sitting still, but more of a tag-along guide when I was moving about.

The sensitivity and awareness carried over into my senses as well. For example, apart from my environment, after I ended my shift and began to come down from the experience, I started craving strongly flavored foods. I ate some very garlicky croutons I'd made a few days before, and a chunk of raw white onion I found in the fridge. The lingering connections to Cat told me s/he was quite pleased by this. I savored the tastes more than usual. It was easy to see why Cat is often associated with sensuality of all sorts. Perhaps the catnip merely acted as an enhancement, or at least relaxed me enough to where I paid more attention to the most basic input.

All in all, I'd say this one was definitely a success. I had never realized before this experiment just how much of a canine person I was. From a shapeshifting point of view, it was one of the most potent mental shifts I've ever had. Taking catnip gave me an entirely different perspective on things, and if I ever want to walk as Cat again, I have a simple and effective way for doing so. Cat certainly seemed to enjoy the process, and while it's not something I want to do on a frequent basis, I can maintain my control enough to get something out of the experience besides a buzz.

Salvia Divinorum

I wanted to take my experimentation a little further to see if I could contact totems through drugs that didn't have any known animals that deliberately sought them out (other than humans). I decided to work with salvia divinorum; while anecdotally domestic housecats may occasionally find salvia intriguing, it doesn't have as strong an association with a particular animal as, say, catnip to cats or amanita to caribou. I was unable to find any animals that specifically sought out salvia as a way of altering their consciousness. At the time I took it in the state of Oregon, salvia divinorum was legal.

I took more caution with salvia than I did with any of the other substances I mention here, partly because it was the only one I had never used before, and partly because anecdotally it was supposed to be intense.[85] While I did all my experimentation with my husband at home, just in case, I made very sure he was my sitter for this experience.

Having obtained a bag of dried leaves (without added extract of the key chemical, Salvinorin A) I made sure the ritual area was clean, and then sat down to meditate and asked for the protection of my guides. I then chewed two leaves, one on each side of my mouth, and settled the chewed leaves in between my gums and inner cheeks. (I knew better than to swallow!) Since this was a more mild form of taking salvia than smoking (plus it didn't have the disadvantage of requiring me to inhale smoke), I figured it would be the safest starting point.

Since I didn't take a very large dose, the effect I got wasn't all that mind-blowing. I didn't get sensory hallucinations of any sort, or float out of my body. Rather, I ended up getting a much stronger mental picture as I meditated, and there was less of "me" in it and more of the spirits taking control and running with me. I didn't let go as much as I could have, but it was more than usual.

The first animal who showed up was coatimundi. I'm not sure which specific species; the coati I saw had traits of both the ring-tailed and white-nosed coatis. The coati was in a desert in what I would guess was Mexico, given that that's where salvia is native to; the landscape was a bit fuzzy, but the coati was in clear focus. I saw the coati the longest, but then s/he ended up getting attacked by a golden eagle, which tore off hir

---

[85] http://www.erowid.org/experiences/subs/exp_Salvia_divinorum.shtml has links to a variety of personal testimonials about salvia use.

tail. Then I got a strong sensation of Nile crocodile, including feeling myself shapeshift from coati to croc. Crocodile briefly turned to anaconda, and then red-crowned crane, finally coming to European rabbit.

I asked why so many animals appeared, and was told that they would all be suitable guides for working with salvia. While coati was the closest to salvia geographically, the others all had traits that would allow them to mesh with salvia. It might be interesting to see if other peoples' experimentations bring them into contact with any of these, or other, animals. I'll also be curious, over time, to see if Coati sticks around, or whether other totems will come to the fore with my subsequent explorations.

Animals as Drugs

In a few cases, the animal is the drug. Beyond the references to toad-licking capers in pop culture, there are several other animals whose bodies contain mind-altering chemicals. Gianluca Toro and Benjamin Thomas report that giraffes, a few species of fish, and the bamboo worm all supposedly contain psychoactive substances in some portion of their bodies. Particularly common are such chemicals as DMT and 5-methoxy-N,N-dimethyltryptamine (5-MeO-DMT). I decided to talk to Bufo Toad, the totem of several subspecies of toad particular known (and used) for their psychoactive secretions.

Since I didn't have access to *Bufo alvarus* or any other psychoactive amphibians, I decided to see what would happen just by contacting the totem without the drug. Since my husband had had good results from working with neurotransmitters that were stimulated by certain drugs, and got similar experiences compared to when he had taken the actual substances, I decided to see if I could get some results from working with the totem, but not the actual drug.

In my first meditation to get an idea of whether Toad was interested in working with me or not, I got an initial negative reaction. However, I calmed myself down, and continued to approach Toad respectfully and quietly. As I did so, he grew larger and larger (or I grew smaller and smaller) until I was about to walk under his belly. I could see him swallowing and breathing, and could smell his skin.

He absorbed me into his skin, and took me through his body to a venom gland. It looked like a huge pool of glowing white liquid. I went to touch it, but he stopped me. "You're so not ready for that right now!" Toad said. He was right, since I hadn't blocked out much time for this meditation, intending only to make contact. "Come back when you're ready, and I'll take you for a ride." He also indicated that he didn't want me taking the actual physical venom, as I was nowhere near prepared for it. I'd be inclined to agree, as my experience with entheogens isn't all that great.

However, before he sent me back home, he made one thing very clear: he is not happy with how his children have been exploited for their venom. Not everyone who uses toad venom to get high (or journey) uses dead toad skins, instead harvesting the venom from live toads. However, Toad did seem perturbed that few people put any thought towards the sacredness of the toads themselves. No one ever seemed to contact him or his children for much beyond the venom and the image; few ever asked him what he could teach them beyond that one trick. While Toad is quite willing to share the entheogenic gift with people, his sorrow is that the toads themselves are commodified, objectified, and taken for granted, and few people ever think to talk to him, even if he makes an appearance in their trip.

I'm guessing that if you can make use of the venom while working with Toad, you'll get a stronger reaction; additionally, if you've taken it previously, the neural pathways created by the experience are already in place and may be easier to retrace if you use meditation/invocation/evocation without the drug. Due to Toad's dislike of the exploitation of his children, I doubt I'll be using the venom itself, though if you choose to do so, I would strongly recommend talking to Toad first and asking him the best way to honor him and his children—as well as find out what he has to share beyond the venom.

Other Forms of Magic

You're not necessarily limited to working with chemognosis totems only for the purpose of talking to them and learning how to use the drugs they're associated with. You can also ask the totems to accompany you on journeys or other forms of magic that incorporate the drug as a tool, but not as the main purpose. You may find that the totem will act as a guide through your journey, and this may be particularly useful when dealing with an entheogen you don't have much experience with. The totem may help you to navigate the journey more effectively and stay focused on the work at hand.

For those who are squeamish about taking various substances into their bodies, it's possible to try meditating with the drug. If it's natural, try contacting the spirit of the plant that bore it. You probably won't get nearly as strong an effect as you would by taking the entheogen, but it is an alternative if you wish to be exceptionally cautious.

Speaking of plant spirits, you may contact them in conjunction with the corresponding animal totem. Try working with them separately before you work with them together to see where each one's strengths and influences are.

Journaling Exercises

Sample Journal Entry:

Date:
Drug/Dose:
Totem:
Physical effects:
Psychological effects:
Other effects: (*energetic, etc.*)
Length of effects:
Purpose/lessons: (*talking to totem, learning how drug feels, other ritual purpose, etc.*)
Other Notes: (*anything else you feel it's important to mention*)

Chapter Seven: Magical Shapeshifting with Totems

Of all the topics I covered in *Fang and Fur*, totemic or magical shapeshifting is one of the topics that I really could have discussed in more detail. While I'm going to try to avoid recycling too much information from the other book, you may recognize a piece of information or concept here and there. Magical shapeshifting is primarily achieved through two means. One involves the invocation of, or other influence from, an exterior totem or animal spirit (or, less commonly, a deity or other spirit who may be associated with nonhuman animals). The other is achieved by building up the energy within yourself and essentially "shaping it" into the form of the animal you want to shapeshift to. This chapter is primarily going to deal with the former method.

Shapeshifting With Primary, Secondary and Tertiary Totems

In a previous chapter, I briefly described a relatively sedentary form of shapeshifting as a method of identifying and getting to know a totem. Shapeshifting is most often done either for magical or celebratory purposes. The former can be anything from practical magic, such as sending energy towards a good outcome in a personal endeavor, to metamorphic magic such as pathworking or rites of passage. Celebrations with shapeshifting are often used simply to celebrate the presence of the totems in our lives, or to give the totems a chance to ride a physical body for a while, though shapeshifting may be incorporated into other celebrations, such as neopagan Sabbats and other holidays.

I generally suggest, if you don't have much experience with shapeshifting, practicing with your primary totem (if you know who s/he is). This is the totem who has the strongest connection with you. Shapeshifting can be a great way to strengthen the bond between you and your totem. It involves a certain amount of mutually shared trust and respect, and it gives you both the chance to get to know each other better on a more experiential, fundamental level. This is true for any totem, though again, your primary's probably the best starting place.

If you haven't yet met with your primary, you might try checking to see if there's a secondary waiting in the wings to practice shapeshifting with you. While many people will notice pretty quickly when a totem or other being is trying to get ahold of them, others may not be as good at catching the signals, or may be distracted. I recommend using the general totem animal meditation with the intent of meeting with whatever secondary totem(s) may be trying to make contact. Or, if you're fairly proficient with the totem cards described in this book, give them a whirl. Don't worry if the secondary who appears isn't a totem commonly associated with shapeshifting, such as Wolf or Fox. S/he may simply be a totem that you may find easier to invoke and otherwise learn from than others.

In the event that there's no specific secondary totem to help you, you can always find a tertiary totem to help you out. Again, either straight meditation or my card deck can be of use here. You may find that the totem you end up with is one more commonly associated with shapeshifting, since this is a less personal relationship than with a secondary, and so the emphasis may be more on shapeshifting in general than on shapeshifting with you, specifically.

However, your best bet will be to start with a totem you're familiar with, whether that's a primary, secondary or tertiary. Say you've worked with Fox for a while as a tertiary on a number of projects, so you've gotten to know hir pretty well over time. You may ask hir for help with shapeshifting since it's one of hir common bailiwicks. Or suppose you've been working with Earthworm to help you find hidden or obscure information. S/he may have some suggestions of totems who may be able to help you out.

Once you're comfortable with shapeshifting overall, you can try shapeshifting with other totems as well. It's a good idea to ask the totem first, rather than just assuming s/he'll be happy to do an invocation with you. If you're not at all familiar with the species, other than maybe a few stories or anecdotes, you'd do well to do your research before you bring that energy into your ritual area—and your body. You want to have a good idea of what it is you're working with, so studying natural history, mythology, and other source material is highly recommended.

Shapeshifting Through Invocation

Over the years, there have been numerous rituals created to help a person shapeshift. Some supposedly aid in the mythical (but ever unproven) physical change. However, even if you never experience a change in eye color, the techniques may still be used for nonphysical, mental/energetic/etc. shapeshifts. While the details vary, the general structure is the same:

* Create or find a setting conducive to being an animal
* Wear appropriate costumery and use appropriate tools (may include hallucinogenic substances in the case of older rituals)
* Vocalize a chant or poem meant to call up the animal self/turn one into an animal/alter one's state of consciousness, and/or dance or otherwise move like the animal
* Shapeshift/work magic/experience altered state of consciousness/journey
* Banish at the end of the ritual and return to everyday consciousness/wake up the next day naked in the woods, bewildered and covered in leaves and mud

This is the same general format used in invocations of all types. Whether you're invoking god-forms, spirits, totems, personality aspects, etc., almost every suggested ritual has most if not all of these elements, or variations thereof. Let's look at the process of invocation in more detail.

Setting: Every magician worth hir salt knows that the reason ceremonialists and other elaborate magical practitioners like to play with sensory effects in their ritual setting is to help heighten awareness and focus on the purpose of the working at hand. It's ritual drama. In an old Russian werewolf ritual that involved circling a tree, the ritual specifically suggests going into the woods and finding a tree stump rather than just any old tree[86]. While there's no obvious connection given, the fact that a specific setting is (supposedly) required automatically triggers the mind into "this is something special" mode[87].

There are a number of elements of setting to consider. Do you have a safe place you can go, either indoors or out, where you won't be disturbed? How could you enhance that setting, especially if it's indoors (and safe from the elements and passerby)? Is there a certain color that you associate with shapeshifting? How about statues and pictures of the animal you'll be shapeshifting to? If you have recordings of sounds that the animal makes or the general sounds of hir environment, you may wish to add that in as well, or if you prefer, a drumming CD. Are there scents that produce primal feelings, or foods that you may associate with that species (or that the totem/other helper specifically requests)? The War God ritual in Carroll's *Liber Null & Psychonaut* is an excellent example of a

---

[86] Anonymous 2007-E

[87] "This is special" mode is not a substitute for understanding magical mechanics. Just because something feels right doesn't mean that there's no reason to know the underlying causes and influences. Hence the reason why so many magical practitioners spend years learning their art.

thoroughly prepared setting, as well as costumery, which I'll discuss next[88]. The ritual involves dressing in military clothing, marching, playing aggressive music, and even shooting firearms. While I don't advise the lattermost activity (at least not indoors!), all of these elements contribute to the martial energy of the ritual, making the invocation that much easier to perform.

Costumery and Tools: This isn't absolutely necessary (neither is setting, for that matter), but some people find it helps. Do you have a particular piece of jewelry or clothing that you can use specifically for shapeshifting? How about a full costume, either made of skins and other parts, or a more vegan-friendly option of fabric? Or would a tail (real or fake) do the trick for you? Putting on a costume helps to signal to your psyche that it's time to switch gears.

Some people may wish to work this ritual in with formal rites from other traditions, such as casting a circle in some neopagan traditions. Do you need tools for this, or can it be done in open-handed ritual? I probably don't need to say this, but you don't need hallucinogens. Unless you're experienced in chemognosis[89], you shouldn't even consider mixing these two types of magic, even if you're using a legal entheogen. In fact, you may want to abstain from all drugs (other than those prescribed by a health care professional), including caffeine, alcohol, and nicotine, for a day or two prior to let your body clear them out of your system. I would not, however, recommend fasting or going without water. You can probably eat a small meal to keep hunger pangs and dehydration headaches (both of which can be very distracting) at bay.

In-Vocation: This is the part where most of the rituals involve a chant or saying of some sort. If you feel comfortable writing something up and speaking it out loud, go for it. I personally find it distracting to try and remember the words, but that's just me. What I generally do instead is active visualization mixed with movement. I've had a good bit of practice with visualization over the years, since it tends to be pretty popular among neopagans. As for dance, it brings me into closer awareness of my body, physical and energetic; through it I can observe how very much like a wolf's body my human body is, or how it may resemble the forms of other animals, and add in the "missing parts" through the energy of the shapeshift.

---

[88] Carroll 1987, p. 43-44
[89] I know that there are numerous practitioners of shamanism and other magical arts who have had a lot of experience with chemognostic shapeshifting. I'm not going to discuss that here, since I don't have sufficient experience to give people good advice on what (not) to do.

If I am going to shapeshift with the totem Wolf, I generally start by formally calling Wolf to join me. Next, I visualize myself as a wolf, and then imitate that animal's movements as best as I can based on previous shapeshifts and observation of wolves on TV and at sanctuaries. I may ask the totem Wolf for help here as I invoke hir, reminding me of what it is to be wolf myself. I may chant a little under my breath or in my head, but it's generally free-form. I might start by repeating "I am wolf, I am wolf" over and over in time with my movements (and the rhythm of any music or drumming accompanying me). Eventually the chant may turn into glossolalia (random syllables making meaningless "words") or animal sounds, and then fall away as I complete the shapeshift.

Due to physical restrictions, too small a space, or other such things, a full dance may not be an option. In this case, you have a couple of options. You can perform less dramatic motions; for example, to shapeshift into Garter Snake, you might try simply weaving your head back and worth, and flicking your tongue out, perhaps hissing. Or if you can dance, but don't have much room, try dancing in place. If there's really no room at all, or if you need to be quiet, visualize the dancing and other motions rather than actually performing them.

What Next: Where you go from here is entirely up to you. Sometimes it's fun to just experience being the animal, and if you're still getting used to shapeshifting I'd recommend keeping it at that. There's a lot to explore in the moment. For example, how does your body feel while you're shapeshifting? Do you feel it should be shaped differently compared to its current human form? What senses do you notice the most? What is most important to you, both in your thoughts and emotions, and in your perceptions of what's around you? Are you aware of the totem "riding" your body? Is there any communication going on between you and the totem? Is there anything specific the totem may want you to do, either during the shapeshift or later? Afterwards you may want to note the differences between your mind and perception as a nonhuman animal and you as human. Don't worry too much about thinking about things in detail and in words while shapeshifted; simply observe, and then record your experiences as soon as you can after the shapeshift is over, while it's still fresh in your mind.

Once you're used to shapeshifting you may try using this state of mind for magical purposes. I've used it in environmental magic designed to help push through legislation that is beneficial to wildlife, though you can do any form of magic that works well with invocation. For example, if I want to create a ritual costume to dance Frog with, and I want to consecrate it for that purpose, I may invoke Frog to work through my body to bless the costume more directly.

If you already have a good relationship with the totem you're working with, you can take this mutual understanding and use it as a basis for pathworkings involving internal work on your part. For example, if you're trying to break a bad habit, your totem may be able to show you some ideas for breaking that habit, or take you on a journey to locate a totem who may be of more assistance. The shapeshifting allows the totem to get past your everyday barriers, and also may allow hir to literally show you what s/he means. For me, it allows a stronger connection between us, so we can get a good stream of consciousness "conversation" going, one that transcends words and instead relies on images, feelings and intuition. It's sometimes easier for the totem to get the message across to me when s/he's "in my head" instead of just in the ritual area with me.

It's best, if you're going to work magic while shapeshifted, to plan out your ritual beforehand, rather than doing the magic on the fly if you aren't that experienced with shapeshifting. Determine what totem you'd like to have help you, and then ask hir if s/he's willing to help before the ritual begins. You'll also want to figure out how you want to work the magic, whether by charging an object, sending out energy for a specific purpose, etc.

However, if you're an experienced magician, are comfortable with shapeshifting, and are working with a totem you're familiar with, there's nothing wrong with creating magic as you go along. You should probably still go in with a specific purpose in mind, but if you or the totem comes up with some inspiration during the ritual, go ahead and modify the magic as needed. Additionally, depending on your endurance and that of the totem, you may try working more than one act of magic during a shift, though be aware that you may need to take a little time out in between each working.

Banish and Finish Up: "If you start it, it's a good idea to finish it" is a good rule of thumb in magic. Banishing involves dismissing or sending away anything or anyone you've invoked (or evoked) to signify that the ritual is at an end. The word "banish" is harsher than it often actually manifests, and can be done with great respect, or with a bit of light hearted fun, all depending on who you're working with and how serious they can be.[90] Internally, it's a way to get yourself back to your everyday

---

[90] You will, of course, have fellow magical practitioners who would have a conniption fit if anyone, anywhere, did a banishing in any form other than the most formal, respectful, and ritualized manner (or however they think it's supposed to be done). If you have better luck with a good laugh (banishing with laughter!) or other irreverent methods, and the power that

state of consciousness. In old rituals, the magic ended when the werewolf turned back into a human, either returning home at the end of the night or, one might imagine, being deposited unceremoniously in the middle of the woods if the change back is unintentional. In this case, though, there are numerous ways to bring yourself back down to Earth, so to speak. Many people like to eat and drink a little to ground, which focuses the attention on the mundane, physical form. You may also consider meditating a bit, visualizing fur, feathers, exoskeleton, etc. sliding back under your skin as the part of you that responded to the totem's presence reintegrates into you as a whole. Try doing something very human-oriented, such as reading, or writing about your experience in your journal.

If you don't banish, the consequences may not be particularly life-threatening, but they can be inconvenient. If you find yourself feeling light-headed or "spacy", or if you can't seem to quite get back to your normal consciousness, you may need to ground a little more. You may want to avoid driving or being around other people (at least those who aren't aware of and/or comfortable with magic and totemism) until you've banished entirely.

Shapeshifting on the Fly (Run, Swim, Etc.)

Shapeshifting isn't limited to formal ritual areas, once you're skilled enough. In fact, with enough practice, you can shapeshift anywhere, any time. However, because you may not have privacy or other safety measures, you should probably have a good reason for this. The stereotypical example is shapeshifting to a big, scary animal when walking down a dark street at night to help ward off troublemakers. However, this is hardly the only possibility. I've shapeshifted with Fox to help me get through woods more easily, and with Bear for healing purposes, for example. These have been in less formal situations than a full ritual setup.

Some people keep certain pieces of jewelry or other costumery with them if they think they may need to shift to a particular animal at a certain point. If you're a marathon runner, you may find it helpful to bring something associated with Horse on the race, then shapeshift if you feel the need for more strength and speed. Many people keep tokens of their primary totems at all times, and may shapeshift if they feel the need for comfort, companionship, or otherwise would like that totem's presence.

---

be haven't indicated any desire to smite you off the face of the planet, then keep doing what you're doing, and alter only as is necessary.

When shapeshifting on the fly, you won't have a lot of time for preparation, so you'll need to be able to focus quickly. If you can't quiet your mind in about a minute or less, then you'll need to practice with meditation until you can. Silently call the totem you wish to shapeshift with (this works better with those you've had more experience with). Then allow hir to enter your body and begin to move with you. This will probably be a more subtle affair than with a ritual dance, but it can still be quite effective. The shift may not be as intense, but in everyday situations you'll rarely need the kind of intensity that comes with an all-out ritual.

Banishing is usually quicker as well. Usually the totem leaves as quietly as s/he arrived. If you have a little trouble shaking off the altered state of consciousness, spend some time paying attention to what's going on around you. Look at the faces of other people, read billboards or newspaper headlines, and otherwise get yourself grounded. Or, if you find you're overstimulated, find a quiet place—even a bathroom stall will work in a pinch.

Suffice it to say, you should not attempt shapeshifting on the fly if you are driving or otherwise need to focus on what you're doing. Additionally, if you have trouble controlling yourself during a shapeshift in formal ritual, you should probably hold off on this type of practice. More subtle shapeshifting actually takes more effort than letting yourself go entirely, because you have to maintain a greater degree of control. However, as with anything, practice makes better, if not perfect.

Troubleshooting/Emergencies

In my personal experience, while totems are powerful beings, working with many of them isn't as potentially dangerous a proposition as, say, invoking Kali or Tiamat. From what I have experienced and seen, most times if a totem doesn't feel that a ritual is a good idea, s/he simply won't show up, or will tell the practitioner that the ritual is a bad idea, and maybe it's better to do something else instead. I've never had a totem sabotage something healthy in my life, or deliberately sow discord for no purpose other than hir own entertainment. For the most part, they'll either help if they think it's worth it, or do nothing at all.

This doesn't mean totems are completely safe to work with, or that they're always nice and sweet and cooperative; they just don't seem to go out of their way to cause trouble for trouble's sake. That being said, they can be difficult to work with, especially if they are either intense beings themselves, or if we're not listening very well to what they're trying to tell us. For a while I was wary working with Bear, mainly because s/he had been one of the "tougher" totems on me, calling me out when I made a mistake or scolding me if she thought I needed it. I found out in time, though, that it wasn't that s/he didn't like me—it was just hir way of working with me. And getting cuffed by a bear, even a spiritual one, isn't meant for fun!

Most of the problems in working with totems tend to stem from the person, not the totem. Our expectations can really get in the way—again, why I really emphasize taking totems on their own terms instead of our preconceived notions about them. I've seen entirely too many cases of people working with carnivorous or otherwise predatory totems who over-emphasized the aggressive aspects of these hunters, and completely ignored the rest. Sure, Bear has big claws and sharp teeth and very few enemies, but s/he was the one who taught me about healing. Additionally, people assume Deer is universally gentle and sweet; however, people have been attacked by bucks and does alike, and antlers and hooves are effective weaponry!

While we're sitting making our assumptions, the totem may be getting frustrated with trying to get through to us, which may cause hir to take more drastic actions to get us to pay attention. While not every bad thing that happens is due to spiritual forces, there are cases of people's lives falling apart for no apparent reason. It may take them a while to figure out that they're sabotaging themselves, and that the spiritual entities in their lives have nudged things along to try to get them to notice what's up, so said entities may give them advice on improving the situation.

However, there are other concerns as well, specific to shapeshifting. Some of these are physiological. If you are in ill health at all, you may want to contact a physician before doing any intense shapeshifting work, or if it's a short-term illness, just wait it out. Make sure you stretch beforehand—nothing kills the mood quite like a pulled or torn muscle. Keep yourself well-hydrated, especially if the temperature is high.

Choose your location wisely; you want to make sure to have access to first aid, a phone, and any other help you may need. If you're dancing around a fire, have water or a fire extinguisher on hand in case things get out of hand. Be aware of other people, especially those who have no earthly idea what you're up to. And while it may be tempting to strip down to your bare skin to get more into feeling like an animal, if you're not on private land with permission, you may end up in a quite awkward situation! Of course, depending on the terrain, running around in the buff may not be advisable anyway…

Occasionally invocation of any sort can lead to a temporary psychological imbalance beyond being a little spacey. Even when we are invoking external beings, we are still also calling on the corresponding parts of ourselves to help the connection manifest more strongly. Since this involves some poking around in our psyches, we may accidentally bring up something we weren't comfortable with. A good example would be someone who has a tendency towards over-aggressiveness invoking a potentially very aggressive totem such as Wolverine—specifically for the purpose of being more aggressive. Unfortunately, such people often have too little control over themselves, and lack responsibility as well. While it's not common, I have heard instances of people doing some really asinine things and then blaming it on the magic they were working. Whether it intentional or not, **the magician is always responsible for the magic that s/he works**.

Psychological imbalance may also come about from improper banishing. Most of the time, even if the initial banishing didn't work, the magic will still wear off after a few hours, a good meal, and some sleep. However, there are rare occasions where effects of the altered state of consciousness involved in magic may linger for days or weeks (or the person may cling to those effects unconsciously, refusing to let go of them for whatever reason).

In this case, a formal banishing ritual may be called for. I am a big fan of the Gnostic Pentagram ritual found in Peter J. Carroll's *Liber Kaos*, but any effective banishing ritual will work. Unfortunately, there will be the occasional individual who on some level is deliberately using the energy from the original shapeshifting ritual as an excuse to act out or to let hirself otherwise lose control, and the banishing may be ineffective. In this case, it's best to let the person be; eventually s/he'll either get bored and find some other way to get attention, or s/he'll wise up to how self-sabotaging s/he's being.

It's more likely that your problem may simply be that you can't get into the shapeshift. There could be any of a number of factors contributing to this. If you're self-conscious about what you're doing, if you're too cold or too hot, if you're too tired or too wired, or if something happened not too long before the ritual that's distracting you, you may simply not be able to get into a good headspace for magic. Hopefully by the time you're attempting shapeshifting you have enough experience in magical practice to have at least a basic idea of what the best setting and schedule works best for you, but this may not be an exact formula. Just be sure that before you convince yourself that you're incapable of shapeshifting that you look at other factors first. More often than not there's something that can be changed to help facilitate your working.

This is far from being an exhaustive treatise on shapeshifting. If you'd like to read more practical information on this topic, I suggest picking up Ted

Andrews' *The Art of Shapeshifting*. It covers much of the same material here, but in much more detail and from his unique perspective; it's a great book if you want to spend a lot of time focused specifically on shapeshifting. Additionally, *Sacred Mask, Sacred Dance* by Evan John Jones and Chas S. Clifton is a wonderful resource for invocation rituals based on animal masks and other costumery, as well as dance and ritual psychodrama.

In the next chapter, I'll explore how magical shapeshifting may aid those who identify as therianthropes with situations specific to the condition of spiritual/psychological therianthropy.

Journaling Exercises

1. Practice shapeshifting with a totem you're familiar with; if you're new to totemism, take time to get to know at least one totem well enough that you trust each other for this sort of work. Use the shapeshifting as a way to get a really up-close-and-personal understanding of the totem and what s/he has to teach you.

2. Try shapeshifting with a totem you haven't shapeshifted with before. How does the experience differ from that with a more familiar totem? Which is more intense? Is either one easier? Does this change as you get to know the less familiar totem better?

3. Use shapeshifting in a ritual for a specific purpose. You might ask Lungfish for help with better endurance in stressful situations, or request that Gadfly give you a hand with "planting a bug" in the ear of an elected official who's about to make an important decision about a particular ecosystem.

Sample Journal Entry:

Date:
Setting:
Totem(s) worked with:
Purpose: *(to get to know a totem better, magical work)*
Props/Costumery:
Other notes:

Chapter Eight: Using Totemic Techniques in Therianthropy[91]

For those not familiar with the concept of therianthropy, here's a very brief definition: a therianthrope is a person who identifies in some manner (almost always nonphysically) as a nonhuman animal. While a good number of therianthropes see their condition as being wholly psychological or neurobiological in nature, others chalk it up to having been a certain animal in a past life, or being a nonhuman animal soul in a human animal body. There are several other theories of how therians explain the whys and hows of their therianthropy, but they almost all involve inherently being a therianthrope, rather than "becoming" one.[92]

Those of you who are not therianthropes should read this chapter anyway. If you suspect you might be a therian, some of the concepts here may aid in reflecting on what, exactly, might point towards you being a nonhuman animal on some level. There are cases (somewhat uncommon) of therians who spend a significant part of their lives being unaware of their therianthropy, and who may become aware of that aspect of themselves when they learn about the concept. There's always the chance that somebody reading this may fall into that category, though as always I urge people to highly question and reflect on themselves before determining that they are, indeed, not entirely human. Finally, you may just find it interesting even if not a single bit applies to you personally, or you may know someone who may get more use out of it on a practical level.

I've tried here to show how some of the material in this book may be used in practices specific to therianthropes. As has been made very clear in the therian community, therianthropy is not the same as totemism. Just because you have a strong bond with your totem doesn't make you a therianthrope. A totem is an external being independent of the magician (though, as I'll explore later in the chapter, the lines here can be fairly blurred in some cases). While some therians have totems (which aren't necessarily the same type of animal that they are), there is a sizable number of therians who do not work with totems or other entities. In

[91] Part of this chapter was originally published in my self-published ebooklet, *Shifting, Shamanism and Therianthropy* (2007).

[92] If you're interested in reading more, my *Field Guide to Otherkin* (2007) goes into much greater detail about therianthropy, Otherkin, and related topics, and additionally has an extensive bibliography. Or, if you'd rather check out a couple of websites, http://www.dreamofhorn.com/therian/ and http://www.otherkin.net are great starting places.

fact, some therianthropes don't even believe in totems, or spirits, or deities, or anything else of that ilk; others subscribe to religions other than pagan ones. Please keep in mind that just because some therians may work with totems, it doesn't mean that they all do. (Additionally, there are those who balk at any combination of the two concepts for fear of confusion.)

Although some therians figure out what their therioside (the animal self) is fairly early in their lives, others may have more trouble identifying exactly what animals they are. It's not that they're not as sincere in their therianthropy; they might have a more obscure therioside, or they may just not have developed as strong an awareness of it yet. The techniques used to find and work with a totem animal can be easily adapted to finding and working with your therioside as well. Instead of working with an external animal, though, you're essentially working with yourself-as-nonhuman-animal. All it takes is a little bit of creativity and patience, seeing reality as multi-layered, and being willing to test your results rather than making immediate assumptions.

Magic and Therianthropy

When I first started using magical techniques in conjunction with my therianthropy, I was utterly clueless as to what I was doing. While I'd been introduced to the concept, I lived in a small town and didn't know anyone else who had experience with this sort of thing other than anecdotes about other people who may or may not actually have been therians. My online interaction was primarily with non-therian Otherkin, and this was before I discovered the word therianthropy (which was crucial to my finding better information later on). As it was, most of what I found while searching for "lycanthropy" and "shapeshifting" was old folklore that didn't fit my experience, so I was pretty much on my own.

While researching I ran across a number of "how to become a werewolf" rituals. These have ranged walking around a tree chanting an incantation[93] to rubbing yourself with hallucinogenic herbs and wearing a wolfskin belt. Supposedly something in the materials you use is what triggers the change, magically turning you into an insta-werewolf. In the case of hallucinogens, one might end up on an accidental trip that, unguided, may lead to all sorts of delusions.[94] But without knowing why

---

[93] Anonymous 2007-E
[94] Though people experienced in chemognosis may have enough control over altered states of consciousness to get genuine nonphysical shapeshifts and other effects.

the ritual is supposed to work, the chance of success is pretty low, especially when shooting for such an improbable goal.

Even more recent ceremonies aimed at increasing your connection to your therioside offer a lot of ritual psychodrama, though they come with the caveat that you can't become a therian if you aren't one already[95]. However, what these rites lack is an explanation of why they're supposed to work. The reason these and older legends attract people anyway is because there are plenty of folks out there, especially newbies, who are looking for a quick, easy fix, not understanding that what they seek is impossible regardless of where they look. Either they want to become a therianthrope, or they are a therian and they want to become the biggest, baddest one of them all. It's a temptation that's common across all forms of magic—and equally fallacious all around.

Go to any big chain book store and head to the metaphysical/occult section. Chances are pretty good that the bulk of what you'll find there are spell books, and basic 101 texts with a lot of rituals (and often not so much content). Part of this is because chain stores pander to the lowest common denominator—in this case, people who are just finding out about paganism and magical topics and who may need some very basic information if they're starting from scratch on their own.

Granted, there's nothing wrong with 101 books in and of themselves. Everybody needs to start somewhere. However, the 101 books that tend to get the best reviews are the ones that actually go into the whys and hows of magical practice, rather than just passing on a bunch of prefabricated rituals and letting the reader figure the rest out for hirself. It's also part of why you don't generally find much in the way of prefabricated rituals and spells above the 101 level. It doesn't matter how big a book of spells you have or how many candles you've burned—your magic will never be as dependably effective if you don't know what it is that makes it work for you.

This is the other reason why most advanced books tend to talk more about techniques and putting theory into practice in an individual manner rather than offering even more complex rituals. Once you get beyond the basics, magic works best when you customize it to your own needs. We each have our own psychological triggers that cause altered states of consciousness necessary for advanced magical practice, and we all make our own personal relationships with the Powers That Be. A book can give you ideas, but it can't hand you the amazing key to adepthood.

---

[95] Noctis 2007, p. 6, 14-22, 35-41

However, attempts at shortcuts occur even among more experienced magicians. My husband has pointed out to me in the past that often, especially in postmodern systems, the results of magic are emphasized over the processes. This is demonstrated by Grant Morrison, speaking of applied magic as divorced from theoretical magic: "we do not need to know HOW magic works, only that it does"[96]. We both disagree with this assertion. While the results are important in that you need them to determine whether what you did worked, you can't adjust your magic for better results or pass on the knowledge for others to use if you have no idea what you did or why it worked. Magic is an intensely personal thing; two people performing the same ritual will still have subtle individual differences in tone, action, and energy. Magic is also partly about personalizing the process to maximize the result, and we each have different needs when it comes to getting the most out of what we do. Otherwise, there wouldn't be a need for so many flavors of magic out there!

Metamorphic Magic

Neophytes often assume that magic is all about making things happen in the world around you. This is certainly true with most practical magic, which is concerned with getting people jobs, healing the sick, and other material causes. There is second branch of magic, though, known as metamorphic (or transcendental, or "high" magic), which is primarily concerned with consciously evolving the individual person on an internal level. This is done spiritually and/or psychologically, depending on what your individual view of magic is.

Traditional forms of metamorphic magic are generally concerned (at least symbolically) with getting the magician closer to God while on this plane of existence. A good example is Qabalistic pathworking focused on studying and climbing the Tree of Life, experiencing and transcending the qualities of each of the sephiroth and paths between them. However, metamorphic magic may also be used on a purely psychological level to reprogram the self, getting rid of unwanted or harmful personality traits and conditioning, and introducing better alternatives. Robert Anton Wilson's *Prometheus Rising* does this using, among other things, Timothy Leary's eight circuit model of consciousness[97]. B.K. Frantzis, on the other

---

[96] Morrison 2003, p. 17
[97] Wilson 1992

133

hand, writes in his books about dissolving energetic (and also psychological) blockages using Taoist water meditations[98].

One form of metamorphic magic, popularized in recent time by Chaos and other forms of postmodern magic, involves deliberately invoking different aspects of the self. Peter J. Carroll, for example, gives a detailed example of how to invoke the War self, one of eight selves based on the colors of magic in Chaos magic[99]. Any system of defining selves may be used, however. Pantheons of gods are maps of the human psyche as well as independent beings in their own right. I've also used totems in conjunction with four aspects described by Wilson in the aforementioned work: Friendly Strength and Weakness, and Hostile Strength and Weakness. By consciously dividing myself up into those personae on a temporary basis, I was able to examine myself in greater detail and understand subtle nuances about my personality I'd missed before—including my therianthropy[100].

The concept of being able to work with different individual aspects is an important one in the material to come. It involves rearranging how you understand your self-image, and isn't always the easiest thing to wrap your head around. But it's something that I've found to be invaluable in my magical work, including that associated with my therianthropy. All of this is a part of the maxim "Know thyself". If you practice magic for long enough, it begins to open you up to yourself whether you like it or not. Once you begin initiating conscious change, that change also affects you. This is not a bad thing. I mentioned earlier that it's a good idea for therians to explore why we believe what we believe about ourselves, and question our convictions. This is a part of "Know thyself", too, albeit not always as intense. If you're going to have full control over yourself, human and otherwise, you have to understand yourself—and that can mean some pretty brutal honesty.

Knowledge is power. Some magical orders deliberately only release certain amounts of information at a time to initiates as a way of letting it sink in at a healthy pace, while saving times of overload for initiatory rituals. Abuse occurs when the knowledge is purposely withheld to make the "elders" seem more powerful. However, even in the case of initiatory traditions, the initiates are given explanations as to why they do the things they're doing. This includes both the mechanics of the rituals and practices they learn, and the reasons behind the metamorphosis that comes with each new level of learning.

---

[98] Frantzis 2001
[99] Carroll 1987
[100] Lupa 2007

You can't progress beyond a certain point without full understanding of where you've been. For example, a few years ago I had someone write out the text for the Lesser Banishing Ritual of the Pentagram since I was in serious need of purification, and she was coming from the perspective of a Golden Dawn practitioner. At the time it didn't make much sense to me because I didn't understand what all those funny words were. I tried the LBRP a few times but didn't get much of a result. However, when I started practicing Chaos magic I read about the Gnostic Pentagram Ritual devised by Carroll. Since by that point I had a decent understanding of Chaos magic, the ritual made much better sense to me and was more effective for me.

That's the difference between doing a ritual because someone tells you to, and doing it because you understand why and how it works. While I have no problem with paradigmal piracy, the art of using elements of whatever tradition of magic works for you in order to get results, skipping over the understanding of the mechanics of whatever you work with is a sign of a sloppy magician. This is especially important if you're going to experiment with magic at all—if you know exactly what elements of a working were crucial to its effectiveness, you know what you need to make sure and include the next time, rather than trying varying combinations and hoping it works.

Therianthropy and the Guided Journey

One thing you'll find in almost any book on neopagan totemism[101] is a guided journey to find your totem. These tend to be based on the power animal meditation in core shamanism, and follow a basic formula:

* Relax and clear your mind of extraneous thoughts
* Visualize a hole in the ground, a tree, etc. and dive into it
* Travel through a long tunnel
* (Option 1) Encounter your totem/power animal in the tunnel itself; if you see it four times from different angles, you've found your animal
* (Option 2) Come out the other end of the tunnel to a natural place where you'll find your animal
* Converse with the animal and learn what its role is
*Return back through the tunnel

---

[101] Including this one—see Appendix C.

There are, of course, numerous variations, but that's the basic structure most of these journeys are based on. There are two primary uses for journeys that I've found specifically in regards to therianthropy (though I'm sure creative people will be able to go even further than that): to help a therian determine hir therioside if s/he's having trouble with identifying it, and getting to know your therioside better once you know what it is.

I do want to re-emphasize that while these techniques are based on working with external totems, your therioside is an internal part of you—you are the (nonhuman) animal. I know some people refer to their theriosides in third person and give them names, similar to what furries do with their "fursonas" (characters). This is actually not conducive to integrating your human and nonhuman aspects; referring to your therioside as a separate being reinforces that idea on a subconscious level, even though consciously you may say otherwise. This can interfere with your attempts at integration. Your therioside is not a separate, possessing being—you are a person who is a therian, a nonhuman as well as human animal.

Keep this in mind as you're working with the magical techniques so that you don't start unnecessarily splitting yourself. In the following exercise in particular, you will temporarily be treating your therioside as a separate being. Note I said temporarily. If you've ever had a conversation with yourself about something you're indecisive about, this is along the same lines. You're taking two viewpoints that you as an individual have and comparing them through dialogue.

Finding Your Therioside

The totem/power animal journey was originally created for seeking external beings. However, guided meditations in general have been used for internal pathworking for a long time. In this case we're going to take the totemic journey and turn it inward, using it to traverse the psyche rather than the external Lower or Other World. The concept is the same, but the intent is what makes the difference. You can get in a car and drive forward, but how you steer it determines where you go. It's the same way with meditation; the structure is just a way to get you where you're going; where that is, is entirely up to you. Although in this meditation you're visualizing natural environments, do so with the intent that this is your mind's way of guiding you into your own psyche; your subconscious mind will choose the best environment to reveal your therioside in.

There's no universal way to interpret the details of the journey, such as the animal's reaction, but you'll want to note it and record it once you're back in normal headspace. Each detail is a symbol, and the best person to determine the meaning of each symbol is you[102]. This is why this is only the beginning of your search for the identity of your therioside.

Part of this is because the animal you find may or may not be your therioside. What you want to do next is simply observe yourself for the next few weeks or even months and see how that animal fits in with what you know of your therianthropy. If you don't know anything about that particular species (or even what species it is) do some research on natural history and the like, not just what you think the animal should be like. Try to remain as neutral as possible, rather than succumbing to wishful thinking; accept that there are equal possibilities that it is or isn't your therioside. In a way, you're "trying on" this animal to see if you successfully got in touch with your therian self, and only you can determine in the end what the outcome was. Not every journey ends in accuracy, so you shouldn't use this technique as the do-all and end-all of your search. If the first animal ends up not working out, try the journey again. You may find your therioside through a process of elimination. You can specifically modify the meditation for that particular purpose. Use it as a way of contacting each animal individually, rather than letting just any animal come up, and then again wait a few months and see if that animal manifests in your therianthropy at all.

The reason that I like this type of journey is because it puts you in direct contact with your own psyche. The potential clutter and confusion of outside sources, such as other people trying to tell you your animal, or pictures and other depictions of animals making you wonder which one you are, is avoided. In this case, it's just you speaking with yourself in a symbolic, structured manner to try to access a particular part of yourself.

A bit of a warning: This isn't a perfect system. As with any form of magic, individual people respond to techniques—including guided meditations—differently. This is particularly crucial since you're dealing entirely with yourself, rather than a dialogue between you and another (ostensibly objective and independent) being. If this sort of journey doesn't work for you, take the basic idea of journeying into your psyche through symbolism and use that to access your therioside.

Also, keep in mind the possibility that you may not even be a therian. You may find that no animal appears which might suggest that you're looking in the wrong place. Or you may find that after you've worked with the animal for a while that it's a totem rather than a therioside. And even if you do determine what you're reasonably certain

---

[102] This does NOT mean your therioside is purely symbolic! Rather, your subconscious mind is using symbols to communicate information to you about your therioside.

your therioside is, using this meditation, that doesn't mean you should stop exploring and questioning yourself. Again, I make no guarantees as to how my techniques will work for people other than me, and this should not be interpreted as a one-size-fits-all solution.

Working With Your Therioside

You can take the journey above and use it in subsequent exploration of your therioside, once you've determined your species. Simply go back through the tunnel with the intent of locating and communicating with your therioside; it generally becomes easier with practice.

I've found this to be particularly useful when I've had some conflict between human-mind and wolf-mind. Since human consciousness is what I'm more familiar with as a result of my body and conditioning, I take on that aspect entirely in the journey while seeking my therioside *as if* it were a separate being. This allows me enough detachment from the situation that I can take a more rational look at it, as well as listen more carefully to what my wolf-mind is trying to tell me. It's like having a verbal argument with a significant other—while you're in the middle of screaming and possibly throwing objects at the wall (though hopefully not each other!) it's hard to really look at the situation with a rational mind. However, if you both go for a walk to cool off and think things through, it's easier to communicate when you talk again.

If you have trouble creating this dialogue, travel through the tunnel to the natural setting. Then visualize yourself as a literally half human, half nonhuman animal, divided right down the middle. Split yourself in half and let each half regenerate itself into a separate whole being, then start a dialogue between the two wholes. When the conversation is done and you're ready to head back, merge both aspects of yourself back into one before you return.

Once you're more comfortable with your therioside, you can try dialoguing, only this time temporarily seeing your human self as the separate being, and visualizing yourself as the nonhuman animal. This is a great way to not only really understand what it is to be nonhuman (at least as much as one can in a human body), but it can also alert you to issues that your therioside may have with the human aspect. For example, let's say I haven't been letting my wolf-self out enough. If I talk to myself as my therioside, I may get the message that that part of me wants to be more active in my everyday life, and some suggestions of what to do. However, by embodying myself solely as my therioside while talking to my human self, I actually fully experience the frustration that the wolf is feeling. Not only does this make the need that much more clear, but it also gives me a clue as to what warning signs to look for if I start repressing my wolf self again.

Keep in mind that you should not find yourself unable to "sense" your therioside outside of meditation! Direct contact such as guided meditation helps you to familiarize yourself with that part of yourself, but you should also spend time outside of meditation observing yourself in everyday life and looking for traces of your therioside as you go about your business. What are some things that you do or think that remind you of your therioside? What habits or traits resemble that part of you the most? In a way, the meditations are like giving a bloodhound a scent from a piece of clothing from a missing person. Once the hound knows that scent, s/he knows to look for it in the environment around hir, isolating it from all other scents. In the same way, knowing the "signature" of your therioside will help you to detect its presence in you as a whole being.

Shifting and Invocation

To some people, the shift[103] is what really makes the therian. Of course, we know that that's not all that there is to therianthropy, especially if you're a contherianthrope who doesn't shift but instead has a stable blend of human and nonhuman aspects at all times[104]. Still, shifting is a large part of the corpus of therian knowledge and a popular topic in the community.

Both therians and non-therians are quite capable of magical shapeshifting; for therians, this is consciously[105] shifting to any animal that s/he does not identify as. A non-therian may identify *with* (but not *as*) hir primary totem strongly enough to say "I am a wolf person" or "I am a turtle person", and even resemble the totem in behavior. But since non-therians generally do not identify as any animal other than human, there doesn't need to be any distinction made as there is with therians who can either A) have a therian shift to their therioside, or B) magically shift to any other animal.

Therianthropic shifting is generally considered to be limited to the inner animal, the nonhuman animal that the therian *is*. This is different than changing your energy/psychology/etc. to something that you

---

[103] A subtle semantic difference—in order to differentiate between magical and therian shapeshifts, I am referring to the latter as simply "shifts", and the former as "shapeshifts". "Shift" tends to be preferred in the therian community, anyway, since it's almost universally accepted that one's physical shape doesn't change.

[104] Lupa 2007

[105] Unintentional shifts to a species other than your therioside is what's known as a cameo shift; I'll cover that later in this chapter.

inherently are not (or do not access on a regular basis, if you believe we have the potential to be all things within us, waiting to be exercised). A non-therian will generally say "I am human"; a therian may say "I am human and [other animal]" or simply "I am a [other animal]".

It's entirely possible that a therianthrope could magically shift with the help of the totem that is the same species as hir therioside. For example, I do distinguish between the wolf that I am, and Wolf the totem who is a separate being from me. If I invoke Wolf, I do not necessarily have to also call on the wolf part of me (though I generally do, whether I intended to or not). Theoretically, I could shift entirely due to Wolf's influence. The same goes for any therianthrope. A heron therian might have a shift induced by Heron the totem, separate from a shift to one's therioside—instead of the shift being induced by whatever internal processes "cause" therianthropy, it can be solely due to the totem.

I'm going to make what some may consider a bold statement, but what others may find more than obvious: therian shifting is a form of invocation (I'll add the *caveat* that this is speaking from a magical viewpoint, and not all may agree.). Allow me to explain.

Traditionally speaking, invocation involves a magician or other magic worker opening hirself up so that an external being such as a deity or spirit may enter hir body for a period of time. Literally, it means "to call in". Invocation isn't quite as intense as the trance possession that is found in certain Afro-Caribbean religions or Heathen mystic traditions. While in trance possession the spirit/deity takes total control of the person, in invocation the magician has some control over the situation and can evict the invoked being if things get out of hand.

However, invocation is not limited to external beings. It is quite possible to invoke parts of yourself in order to bring them to the forefront[106]. We tend to think of ourselves as singular beings (most of us, anyway). We're conditioned to identify primarily with our egos, because in order to communicate we need to present a relatively constant persona to the rest of the world.

This persona isn't as singular as you might think it is. Look at how you act when dealing with your parents, with a police officer, and with children (whether your own or others'). There are subtle differences in how you act in each situation. This effect can be more dramatic if we consciously work to bring out the different personae we wear in each situation. If we explore each one on a temporary basis, we can understand what makes each one unique.

---

[106] Some might argue that this is actually evocation, calling out of. However, since the part of you that you're calling up is not actually being sent out of your body, I choose to refer to it as invocation.

Practice Makes Perfect...

There's not much practical information on shifting in this chapter because I primarily covered it in the last one. However, what I would like to focus on is using magical shapeshifting techniques to help get better control of shifting in therianthropes.

Roughly speaking, involuntary shifts are to stereotypical possession as more controlled shifts are to invocation. It is my belief that many (though not necessarily all) involuntary shifts are a result of a therian not having as much control over hir therioside as s/he could, as well as not giving the nonhuman self enough "space", as it were. In my own case, while most of the activities I take part in on a daily basis are "human" ones, such as being at work, riding the bus, etc., I allow myself to be wolf as well as human, though the wolf-mind tends to be a very subtle overlay rather than a major influence in situations where being too wolfish would be inappropriate. I rarely shift any more as a direct result of being able to access my wolf self almost any time I want (or need). Most of the time I walk around perceiving the world with both human and wolf perceptions, at just the right balance for each situation. That balance may shift subtly depending on the specific situation and what's called for, but both are present almost all the time. The only times I generally have involuntary shifts any more are either when I'm under a lot of emotional stress and don't have as much self-control, or when I've been repressing my wolf-self more than is healthy (anything we repress lets us know that it doesn't like that treatment!).

It took me years of work to get to this point, and there were times of backsliding and frustration. This isn't something a ritual or three can magically "fix". People in general are complex beings, and exploring the self literally is a lifelong process as we continually add to our experiences and how they affect us. The techniques I have described here are some of the tools with which I have managed to balance myself out as both wolf and human, and I haven't just set them up on a shelf to collect dust now that I am where I am. I continue to improve myself, and this is one manner of doing so.

To get better control of shifts involving your therioside, use the basic ritual format described in the previous chapter to deliberately provoke shifts. (Keep in mind that you are calling on your therioside, not an external being such as a totem.) Done over time in a safe setting, you can figure out what tends to trigger shifts, and learn to not only deliberately shift, but also prevent an unexpected shift. Some might argue that this is impossible, that a shift is more like an epileptic seizure. Again, I remind readers that your mileage may vary, and these techniques are not one size fits all. As a therian, I have gained control (for the most part) over my shifts, certainly more than I had before I began exercises like these. And I know other therians who have increased their ability to start or stop shifts. Does this completely negate the possibility of involuntary shifts? Not necessarily. But this material can help in minimizing the chance of them occurring in some therians.

Once you're more comfortable with shifting you may try experimenting with going outside of the ritual area still shifted. The ritual area is a training ground, but you shouldn't associate it with shifting so much that you can't induce a shift anywhere else. Be cautious, of course, when taking your environment and the people and things in it into account. This shouldn't be attempted until you are capable of banishing at will, in case of an emergency. Additionally, be aware of what your motivation for the shift is. While I tend to trust most people to have good common sense, there are always those who think that therianthropy is about being big and tough, and who may wish to use the shift as a way of getting revenge on someone else, or otherwise partake in sheer stupidity. If you do not have control of yourself and your emotions in the "human world", shifting isn't going to help. So if you happen to be one of those deluded folks who decides that shifting would be a great way to enhance your chances if you pick a fight, you're better off dealing with your internal issues before working with this sort of material.

Eventually you'll find you no longer need all the props and such to shift consciously. At this point you can experiment with integrating your nonhuman animal-mind with your human-mind until both are present to some degree at all times. You might try thinking of it as adjusting the hot and cold water in the shower to get it just the right level of warm. Or, after a shifting ritual, imagine the therioside melding with your human body rather than sliding away underneath. Again, you should be able to completely undo the shift at will before attempting this in case things get out of hand.

Just remember that this exercise is meant to help you gain more control over yourself as a whole. It's not meant to make you a ferocious beast 24-7. Rather, your goal should be to find the happy medium between human and not-human so that both can be a part of your perception and mindset at all times. Each person's balance varies; you have to determine that one for yourself. You may still shift sometimes, but this will help you to have better control over them for the most part.

Finally, I would highly recommend picking up a copy of William G. Gray's *Magical Ritual Methods*. It's by far the best explanation of the mechanics of ritual magic I've read. As I mentioned earlier in the chapter, it's essential to know how magic works, rather than just the fact that it does. Gray does an exceptional job of essentially walking the reader through the process of creating a magical cosmology, while at the same time going into great detail as to why each thing he describes is important for making the magic work. The writing style may be a little difficult for those not used to denser writing, but with a little time and patience it's definitely worth the effort.

I won't guarantee you instant results or even any results at all. If these exercises sound like something that may work for you, by all means give them a try. If you need to alter them to fit your personal needs, there's nothing wrong with that. As with any form of magic, all I (or anyone else) can do is offer ideas. It's up to you to find your own best path.

Cameo Shifts and Totemism

Not surprisingly, totemism and animal magic have been major parts of my magical practice. I would probably attribute this at least in part to being aware of something lupine in me at a very young age, though I didn't know what it was until my late teens. Whether my therianthropy is a result of a psychological quirk, a spiritual experience at a young age, or simply a matter of lifelong conditioning, I have always cultivated an awareness of that within me which wasn't the human animal.

Part of my earliest therian experience involved the totemic Wolf coming to me as a very young child, which was what made me first aware of the wolf inside of me. While, once again, I didn't necessarily understand what was going on, I developed that relationship over time. I found that the more I allowed myself to be lupine, the easier it was to relate to Wolf on hir own level. This became a very valuable lesson later on.

When I had been practicing totemism for a few years, I began working with invoking totems other than Wolf. I started with the totems I called on for the four directions; while Wolf is North, Hawk has always been the East, Bear(s) the West, and various animals have held the post in the South, as it represents change. I first noticed that I would shift when I would call the directional totems—not just holding the totem inside myself, but noticing a definite response in my own (nonphysical) body. As each one entered the ritual space, s/he would use my body as a temporary conduit, and I would experience a brief but strong energetic shift to whatever animal energy was being called in. So I began experimenting with invoking other totems in my magical work.

Before that point, I had only evoked totems outside of myself, other than Wolf. Invoking different totems was definitely an experience!

Each one, of course, has hir own personality and energy, and so provided a different area of influence to work with. Instead of evoking the totems and trying to coordinate the magic we were working with outside of my body, the invocation allowed the totem to "shadow" what I was doing so we could work together more easily. In addition, I found myself experiencing what are known in the therianthropy community as cameo shifts, shifts to an animal other than one's therioside[107]. (I am admittedly using that definition in a very broad manner in this section; generally speaking most cameo shifts occur without any outside influence, but as I will explain shortly it's possible to shift without invoking a totem or other being.)

This was a bit of a breakthrough in my practice overall. Not only did it help to get me out of a very lupocentric mindset, but it also showed me that shifting helped me communicate with and relate to totems with more ease. While I hadn't had the lifelong relationship with the others that I had with Wolf, I found that the bond strengthened with practice. The shifts helped them to get the message across easier, and it gave me the additional experience of learning in more depth what these totems had to teach.

These days, even if I'm only evoking a totem, I will energetically shift to that animal temporarily as a way of reaching out to hir. After all, we're both working together, and s/he shouldn't have to do all the work hirself! If the totem is an animal unfamiliar to me, I may do a preliminary journey to introduce myself to hir, so s/he knows who I am and so I can get a sense of hir energy. I find, though, that the totems generally appreciate my efforts to reach out to them and communicate on their terms as best as I can in this body.

Inducing a cameo shift, of course, is easier if you already have practice with shifting. I would recommend using invocation to help with your initial attempts. This allows the totem to show you what it feels like to be that particular animal. Don't skip this step—just because you routinely shift to one particular species of animal doesn't mean that you'll automatically be comfortable shifting to a different one. Wolf and Fox may be similar, but I had to learn how to be Fox; it didn't come as easily to me as Wolf. You can use the same general sort of shapeshifting ritual that I explained above, though you can change the trappings to reflect the specific totem you're invoking. A statue, picture, or other image of the totem may serve as a focus, or you can wear costumery that reminds you of that animal.

---

[107] Lupa 2007, p. 126

Once you've gotten comfortable with the totem's energy, you can induce a cameo shift without invocation. Use the same ritual as above, but instead of calling on the external totem, call on the energy of yourself that you felt when you shifted to that totem. Then when you want to work with that totem again but don't want to do a full invocation of hir, you can call on the corresponding part of yourself and use that as a method of easier communication with the totem. Ellwood theorizes that when you first invoke a totem or other entity, s/he leaves a bit of hir energy within you, while you give a piece of yours to hir. Later, when you go to invoke hir again, that energy in both of you acts as a mutual homing signal to make the process a little easier[108]. If you want to try cameo shifting without invocation, simply draw on that energy within you; you might try visualizing it as being in the shape of the animal that gave it to you, buried deep in your body and then brought out for the shift. Or you might associate it with a particular color and imagine your energy turning that color to make the shift happen.

Additionally, if you still experience involuntary cameo shifts at times, having had experience with shifting to animals other than your therioside can help you gain control of the situation sooner, or at least be able to analyze what's happening so you can then figure out why you've shifted to that particular animal. I figure it's at least worth contacting the corresponding totem afterward to help determine whether the cameo shift was a message, an indicator of something going on internally on your part, or just a fluke. I'm not satisfied with the idea that all cameo shifts "just happen" for no real reason, and I think that when they do occur that we should at least consider the possibility that they were more than a cosmic "oops".

While this chapter has primarily been written for therianthropes, anyone can shift, though therians may be more comfortable with the concept through practice. Therians might find that shifting to animals other than their theriosides is more difficult at first, and doesn't as natural as shifting to their therioside. Non-therians, on the other hand, may not notice any difference, unless they're particularly used to working with a specific totem. Functionally, there's really no difference between a cameo shift in a therian, and a deliberate ritual shift brought on by a magician (therian or not) other than one is unexpected and the other is planned. Both involve a person shifting to an animal that s/he doesn't identify as (since non-therians don't identify as any animal except for human). And that brings me to my last point for this chapter...

---

[108] Ellwood 2007, p. 166-167

Journaling Exercises

1. If you are a therianthrope who is having trouble identifying your therioside, or if you suspect you may be a therian, try using the guided journey and subsequent research to see if you can figure out your therioside (if there is one). Try recording your daily thoughts on the animal that appears in your meditation as a way of helping determine whether that's what type of animal you are.

2. Use the shapeshifting ritual to work with your therioside.

3. Work with the totem of a species other than your therioside. Use the shapeshifting ritual as above. You can use the same journal entry as in exercise two, except add in a line for "totem worked with". Your "other notes" can be used to compare your experiences with the totem with experiences with your therioside and the corresponding totem, among other miscellaneous information you deem important.

Sample Journal Entry:

Date:
Setting:
Props/Costumery:
Purpose: (*to work with a totem, to gain control of therian shifts, etc.*)
Totem(s) worked with (optional):
Other notes:

Chapter Nine: Ask Not What Your Totem Can Do For You...

A Brief Theory About Archetypal Totems

Here's where I delve even more deeply into Unverified Personal Gnosis (UPG) territory. I am a big fan of the idea that totems are archetypes akin to the Animal Master that Joseph Campbell talked about. One possible theory regarding Paleolithic art, including cave paintings, is that they were a part of rituals designed to entreat the Animal Master of a prey species to release a few of his herd for a successful hunt[109]. This was primarily derived from Henri Breuil's hunting magic hypothesis of cave art that he developed in the early 20th century and maintained throughout his life. Although there have been other theories explaining the paintings, and some convincing evidence to disprove Breuil's ideas, we can never truly know for sure that there was no connection whatsoever[110].

Regardless of the original intent of the cave paintings, the archetype of the Animal Master is one that, on a spiritual level, resonates deeply within me. It makes sense on certain levels, and has meshed with some of my UPG, in particular my perception of what totems are. I believe that they are intermediaries between humans and animals. I also believe that just as totems teach us about the animals they protect, they can also convey information about us to their children.

The reason I believe this is because certain species seem to have learned to adapt to humanity better than others. Part of this is due to mundane reasons, such as the need for a specific type or size of habitat, or having a relatively limited diet. However, certain species seem to display particularly adept adaptation in the face of human encroachment. For example, squirrels, rabbits, possums, raccoons, and numerous songbirds have become familiar urban inhabitants in many U.S. cities. Even coyotes and deer are encroaching on the suburbs (and in the case of coyotes, even deeper urban areas). However, wolves and elk are scarce, and bears and cougars only make occasional (and often disastrous for them) forays into human territory as their habitats are chewed up by suburban sprawl. While I think that some of this can be attributed to the physical and behavioral adaptability of the species, that adaptability also feeds into the very

---

[109] Campbell 1984 and 1988
[110] Curtis 2007

essence of what the totem is, and is something the totem can help to promote.

In this manner, some totems may be more successful than others. However, sometimes the extenuating circumstances may be too great for the species to overcome. In that case, I believe that this is when the totem may turn to us for solutions, having taught hir children all that s/he possibly can. I don't believe that totems exist solely to teach us things; rather, I see them as beings whose primary purpose is to protect their physical "children". In that respect, it can be beneficial to aid humanity to higher forms of consciousness so that we don't end up blowing the whole planet up!

When we work with totems, it isn't just beneficial for us. We have the potential to be incredibly helpful to them as well. While they may have more influence than we do in spiritual realms, we have a unique advantage in the physical realm. Physical animals can't speak for themselves, and totems only reach a relatively tiny portion of the human population. That means that those of us they can speak to have the ability to act as intermediaries between the world of totem and their children, and humanity. This doesn't necessarily have to be proselytizing to people to convert to animism and find their totem animals. Rather, it means that we can communicate the needs of animals to other people better than those animals ever could.

Giving Back to the Totems

Remember earlier in the book when I talked about the relationship humanity as a whole has to wolves? We tend to take all animals for granted (ourselves included). Yet here we are at a time when many species, including some with popular totems, stand on the brink of extinction, never to be seen again in this world. Pretty shrines and offerings of trinkets may be aesthetically pleasing, but they do no good to the physical animals. Some of the greatest offerings we can make to our totems are aimed at preserving their children.

With regards to extinct totems, their physical counterparts are gone from this world, and in many cases this is a sad reminder of the impact humanity has on other species. It also may lessen their power and impact on this world, which means they need our intervention more than ever. They may appreciate attempts to preserve their living cousins, or to prevent further extinctions overall.

We are not the only beings affected by pollution, climate change, and other environmental problems. We are, however, the cause of them, and we are the only ones who can reverse them. They are our responsibility. For every species lost, there is power lost on both ends of the equation. The totem of that species loses power and influence on this world. And the physical world suffers the loss of a vital piece of itself. It is as though a chunk of the earth's DNA is removed with each extinction. By working with the totems of extinct species in particular, we can help to reintroduce at least some of that power, if only temporarily, to both the totems and to this world. This power can be used to help heal the world and prevent further degradation and loss.

Making conscious choices about the impact we have can help animals by giving them a healthier environment to live in. Buying local, organic and free range food reduces the amount of pesticides, fuel exhaust and other poisons in the water, land, and air, and promotes better living quarters for livestock. Recycling and reducing the amount of resources you use in general cuts down on the amount of garbage (and resultant toxins) as well as easing the pressure on natural resources.

It doesn't take much time to contact your elected representatives on key legislation and causes. The Endangered Species Act in the U.S., for example, seems to be constantly under threat as various administrations attempt to weaken it in the name of placating anti-environmental interest groups. Various nonprofit watchdog organizations keep a close eye on this important law and notify their membership (and anyone who happens across their website, as well as what media contacts they have) of potential changes for the worse. Regardless of where you live, though, stay abreast of legislation that could potentially impact animals. When it comes up for a vote by your elected officials, contact them (even email will work) and let them know your thoughts. And, of course, anything you can vote on yourself is a chance to really let your voice be heard.

One of the most effective—and simple—offerings is to donate a certain amount of money to a nonprofit organization[111] that works to protect and/or rehabilitate wildlife, or that helps place homeless domestic animals into "forever homes". Even local shelters can always use extra funding for various projects and needs. If you don't have extra money, consider donating your time through volunteering or writing letters. And, of course, if you're in the market for a domesticated pet, adopting a shelter animal is a great way to honor both the critter you bring home and any totem you want to make an offering to. Adoption fees are crucial to helping shelters stay in business, and of course one more adopted pet means a little more space to bring another rescue in.

---

[111] Appendix A has contact information for just a few of the many relevant nonprofit organizations out there.

Pagans love pets for the most part, and we aren't always content with dogs and cats. Exotic pets like parrots, snakes, and certain fish are often caught in the wild and forced into captivity, with a fairly high mortality rate before the animals ever make it to the pet store. Many people in general, including store employees, are inadequately educated about the specific needs of these animals (or, for that matter, cats and dogs). If you must have an exotic pet, insist only on buying captive bred animals that have been properly socialized and don't have the diseases and parasites that wild caught animals often have. Better yet, look for a local shelter that specializes in exotics. Reptiles, birds, and ferrets are particularly common in species-specific shelters.

Even if you just have a cat or dog, there's another very good reason to look to shelters first. If there's less of a market for puppies and kittens, then breeders will breed fewer litters, and lead to fewer unwanted animals euthanized in shelters. Spaying and neutering are pretty much a given, though another reminder won't hurt, especially since there are still people under the misconception that "just one litter" won't matter. One female dog and her pups can produce almost 70,000 offspring in less than a decade; a female cat and her young can have well over 400,000 kittens in the same time period[112]. If you absolutely have to have a purebred dog or cat, look for breed rescue groups first; while greyhound rescue organizations are the best known, there are breed-specific rescues for others as well. **Under no circumstances** should you get a puppy from a pet store—the vast majority of them come from puppy mills, huge collections of tiny cages holding abused, ill-socialized bitches that are bred at every heat, and otherwise maltreated dogs. The breeding itself is done without any regard to genetics, and so congenital defects from poor joints to neurological problems are commonly passed down from generation to generation. In recent years, the puppy mill industry has even tried to legitimize accidental breedings by inventing such "cute" names as peekapoo (Pekingese/Poodle cross); another glorified catch phrase is "designer dog".[113] You want a designer dog (read: mutt)? Go to your local shelter, and you'll find all sorts of wonderful one-of-a-kind pups of all ages there, without dropping a thousand dollars or more for some poor pup with numerous health issues. If puppy mills don't get money, they go out of business.

Make sure your home is critter-friendly, too. Look out for toxic houseplants that cats may like to chew, and don't put chemicals (the blue stuff) in your toilet bowl if that's where your dog likes to get a drink. Be

---

[112] Goldstein and O'Keefe 2003
[113] Sidy Boys Web Design 2007

sure that your house or yard is safely secured so that your dog can't get out; if you have an outdoor dog, only leave hir on a chain for a very short time to do hir business if you don't have a fence or large pen. Being chained can make dogs aggressive and make them feel unwanted and detached from the family. Keep your cat inside where s/he'll be safe from cars, dogs, and—most dangerous of all—people who think that hurting animals is fun. If you must let hir out, do not declaw hir; and any outdoor animal should have a collar and tag in case s/he gets lost.

Depending on your preference, you may also choose to be a vegetarian or vegan as an offering to the totems. I personally am omnivorous for health reasons, and also because I see plants as being every bit as alive and important as animals. However, I do try to stick to free range meat and sustainably harvested seafood as much as my budget will allow. And, as noted in *Fang and Fur, Blood and Bone*, I work with animal parts as part of my magic and spirituality. Avoiding meat, however, helps to ease up on the massive resources required to raise domesticated animals, and not buying meat from factory farms keeps money out of the pockets of conventional meat sources, which stuff livestock full of antibiotics and other such things, and keep them in horrific living arrangements. Carefully choosing seafood from sustainable populations can help prevent the collapse of entire species due to overfishing. On the other hand, even a vegan diet can have a negative impact if the vegetables, fruit, and other plant matter are grown in nonorganic, non-sustainable conditions.

Everyday Offerings

It may be more impressive for a person to donate $100,000 to an environmental nonprofit, but this isn't realistic for most of us (as nice as it would be to have that kind of money to drop!). However, little things do add up, especially over time. This is regardless of whether you're rich or poor, old or young, urban or rural. It's all about changing your habits, one at a time.

Start with your shopping habits. You may not be able to buy organic produce or free-range meat and eggs every week, but try buying one such product once a week. A large package of free range chicken usually only costs a couple of dollars more than a conventional one, and may even be comparable depending on where you live. If you're fortunate enough to live near a farmer's market where locally-raised chickens can be bought, you can ask the person who raised them how they lived and what they were fed (The same goes for produce.). Don't buy more food than you need, to avoid waste—planning your meals a week at a time can help you decide what you need, as well as minimize the number of trips you take to the store. Regardless of what you buy, too, carry your groceries home in canvas totes or other reusable bags, rather than paper or plastic (I occasionally get plastic bags as trash can liners and paper bags for cat litter and recyclables, but other than that it's canvas or carry-out.). In fact, items with less packaging are better, and if you have the choice between recyclable or nonrecyclable packaging, go for the former (Check with your local recycling facilities to find out what they can take—not all plastics or paper types are acceptable.).

With other consumables, including everything from clothing to dishes, furniture to books, buy used when you can. It's cheaper, and it means fewer resources used (If you bought this book used, so much the better!). If you must buy new, try to look for "green" products, such as clothing made from organically-grown plant fibers, or paper products made from recycled material—the latter is especially important since it makes recycling profitable for the recycling companies. And when you're transporting what you buy, use public transit, bike, or walk when possible. Gas is expensive anyway, and I've found that since I moved to an area with good transit I've been able to save money and get more reading time!

I think you get the idea with changing your shopping habits. But what about when you're not shopping? How can you help when you're just sitting at home? The first obvious answer is to cut down on energy consumption. I think we're all heard the benefits of turning off lights that aren't in use, and not letting the water run while we brush our teeth. But we can also help by using fans and open windows instead of air conditioning, and wearing warm sweaters and long underwear while turning the thermostat down. Next time you go to the refrigerator, check to see if you really need it as cold as it is—unless you're in a really hot climate, you can probably get away with having it on the (relatively) warmest setting. And how about a candlelight supper, complete with cloth napkins?

You can even help when you're just sitting at your computer. Most politicians have websites and email these days, and their constituents can easily contact them without using a single stamp (On the other hand, some people argue that emails are easier to ignore—make sure you make your subject line neutral so that the politician—or hir aide—doesn't immediately delete it.). Additionally, while online petitions have limited effectiveness, passing them on can help inform others of issues at hand. And thanks to the joys of Paypal and online shopping carts, it's incredibly easy to make a donation to an environmentally-friendly nonprofit organization (Appendix A has some suggestions). Next time you're about to order a t-shirt with your totem on it, or a similar unnecessary (though

SHINY!) item, take the money you would have spent on it and instead make it into a donation. It'll do a lot more to help you totem than contributing to the use of even more resources.[114]

On Food Offerings

I know I touched on this in *Fang and Fur*, but I feel it's important enough to bring up again. I personally do not believe that it's a good idea to offer food to physical wildlife or, under certain circumstances, domesticated animals.

I remember when I was a kid, my mom took me to a park where we fed bread to the ducks. This is a common practice, and people think it helps the ducks. However, bread is "human food". There are preservatives and other ingredients that are not made for animal consumption and which may upset the birds' stomachs. Also, since bread lacks a lot of the nutrients that ducks and other waterfowl need, it can cause them to starve to death by making them feel full before they've eaten enough of real food. In short, feeding bread to birds is like feeding your child nothing but Big Macs and fries. Additionally, feeding wildlife can discourage them from finding food on their own or from teaching their young how to forage for themselves. If the humans stop feeding the animals, the animals starve.

This is not a reason to continue feeding them anyway. Along with the dietary issues, feeding wild animals causes them to lose their fear of humans. This is invariably bad for the animals. Coyotes and bears in Yellowstone National park have had to be euthanized because they were too eager to get into cars to get human food (and in occasional cases have injured humans in their quests). In her book, *God's Dog*, Hope Ryden tells the tragic story of Elsa, a coyote that she attempted to rescue; Elsa had been raised by humans, and then released into the wild by people who ignorantly thought she'd be able to survive. She was half-starved and trying to climb into people's cars by the time Ryden found her (even leaping into the author's vehicle), and was shot and killed just hours before a rescue attempt was made.[115]

Deer routinely get hit by cars, which can lead to serious injury or death on the part of both the deer and humans. This is an especial danger with deer in suburban areas seeking gardens as their natural territory is

---

[114] Admittedly you bought this book, which wasn't necessary to your survival. However, just as a side note, Immanion Press uses print-on-demand technology to print the books. This means that we only print books as they're needed, which translates into no remainders, and no wasted leftovers to be turned into pulp.
[115] Ryden 1979

destroyed by development. Well-meaning people who put out corn and other food are only making the problem worse.

Even bird feeders can cause problems. You might think that the only animals you're attracting are pretty, harmless songbirds, and occasional squirrels. However, mice and rats may be encouraged to invade houses near bird feeders once the seed and suet is gone, and highly omnivorous raccoons and possums can wreak havoc on trash cans. And, once again, what happens when there's no food left?

If you must give a food offering, make it a donation of pet food to a local animal shelter, or check with your local wildlife rescue as to desired supplies. Don't feed your domestic animal friends offerings that weren't meant for their stomachs; the digestive system of a primarily carnivorous dog or cat is very different in many ways from that of omnivorous humans. And do not leave food outside where wildlife may get to it. One practice I have adopted with human food is to invoke the totem, allowing hir to enter my body, and then eating the food, letting hir taste it through my senses. This way the food is offered, but doesn't go to waste.

Activist Magic

Another offering that I've found pleases many totems is magic aimed directly at helping animals survive in this world. I've cast sigils and burned candles to help boost the likelihood that an animal-friendly law will pass, or that individual animals threatened by illegal hunting, animal abuse, or other problems will just happen to escape to better circumstances. I've danced to raise energy to send for my purpose. I may not ever see these individual animals, but I may send out energy or servitors for the purpose of finding a single animal, any animal, in need, whether from a particular threat or whatever is the most pressing need.

For example, in 2007 there was a massive coyote hunting contest in Montana. Not only did I contact the ironically named then-Governor Otter and voice my displeasure (even though I was a resident of Washington at the time) but I also sent off energy to help coyotes stay out of the crosshairs—and to cause hunters to injure themselves or otherwise have a fruitless hunt. There was no way to physically determine the efficacy of this work, but subsequent divination showed success. With regards to laws, it's easy to find out how your officials voted and whether the law passed or not. Even an apparent failure in the short term may cause change later on down the line; an official may later discover information that causes hir to vote in a more positive manner from then on.

Earlier I mentioned the work I did with Bachman's Warbler, a totem whose children are exceptionally close to extinction. The first ritual I did was a simple candle burning, still one of my favorite forms of magic after all these years. I visualized Warbler's nest in the center of a wooden bowl I use as an offering dish, and placed a candle holder in the center. I then took a green candle and, with the help of several of my spiritual friends, family, and guardians, charged it full of energy for the purpose of helping that single egg of Warbler's hatch and bring more hope for the species as a whole.

There was a little bit of wax left over from the candle, so I decided to incorporate it in a series of servitors meant to further aid Warbler in her hopeful recovery. I took some air-drying clay and created four small bird figurines, each with a piece of the wax in its belly. Once the clay had dried, I did a ritual to evoke Warbler into the ritual area. Once she arrived, I breathed "life", for lack of a better word, into each one of the figurines, bringing them awareness. I then asked all of my spiritual allies who were willing to donate some of their own energy to help, and directed the energy into the figurines by shaking a rattle with increasing speed. Once the energy was sealed into the spirit birds, I told them to follow Warbler back to her home, and I told Warbler that they could take care of tasks that she couldn't. As with all servitors I create, they were to feed on ambient energy, though if they got too depleted they could come back to their individual figurines, which I set on my altar.

It's a much better idea to keep your magic focused. Think of magic like shooting a gun: a shotgun may have a wider range, but a rifle's bullet will penetrate much more deeply. Instead of a vague spell aimed at "saving the Earth" or "wrapping the world's wildlife in white light" (which will end up quickly dissipating due to being spread too thinly), let your intent be something very specific. Try to help an animal-friendly law pass, or put protective energy into a green space that you remove litter from.

Turning Actions into Rituals

Ritual is about intent. It's also designed to get us to be consciously aware of what we're doing above and beyond our everyday state of consciousness. When we perform a ritual, regardless of how simple or complex it may be, our actions are focused on that specific intent, and (ideally) nothing else. However, a ritual doesn't have to be a formal affair done in a specially blessed room with eighteen different colors of candles, a special chalice that we never touch except on special occasions, and that one robe that cost more than a week's pay. Any action can be turned into a ritual. I once turned a trip to the shoe store to get a new pair of Chuck Taylors[116] into a prosperity ritual. I was jobless, and I made the purchase a statement of intent that I would soon be employed. In less than two weeks I had a new job.

Rituals also change us internally by helping to clear out distractions and letting us focus on what's really important. The experiences we have in ritual open us up more to the intent we designed the ritual for, and make us more receptive to them. The altered states of consciousness we achieve make us more receptive to the ideas; in a way, a ritual is a way of programming ourselves. (This is why it's very important to know what's involved in a ritual before you participate in it!)

Rituals also change the world around us. Not only do they reshape our actions after the ritual, which have an impact on the world, but according to some models of magic, they directly influence the macrocosm. From an energetic perspective, the ritual sends out a specific frequency of energy attuned to the initial intent which can change the energy of people, places, events, things, and so forth that it comes into contact with.

By turning activism into a ritual we can have extra impact. Say, for instance, that you make an offering out of picking up garbage in a nearby piece of wilderness. Obviously you're helping by cleaning the physical area. However, you are also impacting yourself by reinforcing the belief that it is important to keep this place clean. Additionally, you're sending out concern, protection and love for that place, which can affect both it and people nearby, or who are otherwise connected to it such as potential developers, decision makers, and so forth.

A very simple form of magic is charging certain items associated with your activism. Say a prayer over a letter sent to a public official who has the opportunity to make a decision for the better (or worse). Add some energy to a check sent to a nonprofit. Imbue a bag of pet food donated to a shelter with healing or a spell to help the animals that eat it get good homes.

To add extra strength to your activist ritual, turn it into a regular practice. This will help build up the momentum and energy around it with each repetition. For example, set aside an hour each week to write letters to your elected officials. Or volunteer a day every month walking dogs at an animal shelter or helping out at a wildlife refuge. Make each repetition occur with the same general intent—to aid the totems. The specific

---

[116] I have since switched over to No Sweat Apparel's sweatshop free look-alikes. Curious? Check out http://www.nosweatapparel.com.

totems you intend to help may differ from ritual to ritual, but the power is still there.

Sacred Ground

It's also possible to "adopt" a wild place to protect. This can be anything from your own back yard to a piece of national forest.

Start by identifying how accessible the place is. If it's close by, then you'll be able to visit more often. If it's on private property, you may want to be mindful of the owner's wishes. Do you have to do some hiking to get there, and do you have health issues that may be a concern? If it's an urban spot, how safe is the neighborhood, and will this affect when it may be wiser to visit?

Assess the condition of the place. Is it relatively untouched woodland, or an urban park covered in garbage? How does it feel energetically/spiritually? Does it welcome your arrival, or do you have trouble connecting with it? Does this change with each visit?

Once you have a good rapport with the place, start spending more time getting to know the locals. What animals and plants do you notice around you? Do they seem healthy? Are there any invasive species competing with native ones? Are there many people there, and do they show the place respect? Do you notice any spiritual presences that manifest as animals that may no longer live there, or never were native there in the first place?

After you have a good relationship with the place and the place is amenable to it, start working with totems there. Depending on how secluded the place is you may like making a small shrine out of organic materials there, though be aware that anything obvious may be susceptible to vandalism, while more subtle shrines may simply be damaged by accident. You may also want to keep any magical workings you do quiet if there are other people around. Still, that doesn't mean you can't make the place into a safe space for totems.

Long-term protection of your sacred ground may take some effort. For instance, if it ends up being threatened by development, can you take action to stop the destruction? Are there other people who feel as strongly as you do? If you have to move away, is there someone you can entrust it to? Keep in mind, too, that although you may leave a place physically, you can still have a connection to it energetically.

The practical reasons for working with your own sacred ground are pretty obvious—you can pick up trash, get to know the place and its inhabitants better, and benefit from having a wild place to retreat to. However, by caring for the denizens of that place you are honoring not only them but their respective totems. Additionally, you can turn that place into a spiritual sanctuary for those totems. Sacred ground doesn't have to be the place that everybody goes to, such as Stonehenge or the coast of the ocean. Even if it's only sacred to you, that's still enough.

Artwork Offerings

It's not always easy to get people to pay attention to environmental issues, at least not in any manner beyond "Oh, that's so sad". Direct action may turn them off, make them defensive, and otherwise be counterproductive. Even I tend to be rather cynical about groups such as the Earth Liberation Front and the People for the Ethical Treatment of Animals. Being "in your face" can often be just as destructive to the environmental movement because it alienates people and makes them less likely to listen to any message. Shouting isn't always the best way to communicate, and more volume doesn't always work.

Sometimes we have to work in subtle ways to let people know why these issues are important to them. One method that I like for creating more awareness, as well as creating offerings for totems, is artwork. Most of the ritual tools and other artwork I create is animal-themed, and almost all of it incorporates bone, fur, feathers and other animal parts. However, the concept I'm about to describe works well with any medium that can be used to portray animals. This includes visual media such as paintings and sculptures, writing of all genres, song, instrumental music, and dance, among others.

On the totemic end of the artwork, each piece of art that I create with one or more species in mind brings honor to those species' totems. Totems are partly "made of" the attention we give them and their physical counterparts; belief is power. Each depiction of a species gives more power through belief and attention to the corresponding totem. Additionally, when I work with the spirits in the skins and bones, this helps not only those spirits but also pleases their respective totems. I can consciously create each piece of artwork as an offering to the totems involved.

With regards to humans, the artwork is a reminder of the existence of those animals. For example, a lot of the jewelry I sell with animal parts or images of animals goes to people who want a daily reminder of their totems or animals that they like. Granted, there are numerous people who buy images of various animals and then treat the physical counterparts poorly; a good example is trophy hunters who will wear t-shirts with deer on them, and then kill a buck only for his antlers. However, this is why I say a blessing over each piece of artwork I create with animal parts during the purification process. I ask that each work will go to someone who will love it and cherish it for who and what it is; I state my intent, and I attach it to the artwork.

I make this intent part of my "selling point" with the artwork. My primary clientele are pagans and occultists who are A) aware of magical practice, and B) generally speaking, aware of environmental issues and their connection to them. This is not to say that I won't sell to other people, but I am pretty selective about where I'll vend. Even the non-magical customers, though, get the full "speech" about the artwork. And while I can't do follow-up with everyone, it's my intent that the very presence of my artwork will subtly coax the customer towards more awareness of animal-related issues.

Of course, it's possible to use artwork to be a lot more blatant. Auctioning off a piece of artwork as a benefit for a particular nonprofit organization is one possibility. Depending on your medium, your artwork could also carry an environmental message in it. A painting could depict the before and after images of deforestation; a story could include themes of preservation of the environment.

Even in private practice, though, your creativity can be a wonderful offering of energy. Part of my therioshamanic training involved developing a drum rhythm, song, and dance for each of my totemic allies. Even if you never share the artwork with any other people, it can be a well-appreciated offering to a totem, as well as a reminder to you of the presence of that totem in your life.

The Human Connection

Why focus on the human animal? Because that is the species that has the most influence over the safety of the world right now. While working to better the cause of humanity may benefit animals as directly as some of the other suggestions, there's good reason to do so.

Some of the biggest dangers to the environment come from mishandling of resources, natural and manmade. This includes everything from dumping raw sewage into waterways, to toxic chemicals released by improper processing of e-waste such as old computers, and even poaching of highly endangered species for food or black market use. These practices aren't limited to huge corporations that should know better. They're also often found in poverty-stricken areas where the cheapest way of getting things done is considered the best, and people will even expose themselves to poisons in order to get enough money to live.

A different angle to the human aspect is awareness. Even among people who may be in postindustrial countries with decent potentials for sustainability, there's still often a low concern for the environment. Again, we run into the issue of poverty. If your biggest concerns are keeping a roof over your head, getting enough food to eat, and paying the bills, buying organic may not be high on your priority list.

Finally, there's the problem of compassion—or, rather, the lack thereof. Not just pollution, but war (including things like nukes and Agent Orange), genocide, and apathy towards famine and other disasters, all may be chalked up in part to a lack of compassion for other people (and other living beings in general). There is a streak of selfishness within human nature that's brought out any time we feel our safety may be threatened. Unfortunately, the perceived threats may not be something material such as a shortage of food, or someone breaking into a home. Skin color, religion, even who someone loves, all may be seen as threats by some people, causing a kneejerk reaction.

While this may sound a bit New Agey, I do believe that it's important to take a holistic look at the environment and related issues— everything is interconnected, and what affects one thing may affect the whole. Racism may not appear to be intimately linked to environmentalism; however, all the energy that is thrown towards racial tensions could be better directed. The same goes towards the energy and attention given to sexism, religious intolerance, and other forms of bigotry. I'm not suggesting that we sweep these problems under the rug and pretend they aren't there. Instead, I argue for finding the best solutions for them and working to bring those solutions around. When we aren't so troubled by bigotry, and when we don't have to worry so much about how others may react to us based on who we are or what we believe, then we can focus more on things that may not involve us directly, but are still important.

The same goes for poverty and economic issues. When people are concerned about where their next meal will come from, the content and origin of that meal isn't too important. If you're starving, you probably won't care if the meat you're being offered came from a conventionally raised cow that grazed on grass that used to be Brazilian rain forest, or from a free range cow raised sustainably in the Pacific Northwest. Granted, this is a generalization, and there are activists who are living hand to mouth, yet who scrape up the money to buy the organics anyway. However, for the most part, poverty is a scourge, and yet another distraction from more "distant" concepts such as "the environment".

I believe wholeheartedly that education is at the heart of the solutions we need. I'm not just talking about formal education, though that's an important part of it. I'm also talking about continuing to make information available on a wider scale, and demonstrating to people from all backgrounds how information has power. Sadly, regimes around the world work to keep people ignorant, and again, horrific living conditions can eclipse any interest or ability to gain necessary education. However, you don't necessarily have to throw yourself into the fight against global starvation, though that can certainly help. Even holding a community workshop on sustainable living or backyard gardening can help. The same goes for writing an article or editorial for your local newspaper or community website. And beyond education, helping people to achieve higher standards of living can help greatly. Try volunteering for, or donating to, Habitat for Humanity (which, by the way, works to create energy efficient homes while conserving resources) to help provide someone with a better place to live.

Bettering humanity may seem a bit contradictory; after all, look at the enormous resource use of the United States, one of the most luxurious countries in the world. However, it is possible to bring the standard of living to a higher point without going to excess. We need to continue to educate on sustainable practices, including in developing countries as well as postindustrial ones. Additionally, the aforementioned education can help in surprising ways; for example, greater knowledge about birth control coupled with better access to resources can significantly lower the birth rate in a given area, thereby reducing the number of humans drawing on resources.

Very few worldwide problems have simple answers. The problem of the environment is no exception. However, by examining all the factors that contribute to the problem, rather than just the obvious ones, we can find more thorough answers and solutions that can, in the long run, benefit all species, not just us.

I know I get pretty preachy here in places; there are some issues I feel very strongly about. Activism is one of those areas where it's best to find your individual comfort zone; better to do a little that you can handle than to burn yourself out trying to do too much. You might try changing one habit a week to start out. Make one week a month an occasion to add a new environmentally-friendly item to your grocery list—for instance, the first month you might start buying only organic apples instead of conventional, then the next month add cloth napkins (which will eliminate your need for paper ones) along with the apples. And so on. Another week each month may be habits to save water, such as using dishwater (with biodegradable soap) to water plants, or not letting the water run while you shave whatever parts of your body you may shave (if any!). Another week could be focusing on contacting your elected officials through letters, calls, emails, or even personal visits depending on the politician; it can also be a week for making a donation (even a small one) to a nonprofit group. And finally, a fourth week could be dedicated to working activist magic of all types.

These are just a few suggestions; as always, make your own ethical decisions. Talk to your totems about what they would like, but if something goes against your ethics, see if you can come up with an alternative.

Chapter Ten: Creating Your Own Totemic System

By now I hope I've made it clear that animal totemism is a much more flexible system than is often assumed. I've provided some ideas about creating a system of totemism for yourself, and I'd like to dedicate this final chapter to fleshing out that concept.

Here are some things to keep in mind.

--What totems will you be working with?

Obviously I encourage people to work with totems besides the BINABM, though even if you choose to only stick to that which is familiar, I'd like to think I've perhaps incited you to think in some new directions. If you find a particular group of totems that appeals to you, such as food totems, try working with them exclusively over a period of time in depth. On the other hand, you may prefer variety, and so work with a wide spectrum of critters. If you're just starting out you may not really know where you want to focus (or what totems may like you in particular), but after a while you may find yourself drawn to some more than others (and vice versa). In some cases, the totems may choose you, so you may find yourself building relationships you didn't really expect.

--What paradigm will you be working in?

You don't have to use drumming, dancing, and medicine wheels to make totems happy. While they originated in cultures that had specific contexts for their spirituality and magic, in my experience totems are pretty flexible. If you're already working within a specific paradigm, try working with your totems as per its parameters. You may have to get a little creative about it, but with time, effort and experimentation you can probably adjust almost any paradigm to allow animal totems. Try substituting a totem animal for another entity you'd normally work with, but use the same kind of ritual, and see what results you get. (If the totem doesn't like it, of course, you can find a good compromise.)

--Is there any other area of magic you'd like to explore in relation to totemism?

Sometimes just brainstorming about a paradigm can give you ideas to play with. If you have thoughts, jot them down and let them simmer in the back of your head for a while if you can't quite figure out what to do with them right now. They might involve a specific totem, a particular group, or they could be for general use.

--What role(s) do totems play in your life?

Your relationships with totems will affect what information is most important to you. For me, totems are the entities I work with the most; they're a very strong part of my spirituality and my magical practice. Therefore, any information involving them is important to me. This may sound familiar; on the other hand, you may have a more occasional practice with them. I would imagine that if you're putting forth the effort to create your own totemic system that you'll probably get rather involved with them, at least temporarily. However, in a primarily practical situation you may be mostly interested in whatever issues the totems are best at helping you with, as well as what they'd like in return.

--What sorts of rituals and other magic do you work with totems?

What types of rituals are most important to your totemic practice? You may prefer a more spiritual relationship, primarily involving meditation and celebrations and only occasionally working with practical magic. The types of rituals may be centered on deepening your relationships with the various totems. You might also like researching traditional rituals involving your totem[117]; for example, David Rockwell's *Giving Voice to Bear* details practices from both North America and elsewhere for honoring Bear and hir children. On the other hand, if you primarily have a practical working relationship with your totems, you may create a personalized series of sigils or spells, or otherwise concentrate on rituals aimed at making active changes in your everyday life. Additionally, if you practice any form of shamanism you may find that different totems accompany you on your journeys to the Otherworld.

--What offerings do your totems like to receive (and what's reasonable for you to give?)? How often do you make those offerings?

---

[117] Keep in mind, of course, that just because you use elements of ritual from, say, Lakota practices, that doesn't make you a practitioner of Lakota religion or a member of that culture.

It's a good idea, especially if you work with numerous totems, to keep a list of offerings each one prefers. This helps avoid confusion, and it also offers you some ready alternatives in case what the totem initially asks for isn't within your current circumstances to give. Be open to new suggestions, of course. However, you may find that certain totems have certain favored offerings. Badger, for example, has come to really appreciate offerings of sushi (especially the fish!).

Some people like to make offerings on a regular basis. Others only make offerings as needed. What you choose to do may depend on your relationships with the totems. While I haven't found totems to be particularly demanding, they do sometimes make special requests. I tend towards a mixture of periodic offerings, and offerings on an as-needed basis.

Your Personalized Dictionary

This is where creating your own totem animal dictionary comes into play. Collect your notes from the exercises throughout the book. Organize them however you see fit. I would suggest collecting information for each species, and arranging it something like this:

Species:
Biological information (habitat, diet, social structure, current population status, etc.):
Mythology and Folklore:
Modern Totemic Lore: (*if you wish, record what other totem dictionaries or magicians have to say about this animal*)
Totem Card Information (if applicable; see chapter four):
Personal Magical and/or Spiritual Qualities: (*these are qualities the totem has conveyed to you directly, not what various authors and other people have written about*)
Rituals and Other Magic Worked With This Totem: (*can include skindancing results, if applicable*)
Misc.: (*dreams, visions, other pertinent information gained while working with this totem, ideas for further experimentation*)

Why collect all this information? As I have mentioned before, a totem embodies all information regarding its species. A lot of totemic information stems from the physical animal's behavior, and while mythology (ancient and modern) shouldn't replace your own observations on totemic qualities, you may find it useful to compare notes with others' experiences. Also, any thoughts you may have on future rituals may be useful when you want to develop the relationship with the totem.

You may want to keep your dictionary in an easy to edit format, such as in a binder or on a computer. I use various blank books for recording raw data and notes from rituals and meditations, but I later compile them into a more condensed format.

Remember, too, that a dictionary is no substitute for actually talking to the totem. If Grasshopper has spent years asking for offerings of lettuce, but then one day requests a ritual in hir honor, don't assume it's a fluke. Ask for clarification rather than assuming that a head of iceberg will do.

One of the most important reasons for compiling your dictionary isn't just so that you can look up information as needed. The process of creating it requires you to really get in touch with the totems and how you work with them. It makes you think about your practice, and may help you find areas to work on, or inspire new experiences. It also helps you realize just how much you do know—which may be more than you expected! It's an excellent learning experience; we can never know everything, and with the many potential totems out there you can spend a lifetime exploring this type of magic.

Creating Your Own Traditions

Beyond this, your decisions are largely a matter of quality vs. quantity. You might like to talk to as many totems as possible, or you may prefer to work with only a few on a long-term basis. Or you could be like me, and do a little of both. While I have worked with a lot of totems during my practice, and particularly in the creation of this book, I still have just a few that I maintain very strong, deep relationships with. You'll probably find that the more you work with a given totem, the more connected you'll become—even if you didn't intend to. And there's certainly nothing wrong with meditating on a totem simply to chat, rather than for any particular purpose. As with any relationship, the connection between you and any given totem is quite personal.

Some people feel that it's necessary to work within a precrafted tradition, such as one stemming from an indigenous culture, or a neopagan reconstruction. There's nothing wrong with that in and of itself. However, as I mentioned before, this can sometimes lead to unhealthy levels of cultural appropriation, and care should be taken to acknowledge one's sources and claims.

As I've mentioned, I have no problem working within a modern neopagan context. I wasn't raised on a reservation, or in the middle of the Amazonian jungles, or on the steppes. I grew up in the rural Midwest United States in a middle-class white family, and I honed my understanding of spirituality both through my own experiences in the woods as a child, and later on within the neopagan, occult, and Otherkin communities. These inform my methods more than any Native American or Australian or other culture does, and I don't think that I'm inferior for it. In fact, if any culture needs an infusion of environmental awareness, it's the very one I grew up in. Rather than jumping ship to another culture, I find I prefer trying to create change from within this one.

Most of my rituals, while sometimes inspired partly by other cultures, are largely my own creation. For instance, the skin dancing wasn't taught to me, nor was any of the rest of my work with animal parts. Rather, this is something that I formulated based on communication with the animal spirits and my own intuition. I've shed most of the elements of other peoples' works and cultures, though I still acknowledge their impact on who I am and what I believe today.

The process by which I developed my own material has been one largely of trial and error. A typical process would involve me getting an idea, trying it out, discarding it after a few tries if it didn't "stick", or developing it further if it was successful. While early ideas were more strongly influenced by others, with time I grew more confident and creative.

This isn't to say there's no value in the work of others.

With or without other books, I'd like to give you some pointers on creating your own system. Some of these I've covered in earlier chapters, but I'd like to bring them all together here. Your methods may not be this organized (my own efforts were all over the place!) but I'd like to at least offer some food for thought, along with the questions I've already asked above. One thing you might use as inspiration is to imagine that you need to put together a tradition that other people can follow; not necessarily something that is one-size-fits-all, but standardized enough so that others can at least understand what you were doing and why. Just don't water down your work in order to make it palatable, unless you actually are taking on students who may be in need of something very basic to start out with. Make sure that the core of it is all yours.

--How often do you want to use formal ritual, meditation, and other practices? Why? Are there special times of the year? Are any of these times associated with specific totems, such as totemic feast days? (The information in chapter five should be particularly useful here.)

--What is the purpose behind your system? Is it celebratory, magical, or both? Will other people be involved, either as participants or patients (as in the case of shamanism)? How will it benefit the totems, as well as yourself and any other people?

--Is there any particular type of totem (such as prehistoric, invertebrate, etc.) that you have a particular interest in or relationships with? Do you want to tailor your tradition to working with them?

--Are there specific ritual effects that you find useful, such as costumes or other tools? Do you find it's better to make them yourself? Do they come from a particular culture, or are they your own individual creations? Can you come up with symbols and other elements inherent in the culture you currently are a part of that are meaningful enough to help create ritual trappings? If you feel your culture is devoid of meaning, can you create symbols from within rather than drawing on another culture that you may not have a connection to? Or do you at least find it helpful to be inspired by other cultures that have active, living totemic and related spiritual systems?

--Do you have to be outdoors, or will a well-decorated indoor temple work as well?

--What about mythology? Can you talk to the totems and ask them to tell you stories about themselves and others? Or are you simply inspired to write myths of your own? What archetypes and motifs are involved? What purposes do these myths serve? Are they simply symbolic, or do you believe that they have a larger cosmic effect on your life, such as taking a creation myth literally?

--What other beliefs are central to your conception of totemism? Why? Do you hold to any personal ethical code? If others are involved, is there any reason to expect them to live up to that code, or can they adapt the tradition you create to their personal boundaries?

--How far are you willing to push yourself as an individual? Are you content where you are, or do you feel the need to explore ever deeper within, and ever higher without? What methods might you use to attain altered states of consciousness for the purpose of this sort of exploration? Can you effectively create ritual psychodrama on your own, or do you wish to recruit the help of others?

--Are there any formal initiations or other rites of passage involved? Or do you simply know the time when it arrives? What do you use to mark these passages? Is this something you intend to keep personal, or will it extend to others?

--Does the system involve any form of activism? How important are the physical animals and their habitats to you? Do you prefer a more abstracted view of totems, or do you see them as spiritual extensions of the physical environment? Can activism be a part of your ritual work?

These are just a few ideas to get you started; no doubt you'll be able to find what works best for you. One thing that really works for me is daydreaming about what sort of path I'd ideally like to follow, and then find ways to make that manifest into my life. For example, as I was writing this book I began thinking more and more about skindancing on a regular basis, including dancing with the skins I hadn't given so much attention to. The more I daydreamed, the more it led me to consciously make time to work with the skins. Eventually, this became a key part of therioshamanism.

The other thing to keep in mind is that you also need to be getting input from the totems themselves. While what I've written above primarily deals with the needs of the practitioner, it cannot be overstated how important it is to listen to the totems and their needs. You may have a fine idea that you think will be perfect, but then the totems come along and say "Nope, we need you to do it this way. Sorry for the inconvenience". (Perhaps not in so many words, but you get the idea!) So always check your needs against those of the totems. You do have the right to question anything they say; if, for example, they want you to do a two hour ritual every day, and your schedule is too tightly packed, there's got to be room for negotiation. I haven't had any unreasonable requests in my experience, though I have had some that were tougher to carry out than others. Still, this isn't just something you're creating for yourself—you're also creating it for them.

Testing, Testing, 1-2-3...

Above all remember that to an extent, creating a personalized system of totemism is about experimentation. You're trying to find something that works for you, as well as the totems you work with—at least, I would hope you are if you're planning on creating something long-term. There's a difference between suffering in a constructive way, such as fasting for spiritual purposes, and suffering due to feeling constrained in your spiritual/magical practices for no good reason.

This may mean that at some point you end up abandoning a practice you've tried for a while with no real results, or diminished effectiveness over time. If this occurs, it doesn't mean you're a failure. Rather, it may be that the practice wasn't a good fit in the first place. Or maybe you've changed enough since first adopting it that it really doesn't fit you any more.

In that case, don't be afraid to try something different. If necessary, go back to the drawing board, start from scratch. That's what I did with therioshamanism—I took the best of what I learned in the first decade of my path, discarded what didn't work, and started all over again. If you find yourself drifting away from a particular totem or group of totems, it would be most respectful to talk to them about it before just leaving them behind. They may have reasons on their end for why things aren't working so well. If it turns out that the relationship is coming to an end, do a ritual of thanks to show your appreciation for their time spent with you.

Keep in mind, too, that spirituality and magic are things that can keep us captivated our entire lives. We are not static, stagnant beings, though. We are continually changing, as is the world around us. You may find that you have a particular core to your path that remains essentially permanent, but the trappings around it change with time. What's most important isn't what you're doing, but what effects it has for you, and for the totems and other beings you work with.

A Challenge to Readers

Some of you have read *Fang and Fur, Blood and Bone*; some of you are only familiar with this book. Either way, you probably have a good idea of some of the ways I've expanded on the subject of animal magic. Now it's your turn.

There's nothing wrong with traditional totemism and other forms of animal magic in and of themselves. And if you're happy with what you already have, no problem! But as I mentioned early on in this book, many animal magicians keep going over the same material again and again, simply because it never occurred to them to do otherwise.

The practice of magic is a key part of my life. Magic, as a discipline, is ever changing as the cultures it inhabits shapeshift with time. In fact, magic *is* change—we create it because we want something in our lives to be different. This is why people are continually inventing new ways to channel and work with magic, whether they view it as energy, as spirit, or as psychology. And animal magic is a realm that has tons of potential for growth.

This doesn't mean you throw out more traditional forms of animal magic. You can be quite an effective magician by working with established paradigms. However, even with the most rigorous regimen of meditation and practice handed down over the years, the individual still tailors it to hir own experience and creates at least a tiny degree of change. What I propose is taking the established paths and preserving them, but also blazing new trails as well. Our ability to cause magic to evolve isn't just limited to tiny incidental increments that are a natural part of the progression of humanity in general. Just as technology has been furthered by those who wanted to see what they could make it do next, so can magic be explored and played with, and brought to new levels of possibility and manifestation.

This doesn't, of course, doom us to the same mistakes that overzealous use of technology has wrought, such as environmental damage. We are able to learn from the errors of the past in any field of study and practice, and apply our understanding of where things went wrong to our own experimentation. It's true that magic is potentially harmful, even by accident, which has led to the creation of cautionary guidelines such as the Wiccan Rede (which are occasionally turned into outright dogma). However, as in *Fang and Fur*, I once again leave the ethics up to you as an individual human being responsible for your own actions and decisions.

So here's the meat of my challenge to you: expand on what I've created here. Play with magic—it likes to play as well as work. Take the concepts of totemism and animal magic (and other forms, if you like) and see how you can build on them to create something new. My goal in all this is similar to that which drove Joshua Wetzel to write *The Paradigmal Pirate*, his groundbreaking work on Chaos magic: "To provide some of the material which will help…magicians…propel themselves past myself and those doing magic now"[118]. We have the potential to take animal magic and improve it, to expand beyond the same dictionaries and attempts to "be just like the Indians!" We are not limited to what already exists, good or bad, but hold in our own minds and hearts the key to creating the wildest magic yet.

Let me tell you more…

---

[118] Wetzel 2006, p. 209

Afterword: The Future of Neopagan Totemism

If I've done my job as a writer well, you've gotten at least something out of this book. However, if you take nothing else away, I ask that you consider the concept of neopagan totemism as a separate entity from traditional totemic systems found in indigenous cultures around the world. I would also add that it is my sincerest belief that neopagan totemism is no less effective than these older systems, and that it can exist without other cultures' trappings.

As I've said before, modern American culture is not spiritually dead. Pessimists would say that all Christians (or in some cases, all monotheists, or even all non-neopagans!) have sucked the spiritual life out of America and replaced it with dogma. I argue that this perspective is just as dogma-laden, because it paints an entire group of people with one broad brush and allows no room for compromise. If America had no spirit, would new religious beliefs, pagan and otherwise, keep cropping up?

We cannot divorce ourselves entirely from the culture we're immersed in. The effects may be subtle, but they're still there. Rather than attempting to distance ourselves entirely, I think it's healthier to at least admit where we've come from and that it does leave an essentially indelible mark on who we are. We can join other cultures and subcultures, but rare is the person who can erase every single trace of hir origins. That doesn't mean, of course, that you shouldn't explore other cultures if that's your preference. Just understand that your perspective will necessarily be at least a bit different from that of someone raised within that culture from birth.

Personally, I'm quite content being a part of American neopaganism, drama, flakes, and all. Yes, we've drawn from other cultures, and we should acknowledge that. However, we've also taken those concepts and made them ours, as well as created new things from them. For instance, look at neopagan totemism. It's primarily drawn from New Age perceptions of Native American cultures' totemic systems, as well as a mishmash of power animal lore and individual spirit guides (again, primarily from Native American sources). But neopagan totemism is different enough from its progenitors that it has essentially become its own entity. It is uniquely suited to the intensely individualistic nature of American culture (and neopagan cat herding), as well as the melting pot ideology of cultural creation. It has combined practices from various cultures, and begun to make them relevant—in practice as well as theory—to this one.

Rather than looking to an often-romanticized past, we need to look at the realities of the present. Much of the New Age material that neopagan totemism is derived from perpetuates a reincarnation of the "Noble Savage" stereotype of Native American cultures. I've yet to see any of these texts address the fact that people are starving on reservations, that Native Americans (as a general demographic) have the dubious "honor" of having the highest rate of alcoholism in the United States[119], and that some of the material presented as "genuine Native American spirituality" has been mixed with New Age concepts such as crystal skulls and Atlantean fantasies. While there are still strong displays of Native American cultures, such as powwows, and certainly not all are in destitute situations, the reality for many of these people, economically, politically, and otherwise, is dire. Yet many of these books would have readers believing that all Native Americans wear buckskins 24-7 and are full of ancient wisdom that they feel honored to dispense to the rest of us, free of charge. These stereotypes place these people firmly in the past, as if they no longer exist as peoples. This is like reading up on Victorian America and then saying that you know everything there is to know about modern Bostonians.

I don't think this means that we have to guilt ourselves incessantly over our theft. Nor does it mean that we have to pretend that indigenous religions don't exist, or that we can't be inspired by them. However, I do think we need to stop using other cultures as escape pods away from the unpleasant aspects of modern American culture and neopaganism. This doesn't necessarily mean looking to non-Native-American cultures, such as pre-Christian European ones (though again this isn't bad in and of itself). Along with the inspiration from those who have come before, I believe we also need to be inspired by what is *now*. We have a unique community of magical, spiritual people who are full of creativity; yet we deface that creativity whenever we say it's not good enough, that the "old ways" are automatically better.

Additionally, we can look at the techniques that indigenous cultures around the world engage in, and see where we can find similar correlations in our cultural context. For instance, when I read about a particular technique in shamanic systems in various cultures, I don't think "Well, I'll have to stitch together the gods from this system with the view of the Otherworld from that one to make this work". Rather, I see what it is that the people are doing, and then I ask myself, "As a modern

---

[119] Szlemko, Thurman, and Wood 2006

American of genuine European mutt stock, raised in a small town and living in a city, how would I go about doing the same thing?"

This is why I so strongly suggest creating your own system, regardless of what your inspiration is. You are yourself. You may have had lives in other times and cultures, but your most recent experience—and therefore the life that almost certainly has had the most impact on you now—is the one you're living right this moment. Your outlook may be somewhat different from other people, but that may have as much to do with your socialization and/or temperament as any effects from past life experiences. It's clichéd as all hell, but people are individuals, and there's a lot more diversity in thought and perspective, even among seemingly "mundane" folk, than is often credited.

It's been said time and again that the best spells you create are your own, that you follow the path that speaks to you, and that you choose what works best for you when it comes to magic and/or spirituality. And if that path is one that's already been created by others, if you're honest about your intentions and experiences, then I see no reason to complain if it fulfills you. However, I also call you to consider what is in the process of being created right now. It's already been determined, for example, that Wicca is only about sixty years old and has as much to do (if not moreso) with the Golden Dawn and other ceremonial systems than with ancient witchcraft. But that doesn't make it an invalid religion; people embrace it in spite of (or, in some cases, because of) its youth.

This is why I have written this book: to give you a resource in creating a system of totemism that is uniquely yours. You may draw on elements of the experiences of other people and cultures, but the bulk of the material hinges on what you, yourself, believe and practice—regardless of where you are, what cultures and subcultures have influenced you, and what path you prefer. I offer this as a way of creating a system that is tailor-made for you as an individual, rather than trying to stuff everyone into the same paradigm.

Neopagan totemism isn't a set tradition with a specific collection of rules and practices. It is simply any totemic system developed by a "new" pagan, whether s/he considers hirself part of the neopagan community at large or not. It's infinitely customizable because it doesn't have a particular set of cultural boundaries to stay within. You, the individual, are the heart of neopagan totemism, and the only person who can judge whether your practices and experiences are valid, is you.

Communicate. Experiment. Create. The only boundaries we set in this adventure are those we ourselves create.

Appendix A: Animal-Friendly Nonprofit Organizations

Yes, I fully admit I lifted some of this list from *Fang and Fur* (though I did update contact info where needed). I still think they're good groups, and I still give a portion of what I make on artwork to the Defenders of Wildlife. They're not the only organizations out there, but they're ones I'm familiar with and have supported in various ways over the years.

Keep in mind, too, that these are just some of the more high-profile groups. Many areas may have smaller organizations that concentrate on local issues, and which may not receive as many donations as better-known groups. The money you give to them could go a lot farther. This includes local animal shelters and environmental groups, among others.

The Defenders of Wildlife
National Headquarters
1130 17th Street, NW
Washington, DC 20036
USA
1-800-385-9712
defenders@mail.defenders.org
http://www.defenders.org

The Defenders of Wildlife work to protect wild species, large predators in particular, worldwide. Programs include not only population growth but also habitat preservation and endangerment prevention.

American Society for the Prevention of Cruelty to Animals (ASPCA)
424 E. 92nd Street
New York, NY 10128-6804
USA
(212) 876-7700
http://www.aspca.org

Royal Society for the Prevention of Cruelty to Animals (RSPCA)
Wilberforce Way
Southwater
Horsham
West Sussex

RH13 9RS
United Kingdom
0300 1234 555/+44 870 33 35 999 (international calls)
http://www.rspca.org.uk

Royal Society for the Prevention of Cruelty to Animals Australia
PO Box 265
Deakin West ACT 2600
Australia
02 6282 8300 (or 61 2 6282 8300 outside of Australia)
http://www.rspca.org.au

The SPCAs in general are aimed primarily towards the welfare of domestic animals, though the various branches do sometimes have campaigns involving wildlife. They do a lot of work towards educating the public about issues and proper domestic animal care.

Humane Society of the United States (HSUS)
2100 L Street, NW
Washington, DC 20037
USA
(202) 452-1100
http://www.hsus.org/

While the Humane Society is best known for pet adoptions, the organization has extensive campaigns for domestic and wild animals alike. If you're in the United States and you're looking for a pet, check out your local Humane Society shelter.

World Wildlife Federation (WWF) International
Avenue du Mont Blanc 1196
Gland
Switzerland
+41 22 364 9111
http://www.panda.org

One of the best-known wildlife preservation organizations, the World Wildlife Federation has spent the past four decades working with issues on a global scale. They focus a lot on both species and habitat based programs, and include the needs of indigenous cultures in their solutions for worldwide problems.

The Wilderness Society
1615 M St., NW
Washington, D.C 20036
USA
1-800-THE-WILD
http://www.wilderness.org

This organization specializes in protecting wildlife habitats; keep in mind that many of the animals facing extinction today are endangered because of habitat loss.

Natural Resources Defense Council
40 West 20th Street
New York, NY 10011
USA
(212) 727-2700
http://www.nrdc.org

Another good organization that lobbies for habitat and species protection, as well as helping more local groups protect areas near them.

Animal Welfare Institute
PO Box 3650
Washington, DC 20027
USA
(703) 836-4300
http://www.animalwelfare.com

A more moderate group than some, this organization nonetheless has been seeking better treatment of animals in the wild, in labs, and in agriculture since 1951.

The Jane Goodall Institute
4245 North Fairfax Drive
Suite 600
Arlington, VA 22203
USA
(703) 682-9220
http://www.janegoodall.org

Founded in 1977 by one of the foremost authorities in biological field research and the behavior of chimpanzees in the wild, the Jane Goodall

177

Institute works to not only protect chimps and their habitats, but to educate people worldwide about animal welfare, conservation, and what we as individuals and communities can do to help animals, both wild and domestic. The JGI features a variety of innovative programs of interest.

Appendix B: All-Purpose Generic Guided Meditation For Totemic Work

I'm dead serious about the title. What this appendix contains is a basic, customizable formula for meeting and working with totems. It can be altered for use for several different purposes as described in this book—and whatever other related purposes you can come up with. I have used it for everything from meeting new totems to visiting familiar ones on a regular basis, and I also use it with the totem cards described in chapter four. I even adapted it for use with Gallegos' *Personal Totem Pole* system. It's been marvelously successful.

You may wish to memorize the basic steps, or you may have someone read it for you. I've put the approximate amount of time you'll want to dedicate to each step, though this can be changed as needed.

First, get yourself in a comfortable position and relax your body. Breathe deeply and slowly, feeling the tension flow out of your body and into the Earth beneath you. Let the thoughts in your head slip away; concentrate on the sound and feeling of your breathing. (Three-five minutes minimum)

Now, visualize a hole—it may be in the ground, or a tree, or the clouds, or ice over an Arctic ocean. Dive into that hole, and it will take you into a tunnel. Travel through this tunnel, whether you walk, run, fly, hop, or swim. (Two-three minutes)

When you come out the other end, you will find yourself in a natural place. It could be a forest or meadow, water or sky, mountain or desert. Take some time to explore this place. (Two-three minutes)

Off in the distance, you see an animal approaching. As it gets closer, take note of its species, or at least what family of animal it is if you're not sure of exact identification (you can always research later). This should be your totem (or whatever other animal entity you're here to meet). (One minute)

Once the animal has arrived, spend a bit of time observing it and, if possible, communicating with it. Why has the totem arrived? What does s/he want to work with you on? How long does s/he intend to be with you? (At least five minutes)

It's time to head back home. Thank the totem for showing up, and that if things are right you'll meet up again. Then head back to the tunnel (if you've lost it, just look down at the ground beneath your feet, or whatever happens to be below you, and the hole should show up. Come back through the tunnel, and give yourself a few moments to "wake up" again. Stretch, get the blood flowing again, and record your results. (Three-five minutes)

Appendix C: Are We Just Splitting Hairs? (Therianthropy and Totemism)

While the shifts to other animals weren't nearly as strong as my usual shifting more towards the wolf side of me, the process was essentially the same for an energetic shift. With practice I also began experiencing an additional mild mental shift, enough to get a taste of the totem's mindset. I found, too, that there were parts of myself that corresponded to those other totems in a manner similar to Wolf. The primary difference was that I had been identifying myself as a wolf inside for so long, and working with Wolf the totem besides, that the bonds with other animals both within and without were nowhere near as strong as the bond with my wolf/Wolf. It's also possible that because I spent such a long time being focused wholly on Wolf, that it took me longer to learn to work with other totems; I'll admit that there was a time early on in my practice that I worried that Wolf would leave if I built relationships with other totems (fortunately that worry was for nothing).

I wonder sometimes if it's possible that the bonds with other totems, and the corresponding parts of myself, could be strengthened to the point where they have as much of an influence on me as my wolf therioside and totemic Wolf do. One argument I've heard brought up quite frequently when discussing therianthropy with magicians who aren't therians is the possibility that we're just misinterpreting an internal bond with a totem or other animal spirit. I hear this especially from Chaos and other postmodern magicians who tend to blur the lines between microcosm and macrocosm, and who may view totems and even entire pantheons as psychological constructs.

Yes, I know that this has gone round and round the therian community numerous times, with the ultimate consensus generally being that a totem is not a therioside and vice versa. However, American culture (which is where the largest numbers of therians come from, me included) lacks a cohesive cultural mythology. We also lack cultural spiritual practices. If anything can be said to be a cultural mythos shared by the majority of people, it's science. When something abnormal happens, we look to science (including the soft science psychology) to explain it before anything else—even those who consider something odd to be an "act of God" are sometimes viewed as being a little off.

We don't have any sort of long-standing mythical explanation to explain someone who feels a spiritual or other internal bond to an animal. We have the popular depictions of lycanthropy, but even this is only a partial match given that it centers on people who physically turn into wolves. The first thought that comes to many non-therians' minds when approached with the concept of therianthropy is "These people are insane!" And some of the explanations laid out for therianthropy as a sane concept deal with it as a psychological condition. In fact, numerous phenomena that were once (and are still sometimes) seen as mystical or magical occurrences are these days packaged away in a nice, neat left-brain-friendly rational package wrapped in science.

Another thing to keep in mind is that since we don't have a cultural mythology, we as individuals may try to make up for that deficiency on our own, whether we realize what we're doing or not. It's my belief that the concept of Otherkin in general is at least in part a manifestation of personal mythology. We internalize anything that doesn't fit neatly into the culture we live in; we either consider it "imagination", or "faith", or "maybe I'm insane".

It's not that far a leap, given the general environment many therians live in, to think that perhaps the mythology of totemism has been subverted by the scientific mindset into a psychological condition (and, according to some people, a form of insanity). If we're conditioned from a young age that the most "true" source is science, and we take that literally, then it's only natural that people will attempt to explain something they don't understand according to the scientific viewpoint. This is especially true when one's sanity is questioned; if a therian can prove that s/he's well-grounded in rational thought, then s/he may feel that s/he is less deserving of ridicule.

So I would like to put forth the possibility that totems, in a form of self-defense, have manifested in some people as theriosides. Since we as a culture are more used to focusing on the individual rather than the society, and because we're raised with such a science-centric perspective, that what may once have been explained as the influence of a spirit guide has become the influence of an abnormal part of psychology. Since we lack a method of understanding and working with this phenomenon, most of us have to figure it out on our own, even if we do have other therians to talk to. It's not impossible, of course; it just takes longer than if there was a support structure in place for dealing with a therianthropic headspace.

Once again, though, I don't necessarily think that this means that totems are only internal constructs of my mind. In my own practice, I view the internal and the external as intimately linked. As Above, So Below = As Within, So Without. I look at the world from a multi-layered perspective where there are multiple correct answers to questions on things like identity. And while it's not my sole explanation for my own therianthropy, I do consider it quite possible that I am a therian in part because of my strong bond with my Wolf totem. I have met several exceptional cases of experienced magicians who essentially became therians through intense rituals that bound them to their spirit guides (or a portion of the guide's energy) so that they were, for all intents and purposes, no longer entirely human. In talking to two of these people in particular who are friends of mine, I have seen no difference in them when comparing them to "born" therians I've met.

This doesn't mean that I think that all you have to do to become a therian is click your heels three times and say the magic word. As I said, these cases are exceptional and a definite minority. But by now I think I've demonstrated that although not identical, there are some similarities in the functionality of therianthropy and animal totemism, and I think that in *some* people the two concepts can be very closely interwoven. Just because the concept of therianthropy originally dealt with people who were "born" therians (often from a psychological viewpoint) doesn't mean that our understanding of the concept can't evolve. A lot has happened in the years since alt.horror.werewolf gave birth to the initial modern definition of therianthropy, and if we're going to understand what therianthropy really is we can't close off possibilities without substantial, irrevocable evidence either way. As it is, what we have is primarily anecdotal, with little universal and empirical data to work with, and so I choose personally to keep my options open as to the final word.

Yes, there are plenty of therians who neither practice nor believe in magic and totemism. And there are therians whose primary totems are an entirely different species than themselves. However, there are also therians for whom therianthropy and totemism are inextricably linked. I don't think any of these people are fake, and that each one has the same possibility of having a "genuine" experience. I don't think we should have to conform to one theory or another just to fit in. If wrapping your psychology in spiritual or magical trappings makes it more effective for you, then there's no sense in stripping it down to the bare bones just to match a more rational image. I believe there are multiple explanations for how therianthropy happens, and I don't think we necessarily have to narrow it down to one; a phenomenon may have both spiritual and psychological implications, for example. How do we prove that the psychological is truer than the spiritual?

One thing that I have learned as a magician over the years is that reality is more subjective than commonly thought. Part of magical practice involves recognizing and using that awareness to shape your reality to your needs and desires. This doesn't mean that you can indulge in outright delusion without harm, such as believing that you can shoot fireballs from your ears or something equally improbable. However, even science is belief-based because we have to trust our senses—and as everything from optical illusions to quantum physics demonstrate, our physical senses aren't always as correct as we assume. "Scientific truths" get disproven all the time. Remember, the best scientists of the day prior to Copernicus (and even some after him) believed the Sun revolved around the Earth.

When you get into something even more belief-based like therianthropy, reality becomes even more subjective. There's no way to prove that there are no cases of therianthropy that are totemic in nature, even if you get ten thousand therians together who say it's all in our heads. And even if we were able to pinpoint a very specific neurobiological quirk common to all therians, that doesn't automatically negate the spiritual realities of individual people. After all, we can measure the chemicals in the brain of a person who's in love and show that they're very similar to a person with obsessive-compulsive disorder[120], but does that undo thousands of years of romance?

Of course, this is all entirely speculation on my part. Belief is a very personal thing, and if you want to believe that your therianthropy is wholly due to neurobiology with nothing spiritual about it, I won't argue with you. I figure you have just as much of a chance of being right as I do, especially at this point when nobody's managed to do any serious research on the brains of therians. I tend to think that there really is no single explanation for therianthropy, and that it's probable that some are psychological, some are reincarnation-based, some are totemic in nature, and so forth. I also want to reiterate that I see things on multiple layers of reality, and that I often perceive "truth" to be multi-faceted, with its appearance changing dependent on perspective.

---

[120] Johns 2006

Appendix D: Shamanic Journeying and the Totem

By Ravenari

Totemism as a contemporary spiritual path creates personal growth and understanding, but it's important to recognise that totemism does not equal shamanism, and being a totemist doesn't make you a shamanist or shaman. While the practice of shamanism is greatly enhanced by a belief in totemism, a totemist can have nothing to do with the Otherworlds, healing others, or acting as psychopomp--all aspects of shamanism--so it is important not to confuse the two. Making a distinction could mean your safety; it can be the difference between relying on one animal in the Otherworlds, and recognising the need for an ensemble of helpers.

One of the primary functions of the "shaman"[121], and in turn, shamanist, is to alter their state of consciousness so they may journey to the Otherworlds in order to heal people, and psychopomp for the dead (Walsh, 2007). This is true of many traditional forms of shamanism, and also true for many dedicated neoshamanists who practice more eclectically.

The work that shamanism requires within the Otherworlds can be dangerous and complicated (Vitebsky, 2001). We do not live in the Otherworlds and are not born with an innate knowing of the places, etiquette and general "how tos" of getting around. We also aren't able to "create our world" as we can in visualisation, and many of the spirits there have no interest in humans, no interest in helping us, and can be malicious and predatory. Because of this, it helps to have an entourage or ensemble of spirit helpers, deities, ancestors and other entities (Vitebsky, 1997). Unfortunately in more contemporary practices, some shamanists have been encouraged to believe--due to a proliferation of more commercial writings--that the power animal, or single totem, is enough of a help on its own to assist in the Otherworlds.

The function of the totem has evolved in contemporary culture. I am a bit of a traditionalist, so I only believe in one personal totem; but equally valid is a belief in more than one, or choosing to use the term to indicate other animals that I would consider "guides". When it comes to

---

[121] For this essay, I have chosen to use the term shaman to indicate a group of healers from diverse cultures (both traditional and contemporary) who journey, psychopomp and use a knowledge of the spiritworld to serve themselves and others; though I am aware of its origins as a culturally specific Tungus term.

such a thorny term, it is very much a matter of semantics. My referral to totem refers to the primary animal guide, or primary animal spirit that comes into a shamanist's life and sticks around for years, often for the lifetime of the shamanist.

I feel it is dangerous to rely on a single totem when journeying in the Otherworlds, because a solo animal can be just as ineffective or powerless as you in certain areas of the Otherworlds. There are many reasons why a single totem may not be a wholistic source of assistance. Not all animals can travel to all places. Hounds, for example, are – in my own experience – much more likely to be found in the underworlds, and occasionally in the middleworld. This is reflected in mythology, where dogs and wolves are commonly the animals of deities of the underworld (such as the Nordic Garmr who guards Helheim in the underworlds, the Greek Cerberus who guards Hades and the hounds of Hekate who walk the crossroads with her). On the flipside, I have never heard of a shamanist ever finding a dove in the underworld; and in my own experience, have only found them in the upper and middleworlds. In addition to some types of animals not being able to travel everywhere, some animal spirits may not be able to negotiate; aggressive animals like the Tasmanian devil do not have gentle charm on their side when confronting other spirits! Some animals may not be able to lend a reliable source of power, especially those who have come into your life to teach you how to master your own power.

Other totem animals simply aren't present all the time, and can't be called back when needed. I have been left stranded in the otherworlds before, because I foolishly thought that raven would come whenever I called him, especially in a time of crisis. I learnt that when he did not come (and I had to fend for myself), that it is not so wise to be a solo agent in the otherworlds, or an agent with only a totem. And secondly, it taught me the value of recognising that totem animals are independent beings, capable of withholding aid not only because they feel it is necessary, but because of reasons we may have little knowledge of. This will mean nothing of course to people who see totems as archetypal beings only, but for spiritualists / shamanists like myself who see the otherworlds and spirits as independent beings, it is important to recognise their autonomy. Just as you wouldn't dump all your problems on one friend, and one friend only, so it can be unfair to dump all your problems on one totem animal. A little bit of balance doesn't hurt.

Don't get me wrong, the totem is a powerful spirit. It can reflect our personality or inner selves back to us, so that we can learn who we are through observation and understanding. It provides challenges to help push our spirit into growth. It can also provide reassurance and comfort during times of stress (depending on what your totem is, of course). Finally, it can be seen as a source of additional help and strength in the Otherworlds. It is this latter that has been warped and changed into a belief that a totem is the *only* source of additional help and strength in the Otherworlds.

When it comes to journeying, there are a few tasks that come to mind immediately, that a single totem or animal helper will not be enough for, such as shamanic healing and acting as psychopomp; both tasks can be quite dangerous. Shamanic healing involves soul retrieval, or the art of knowing how to look for soul fragments, locating them and bringing them back safely. It also involves knowing how to banish unwanted energies and spirits that could be plaguing a person. Acting as psychopomp involves safely shepherding a spirit of the dead into a place of rest and rejuvenation. A single totem is not enough to do this, and convincing yourself otherwise is reckless and irresponsible, *especially* if you are attempting to heal others. I will use the act of psychopomping the dead as an example; while shepherding the dead, one requires spirits to help keep a look out for danger, show the way (not all spirits of the dead are taken to the same place, and some places and paths will be unfamiliar to you), negotiate with spirits or gods that you may be unfamiliar with, tend to the spirit itself (which may be distressed or unhappy), and then facilitate as safe a passage for that spirit as possible. Theoretically, you *could* place all your trust in one totem, but I feel this is irresponsible when one considers the different things that need to be monitored, and the fact that an individual spirit is involved. You are not just attempting a solo act here, but working with another spirit, one that is sometimes scared and needs reassurance. A surgeon has a team of nurses and aides to help him do the surgery in the most responsible way possible; having a team of spirits or totems in the otherworlds ensures that you can assist others in the most responsible way possible. Putting yourself in danger is your choice, but putting others in danger is not what being a shamanist is about, in my experience.

The benefits of a group of animals is immediately evident. From a logical perspective, it always helps to have a group of people or entities who possess a diverse range of different skills. There is no omniscient helper out there who can do everything; it would be nice, but it would also be a little lonely too. It is safer to travel with an ensemble and from a personal perspective, also a lot more enjoyable too.

So what sort of things is a totem suited for, from the perspective of a shamanist? I personally feel that they are excellent support during extensive visualisations, internal pathworking, and work on the self. They can also be a help for less intensive journeying; for example, as a start out guide before you meet others, as a helper while you are just learning how to get to the Otherworlds in the first place, and also for exploring some of the safer places in the middleworlds that you might want to have as your "starting point" when you journey in the future. They are certainly very helpful to those who want to begin potentially exploring a shamanic spiritual path, or shamanic techniques and tools.

Totems are extremely helpful in many facets of spirituality, and even in some aspects of shamanism. I work with them frequently, because I feel I get a level of spiritual enjoyment and growth with animal totems that I don't get anywhere else in my practices. Shamanic journeying with a single totem has its risks, particularly as your path intensifies and you choose to start healing more, or going to different realms. Remember to distinguish between totemism and shamanism, whether you are a totemist, shamanist or both! Totemism does not equal shamanist/shaman. Recognising this will help you to best realise what path you are on, and facilitate a greater understanding of your beliefs.

References

Levi-Strauss, Claude. (1962). *Totemism*. London: Merlin Press.

Vitebsky, Piers. (1997). "What is a Shaman? – Worlds of the Shaman". *Natural History Magazine* (March 1997). Retrieved from: http://findarticles.com/p/articles/mi_m1134/is_n2_v106/ai_19360545.

Vitebsky, Piers. (2001). *Shamanism*. Oklahoma: University of Oklahoma Press.

Walsh, Roger. (2007). *The World of Shamanism: New Views of an Ancient Tradition*. Minnesota: Llewellyn Publications.

Appendix E: Working with Extinct Spirits
By Paleo

Can modern animists work with the spirits of extinct beings? Can an extinct animal be a totem? My answer to the first is most certainly. One can find all that ever was, is, and will be in the Otherworlds. It is simply a matter of the animist's knowledge, skill, and dedication whether or not they can find and access the right realms to visit these beings. My answer to the second is a hesitant yes…but any given person is far more likely to have an extant totem(s) for reasons I will explain later.

Understanding extinction from a spiritual point of view can be tricky. Like death, it is not something Western minds like to dwell on wrapped up in feelings of fear, denial, and misunderstanding. I feel that today's society is even more deluded about the nature of extinction than the nature of bodily death. Because of the obvious and personal nature of individual death, more people seek to come to terms with it, understand it, and possibly even accept it. Most modern humans though, never think about or deny completely the inevitable extinction of the entire *Homo sapiens* lineage. True, there is anxiety, and this often shows up in books and on the screen in grand dramas of humanity being beset by possible extinction by everything including virulent microbes, hostile alien races, and, of course, humanity's own hubris in relation to our environment. However, while I can think of many movies and television shows that portrayed the death of heroes and protagonists, I can only recall a very few times where humanity itself ultimately fell. Even documentaries exploring possible futures for humans paint an illusion of the race going on and on forever into space and time.

So, what does this have to do with animism? I personally believe that the longer a dedicated animist explores the spiritual realms of Nature, the more likely s/he will encounter energies, landscapes, and creatures from Earth's bygone eras. There are many reasons I say this, perhaps the most important consideration being a mere matter of odds. When one considers the fact that more than 95% of species that have ever lived on Earth are already extinct, one realizes that the more familiar extant species comprise but a fraction of the beings connected to Earth's sphere of physical and spiritual influence. If one studies Nature long enough, one realizes that extinction doesn't mean a species is suddenly irrelevant to the life that continues on. If we look at life from a standpoint of all things being connected, we can begin to see that looking at Nature from a single point in time limits our ability to understand the whole picture. The speed of pronghorn antelopes, the fastest land mammals in North America, cannot be understood without knowledge of the American cheetah, an extinct Ice Age feline who put great evolutionary pressures on pronghorn during that era. Human evolution cannot be fully appreciated without understanding the contributions of numerous species of primates and other mammals, not to mention dinosaurs, fish, amphibians, and insects who created environmental conditions that shaped the lives of our ancestral species.

Another issue that may lead to contact with extinct species is the fact that, sadly, we are living in a time when humanity itself is the greatest cause of rapid extinction. Dinosaurs and Ice Age totems may come to bring wisdom on the nature of extinction and on ways of dealing with any strong emotions we may have surrounding it such as sorrow, fear, or anger. More recently extinct totems, such as Dodo or Thylacine, may wish to tell of their species' human-caused annihilation in the hopes of awakening human concern for species who are in grave danger of joining their ranks and helping humanity learn from past mistakes so that we can turn from the path we are currently on toward one of better coexistence with the rest of Earth's creatures and fauna.

Another reason for contact with extinct totems is that some people simply may be naturally connected to extinct times, landscapes, and critters. This was the case for myself, as I consider myself a dire wolf therianthrope and consider Ice Age North America to be a "true home" of sorts, spiritually speaking. Also, my spirituality heavily involves research into and inspiration from our Paleolithic heritage, and I have found it useful to contact totem spirits who lived with the peoples of those times such as Short-Faced Bear and Auroch. For folks who identify as extinct therians, or those whose spirituality delves heavily into Paleolithic realms, working with totems of the species from the eras you feel drawn to may help enrich your knowledge and understanding of yourself and/or your path.

I feel I must make a small note about one of the potential drawbacks of working with extinct totems. Their living representatives are no longer around to help give direct understanding and knowledge of their behaviors and lifestyles. Because totemism often involves a relationship where important life lessons are learned in part by emulation of the totems' viewpoint and energies, this lack of knowledge has a tendency to cause extinct totems to be somewhat less viable as a primary totem to work with. Because of this, it is my view that most people will have extant totems as their primary teacher.

Exceptions do exist, and there are no rules in neopagan totemism that say you can't seek out lessons from animals beyond your primary and secondary teachers (in fact, I encourage it). If you find an extinct totem you want to work with or who wants to work with you, there are a few ways you can make the relationship run a little smoother.

The obvious first step would be to start researching the knowledge that paleontologists, biologists, and other scientists have amassed on the species. During this research, don't neglect to learn about the world surrounding that species as well. The plants, weather systems, and landscapes that made up the species' home will provide important clues into how it behaved and what motivated it. On the spiritual side of things, some may find fossils to be great aides in contacting extinct totems. Fossils and fossil clones are available on the internet, and access to one may help in finding a direct way to connect to the spirits they represent. If you have access to a natural history museum that displays fossils, you may also try contact there. If you practice shapeshifting, why not take some of those glorious skeletons out for a test drive? I recommend focusing on matching your own skeleton to that of the dinosaur or other critter, allowing muscle and flesh to form around it. The reason I prefer this shapeshifting method for dinosaurs is in hopes of limiting the chance of fictional dinosaur archetypes (such as the monsters of *Jurassic Park*) from popping up instead.

Another method of gaining more knowledge about an extinct totem is contacting and studying extant totems who are directly connected in some way to them. You may contact evolutionary descendants and relatives. For example, I have talked about Dire Wolf with both Grey Wolf and Coyote to get their perspectives. I am currently preparing to work with Auroch and have contacted the energies of Musk Ox, Water Buffalo, and Domestic Cattle (specifically Longhorn) to help me understand the bovine energies I will be working with.

Animals that fill a similar niche or are examples of convergent evolution also hold possibilities. I discovered my therian species in part because of Spotted Hyena's help. I knew that Grey Wolf didn't exactly match my inner-critter and was baffled when I accidentally discovered that Spotted Hyena held some things that "filled some of the holes". And yet, I knew I wasn't hyena. When I later learned that dire wolves played a similar role in their biome that spotted hyenas do in theirs, the connection made sense and Spotted Hyena has had much influence on how I understand my nature as a dire wolf therian. The connection may be obvious, but learn to think a bit outside the box as well. Giant Ground Sloth/Megatherium holds roughly the same niche as Giraffe, though one might not think there was much in common between them at first glance.

One may also look to the totems of any extant predators, prey, or competitors of the extinct totem in question, a good example being the relationship between American Cheetah and Pronghorn.

Lastly, I would like to direct attention to the possible use of ancient living creatures as guides to extinct times and places. Some folks seem to have trouble accessing eras that existed long before the humans existed. In that case, it may help to seek out a being such as Crocodile, Shark, Horseshoe Crab, or Coelacanth. These ancient beings often exude a sense of "I've seen it all" and know exactly how to find the many, many eras they have witnessed and, thus, may be worth seeking out should you want to do a little time-traveling.

Working with extinct totems makes me fall in love with Nature all over again. The beauty, diversity, and drama we witness today all across the world is but a small fraction of Earth's creation, and a tiny taste of the possibilities Earth has to offer. Extinction is an important and inevitable part of Nature's cycle, yet because humanity is the direct cause of today's current mass extinction, now more than ever we need to understand and respect our ability to end the existence of whole species. More importantly, we need to understand and respect our ability to *not* end their existence by making sane and respectful choices on how we coexist with the animals and plants that are with us today.

Working with extinct totems can be fun, frustrating, mysterious, and enlightening. This "spiritual paleontology" helps connect us more firmly to our roots and evolutionary ancestors. It helps us to appreciate the fact that existence is a gift that can be fragile and fleeting or tenacious and long-lasting. I hope that this essay encourages some of you to seek out the totems of times beyond our realm of here-and-now. I can't promise that they all will welcome human inquiry, but I do know first hand that many of them appreciate being remembered and are eager for their voices to be heard again.

Appendix F: An Introduction to Therioshamanism

Over the years, I've run across references to shamanism throughout my animal magic studies. While I was enamored of the concept when I was a newbie, I soon discovered that having a deerskin pouch and some herbs did not a shaman make. So I put that title aside and began exploring neopaganism in general in more depth. While I occasionally had other people try to apply the "shaman" label to me, I didn't take it for myself, knowing that what I was doing, while animistic and somewhat primal, didn't really count as shamanism. I didn't journey to retrieve souls, nor did I have as intense a relationship with the spirits I worked with that I would need for such endeavors.

In 2007, things began to shift in my practice. For years the totems and other spirits I worked with (heretofore known as "the spirits") had done a lot to help me in my everyday life as well as in more esoteric pursuits. As I grew older I began to feel a greater urge to give back to them, to do something for them as a way of showing gratitude for all the ways they had helped me. I also began feeling the need for a more formal spiritual and magical practice. While my exploration over the years had yielded me a lot of good experiences, I was ready to settle down into something deeper.

For a while, the spirits had been poking, prodding, and hinting at me that I should start looking into shamanism. This intensified as 2007 unfolded. Once I figured out what it was they wanted, I was hesitant to go forward with it. I had years of self-conditioning telling me, "You don't know enough to be a shaman, you don't have any ties to any indigenous cultures, and you have a day job that keeps you from communing with the spirits 24-7". But the spirits kept on nudging me.

Finally, I gave in. I told them I'd give it a try. If it worked, great. If not, we'd try something else. So starting at the Autumn Equinox of 2007, I started on a six-month training course developed and guided both by myself and the spirits. Along with their guidance and my trial-and-error learning, I also read voraciously about shamanism—not just how-to books, but also anthropological texts. I also talked to a few neopagan shamans I knew, as well as Ravenari, whose background includes traditional Russian animism/shamanism, as a way to keep myself grounded and make sure I wasn't jumping off the cliff of insanity.

The first six months of training focused primarily on creating/discovering cosmology—my understanding of how reality is put together, as well as the positioning of various beings and features throughout. Since I was drawing heavily on my neopagan background in lieu of any indigenous cultural heritage, my cosmology centered on the four directions, elements and other correspondences associated with neopagan and other forms of modern magic. My guides were the four totem animals I associated with each quarter. The first month was spent reacquainting myself with all four quarters in detail, strengthening my awareness of them. Then I dedicated each of the next four months to studying a quarter and its associations in more depth. My final month revisited all four, but with the experiences of the previous months to give me more perspective.

I found that my lessons weren't limited to just studying correspondences. I spent a lot of time bringing the lessons of each quarter into my everyday life. Sometimes this wasn't planned—at the beginning of my Earth month, and at both ends of my Water month, I caught colds that turned into respiratory infections. Each time was a reminder of things that my body (Earth) needed to stay healthy (Water). Granted, they weren't pleasant lessons, but they brought the message home. I also had a critical breakthrough in my communication with my husband occur during my Air month, and cleared out a lot of unnecessary personal "underbrush" while working with Fire. And I brought these lessons into my interaction with the environment as well, as I started a compost bin, increased my use of organic and free-range food, and altered a lot of everyday habits to be more green.

Along with the totems, I also worked with the skin spirits on a more regular basis. At least once a month I would take the time to get to know one of the skins I didn't know so well, meditate and/or dance with it, and otherwise improve our relationship. After my first six months were over, I dedicated a week apiece to them, coming up with a drum beat, dance and song for each one. I primarily worked with one deity during my training. My patron goddess, Artemis, had told me in February of 2007 that she would be "handing me over" to a god soon. Shortly before I began my shamanic path, the god I know as the Animal Father made himself known to me. He revealed himself through the Paleolithic cave painting in Les Trois Freres known popularly as the Sorcerer, a human-animal hybrid with great branching antlers, a long tail, animal paws, and male genitalia. Whether he was an actual deity worshipped by the people who created that painting, a god who took the opportunity to channel himself through that painting, or a construct birthed from the wonder of those who saw it, I was never completely sure. He was, however, an embodiment of the Animal Kingdom, from the tiniest microscopic beings to the great Blue Whale.

At the end of my six months, I traveled down to Sedona, Arizona to go through the first two initiations offered by James Endredy, author of several books including *Ecoshamanism*.[122] Each took up two days, with a day in between that just happened to be the exact six month marker for my path. During the first initiation I reopened an innate connection to the Land that I had not had since I was much younger, and this came strongly into play on the day in between, when I went on a personal journey out into the desert on my own. The second initiation, the Embrace of the Earth ceremony, helped to strengthen the things I had learned. As it involved being buried in a hole in the ground, it gave me time to really meditate on the changes that had occurred, and talk to the Land about where I had been and where I was going.

These experiences helped me to open up my perception of my path quite a bit. While the animals remained important, I learned that in order to help them I also had to have a good connection to the entire system that they—and I—relied on. So I began working more with the Land back in Portland, where I live, spending more time connecting with places that were sacred to me in various ways, and communicating with the spirits there. I also had started a garden shortly before I left for Arizona, and working with the plants as they grew helped me to connect more with the Plant Kingdom. In addition to working with the Animal Father, I began to connect more with the Green Mother, Father Sun and Mother Moon[123], and other such beings.

Since then I've been working on creating deeper relationships with the Land and its denizens, and finding out what they need of me. While "therioshamanism" translates to "animal shamanism", and my primary interaction is with the animal spirits and totems, I'm finding that it's not only helpful but absolutely necessary to not limit myself. There are numerous definitions of "shaman", ranging from "spiritual practitioner of certain Siberian indigenous tribes" to "anyone who works with the spirits and journeys to the Otherworld on behalf of the community". The

---

[122] You can find out more information at http://www.jamesendredy.com. I highly recommend working with him if you can; he's one of the most down to earth people I've met, and his *Ecoshamanism* is wonderfully suited for modern nonindigenous cultures that may lack a traditional shamanic role. Additionally, I've never met anyone quite so closely linked to the Land he lives with, something that I find incredibly inspirational.

[123] When I refer to these entities by familial terms, such as Mother or Father, it is not because I am attempting to be "more like the Indians". Rather, it is a practice that, having dealt with these forces as living beings, not just unconscious phenomena, makes complete sense. These are terms of respect and honor, as well as acknowledging connection, that aren't culturally specific. We all can work with the Sun and Moon, Wind and Water. They seem to like the familial terms.

working definition I find best for now is, "I serve the Land". All else is in the details.

Appendix G: My Frank Appraisals of Totemic Literature

I am a semi-professional book reviewer. I specialize in pagan and occult nonfiction, though I've branched out into magic-themed fiction as well, on occasion. One of my specialties, not surprisingly, is books on animal magic. While I haven't read every single book on the topic, I've read the majority of the ones I know about—and I do a lot of searching for obscure titles. Granted, reading and reviewing isn't the same as reading, doing all the exercises, and incorporating the material into one's everyday life. However, after you've read a certain number of books on a topic—especially if they follow a particular basic formula—and you've done enough practice on your own, you get a pretty good idea of the material just through reading it.

This appendix is dedicated to brief reviews of some of what's out there as far as further reading goes, mainly from a neopagan rather than anthropological perspective. I'm not entirely against totem animal dictionaries, but I'd like to offer my opinions on what dictionaries and other books may be particularly useful if you feel the need to research others' viewpoints. As they are my opinions, they are wholly subjective, and you are more than welcome to agree or disagree as you please. Also, these are very brief opinions; for more complete reviews, please surf over to http://lupabitch.wordpress.com. I've also not included all the books I've read, just a selection; my book review blog at the address above has a more complete collection.

Andrews, Ted: *Animal-Speak* and *Animal Wise*. These are pretty much considered to be the classics on neopagan totemism (at least as classic as something dating from the early to mid 1990s can be). Both dictionaries cover a wide variety of animals, though most of the invertebrates are insects. Well-written, with some good exercises; Andrews' *The Art of Shapeshifting* is a good supplement for magical shapeshifting.

Anonymous: *Your Spirit Animal Helpers*. This is a rather obscure book; it has a dictionary of thirty animals, and some basic totemic information. It's a good 101 book, and one I'd recommend. I also have to rave about the wonderful illustrations by an artist named Marc Brinkerhoff; definitely one of the most visually appealing books out there!

Bennett, Hal Zina: *Spirit Animals and the Wheel of Life*. I really enjoyed this book. Rather than rehashing the same totemism 101 information, this book takes a fresh approach based on the author's own experiences. Additionally, it's highly ecospiritual, and also provides an effective psychological pathworking system. One of my favorite introductions.

Bruce, Marie: *Magical Beasts*. I wasn't particularly thrilled with this book, which wasn't so much a dictionary as an animal spell cookbook. Some of the material is poorly researched, or downright silly. However, there's also some good information in there, and it's one of the easiest books to read, with an inviting writing style. It's not high on my recommended list, but it's also not the worst I've seen. So-so.

Buffalo Horn Man and Firedancer: *Animal Energies*. This is a small self-published booklet that's essentially all dictionary. Mostly BINABM, though with a few exceptions, and it's pretty well-written, if a little sparse. It's available primarily through the authors' website, http://members.aol.com/danceottr6/aetsc.html.

Conway, D.J. *Animal Magick*. I recommend not picking up this text. It's one of the earliest dictionaries, and while it has a decent variety of animals, it's poorly researched. I'd recommend some of the other dictionaries in this list over this rather mediocre selection.

Dolfyn: *Shamanism Volume III* and *Shamanic Wisdom II* (with Swimming Wolf). The former is an earlier thirty-page booklet that was the precursor to the latter, a proper book. Lots of BINABM, and I really didn't care for the "Indian this" and "Native that" New Age tone. However, they still have good information, and if you can look past the tone they're worth reading.

Farmer, Steven D.: *Power Animals* and *Animal Spirit Guides*. This is a pair of animal totem dictionaries. Both are decent, and the former comes with a guided meditation CD. The latter, though, makes me think of the potential race to have as many unique totems in a dictionary as possible, since there were a lot of entries, and a wide variety beyond the BINABM. While it's nice to see branching out as far as what totems are listed, I'd like to see more exploration in ways to work with totems. These are good additions to a dictionary collection, either way.

Franklin, Anna: *Familiars*. This is a British perspective on totems (which Franklin refers to as familiars). It has a good dictionary, lots of entries, and her information is good to compare to other authors'. A good addition to a collection of dictionaries.

Galenorn, Yasmine: *Totem Magic*. I have to comment the author for writing a book on animal magic without a dictionary. Well done! She goes through a lot of topics on animal magic, backing them up with anecdotes from her own practice. An impressive work, and a must-have.

Gauding, Madonna: *Personal Power Animals*. I was really unimpressed with this one. Along with a very basic totem dictionary, there was a smattering of information on related systems such as the Chinese Zodiac. However, there was nothing unique to make it stand out from the crowd, and really not all that much information in there. Unless you're a serious collector, there's not much of interest here.

Green, Susie: *Animal Wisdom*. Not to be confused with Palmer's book of the same title. It's one of my favorite dictionaries, largely because she includes a lot of environmental awareness amid the information. There's a good variety in her dictionary, though the book is primarily dictionary entries. Still, it's a good one to have.

Nitsch, Twylah: *Creature Teachers*. This one just confused me. It's supposed to be Seneca totemism, but the author wrote a collection of parables with no real explanation of their original context. The method of finding your totem consists of picking a number and them seeing what animal corresponds to that number on a wheel in the back of the book, which really didn't impress me.

Palmer, Jessica Dawn: *Animal Wisdom*. This is probably the best dictionary in the bunch, apart from other information. That's saying quite a bit, but this book has a lot to offer. The entries are many, and well-written, rather than being a couple of brief paragraphs and correspondences. If you want just a solid totem dictionary, this is one of the best.

Pennick, Nigel and Helen Field: *A Book of Beasts*. I really liked this book, mainly because it focused in detail on sacred animals in Britain. You don't really get that kind of in-depth exploration outside of attempts to explain "Native American" totemism. It's useful even if you don't live in the U.K.

Roderick, Timothy: *The Once Unknown Familiar*. This book has some of the best psychological pathworking in it. The totem dictionary and other information seems a bit like an afterthought, and there's some filler, but the exercises and rituals in it are worth the cover price alone.

Sams, Jamie and David Carson: *The Medicine Cards*. I know, I already said it before, but—I don't like this book. The deck is pretty, but the book has a lot of New Age wannabe-Indian material. Last I checked, no Native American tribe ever talked about Atlantis or Mu in its traditional lore. If you want a totem deck (besides the one in this book) I suggest Susie Green's *Animal Messages* or Ted Andrews' *Animal Wise* deck (not the same as his book of the same title).

Scully, Nicki: *The Golden Cauldron/Power Animal Meditations*. Published under two different titles, this book has a wealth of pathworkings involving different totem animals in it. It's highly recommended if you get a lot out of guided meditation, or if you want more ideas on how to actually work with totems on a more personal, internal level.

Steiger, Brad: *Totems*. It has a decent dictionary, with good variety, though not as much as Andrews or Farmer. Good 101 totemic information, though it's a little too "trying to be Native-centric" for my tastes. Good bibliography, though no internal citations.

Telesco, Patricia and Rowan Hall: *Animal Spirit*. This is a really good introductory book to animal magic in general. The dictionary is so-so, but the authors cover a lot of ground on other types of animal magic, including working with animal parts.

Bibliography

Books

American Indian Movement (1984). "AIM resolution sovereign dine nation, window rock, AZ, May 11, 1984". In Harvey (2003). *Shamanism: A reader*. New York: Routledge.

Andrews, Ted (2005). *The art of shapeshifting*. Jackson, Tennessee: Dragonhawk Publishing.

Campbell, Joseph (1988). *The way of the animal powers, part 1: mythologies of the primitive hunters and gatherers*. New York: Harper & Row.

Campbell, Joseph (1984). *The masks of god: Primitive mythology*. New York: Penguin Books.

Carroll, Peter J (1987). *Liber null & psychonaut*. York Beach, Maine: Weiser Books.

-- (1992). *Liber kaos*. York Beach, Maine: Weiser Books.

Curtis, Gregory (2007). *The cave painters: Probing the mysteries of the world's first artists*. New York: Anchor Books.

De Mille, Richard (1976). *Castaneda's journey*. Santa Barbara: Capra Press.

Ellwood, Taylor (2008). *Multi-media magic: Further explorations of pop culture and identity in magic*. Stafford, U.K.: Immanion Press/Megalithica Books.

Ellwood, Taylor (2007). *Inner alchemy: energy work and the magic of the body*. Stafford, U.K.: Immanion Press/Megalithica Books.

Endredy, James (2005). *Ecoshamanism*. Woodbury, Minnesota: Llewellyn Publications.

Frantzis, B.K. (2001). *Relaxing into Your being: The water method of taoist meditation series, volume 1*. North Atlantic Books.

Gray, William G. (1980). *Magical Ritual Methods*. York Beach, Maine: Weiser Books.

Hemachandra, Ray A (2003). "Selling the sacred? American indians and the new age". *New Age Retailer*, November/December 2003.

Hook, Patrick (1998). *Wolves*. New York: Gramercy Books.

Johns, Chris (2006). Editor's note. *National Geographic*, 209 #2, no page number given.

Jones, Evan John and Chas S. Clifton (1997). *Sacred mask, sacred dance*. St. Paul, Minnesota: Llewellyn Publications.

Heaven, Ross and Howard G. Charing (2006). *Plant spirit shamanism: traditional techniques for healing the soul*. Rochester, Vermont: Destiny Books.

Kelly, Jane Holden (1991). *Yaqui women: Contemporary life histories.* Nebraska: University of Nebraska Press.

Laurie, Erynn Rowan (November 2008). "Dead Religions, Living Cultures: The Reconstructionist Research and Visionary Blues". In Lupa (editor), *Talking About the Elephant: An Anthology of Neopagan Perspectives on Cultural Appropriation.* Stafford: Megalithica Books.

Levi-Strauss, Claude, Rodney Needham trans. (1963). *Totemism.* Boston: Beacon Press.

Lopez, Barry Holstun (1978). *Of wolves and men.* New York: Charles Scribner's Sons.

Lupa (2007). "Totems and Transformation". *Magick on the Edge: An Anthology of Experimental Magick.* Stafford: Immanion Press/Megalithica Books.

Morrison, Grant (2003). "Pop Magic!" *Book of Lies: The Disinformation Guide to Magick and the Occult.* New York: Disinformation.

Noctis, Natassja (2006). *The Therian Bible* (third edition). Self-published (Lulu.com).

Perrins, Dr. Christopher M. (1990). *The illustrated encyclopedia of birds: The definitive reference to birds of the world.* New York: Prentice Hall Editions.

Pike, Sarah M. (2001). *Earthly bodies, magical selves: contemporary pagans and the search for community.* Berkeley: University of California Press.

Root, Deborah (1997). "White indians". *Borrowed Power: Essays on Cultural Appropriation.* New Jersey: Rutgers University Press, p. 225-233.

Ryden, Hope (1979). *God's dog: A celebration of the North American coyote.* New York: Lyons and Burford, Publishers.

Samorini, Giorgio (2002). *Animals and psychedelics: the natural world and the instinct to alter consciousness.* Vermont: Park Street Press.

Sams, Jamie and David Carson (1999). *The medicine cards: The discovery of power through the ways of animals.* New York: St. Martin's Press.

Vitebsky, Piers (1995). *The shaman.* Boston: Little, Brown and Company.

Wetzel, Joshua (2006). *The paradigmal pirate.* Stafford: Immanion Press.

Wilson, Robert Anton (2004). *Sex, drugs & magic.* Tempe, AZ: New Falcon.

Wilson, Robert Anton (1992). *Prometheus rising.* Tempe, AZ: New Falcon.

Websites

Aldred, Lisa (2000). *Plastic shamans and astroturf sun dances: new age commercialization of native american spirituality.* Retrieved 24 September, 2007 from http://muse.jhu.edu/demo/american_indian_quarterly/v024/24.3aldred.html.

Anonymous (2008-A). *Amoeba.* Retrieved 29 June, 2008 from http://en.wikipedia.org/wiki/Amoeba.

Anonymous (2008-B). *Dodo*. Retrieved 16 March, 2008 from http://en.wikipedia.org/wiki/Dodo.

Anonymous (2008-C). *Euglena*. Retrieved 29 June, 2008 from http://en.wikipedia.org/wiki/Euglena.

Anonymous (2008-D). *Paramecium*. Retrieved 29 June, 2008 from http://en.wikipedia.org/wiki/Paramecium.

Anonymous (2007-A). *Chicken*. Retrieved 23 May, 2008 from http://en.wikipedia.org/wiki/Chicken.

Anonymous (2007-B). *Lungless salamander*. Retrieved 23 May, 2007 from http://en.wikipedia.org/wiki/Plethodontidae.

Anonymous (2007-C). *Metynnis argenteus*. Retrieved 23 May, 2007 from http://en.wikipedia.org/wiki/Metynnis_argenteus.

Anonymous (2007-D). *Unverified personal gnosis*. Retrieved 23 May, 2007 from http://en.wikipedia.org/wiki/Unverified_personal_gnosis.

Anonymous (2007-E). *Werewolf*. Retrieved 23 May, 2007 from http://en.wikipedia.org/wiki/Werewolf.

Anonymous (1973). *Don juan and the sorceror's apprentice* (TIME magazine). Retrieved 25 September, 2007 from http://www.time.com/time/magazine/article/0,9171,903890,00.html.

Beetham, John. *A D.C. birding blog: Bachman's warbler in cuba?* Retrieved 4 July, 2007 from http://dendroica.blogspot.com/2006/08/bachmans-warbler-in-cuba.html.

Carson, Roy S. *Government sanctions amazon genocide*. Retrieved 20 September, 2007 from http://albionmonitor.net/10-30-95/amazongenocide.html.

Cole, Joan Schraith (2004). *Pseudo native american tarot decks: a picture is worth 1000 words*. Retrieved 27 June, 2007 from http://www.lelandra.com/comptarot/tarotindian.htm.

Finley, Klint (2006). *Fang and fur, blood and bone: A primal guide to animal magic*. Retrieved 10 November, 2007 from http://www.technoccult.com/archives/2006/06/13/fang-and-fur-blood-and-bone-a-primal-guide-to-animal-magic.

Goldstein, Laurie D. and Christine O'Keefe, Ph.D. (2003). *The need for low-cost spay-neuter programs: $aving tax dollar$!* Retrieved 4 May, 2008 from http://www.straypetadvocacy.org/PDF/NeedLowCostSterilization.PDF.

Kaldera, Raven (2003). *Day 6, jotunheim: "I am the lost child of the iron wood"*. Retrieved 23 September, 2007 from http://www.cauldron.jovi.net/nine/day6.html.

Lavey, Anton (unknown). *How to become a Werewolf - The Fundamentals of Lycanthropic Metamorphisis; Their Principles and Application*. Retrieved 22 March, 2007 from http://www.playspoon.com/twi/howto.html.

Mesteth, Wilmer Stampede, Darrell Standing Elk and Phyllis Swift Hawk (1993). *Declaration of war against exploiters of lakota spirituality.* Retrieved 27 June, 2007 from http://www.aics.org/war.html.

Sidy Boys Web Design (2007). *PuppyMills.* Retrieved 4 May, 2008 from http://www.sidyboysfoolin.com/PuppyMill.html.

Szlemko, William, J., Pamela Jumper Thurman and James W. Wood (2006). *Native americans and alcohol: past, present and future. (Clinical report).* Retrieved 26 September, 2007 from http://www.encyclopedia.com/doc/1G1-154391007.html.

Van Ravestein, Pia (2007). *Wolf.* Retrieved 27 June, 2007 from http://www.wildspeak.com/vilturj/totems/wwolf.html.

Index

About the Author

Lupa lives in Portland, OR with hir mate and fellow author, Taylor Ellwood, their cats Sun Ce and Ember, and entirely too many books and art supplies. S/he enjoys the progressive social environment there, as well as being in close proximity to both the Cascades and Columbia River Gorge, and the Pacific Ocean. While biologically female, Lupa identifies spiritually as genderfluid androgynous, and is perfectly happy with whatever pronouns you throw at hir (though s/he may default to female pronouns to avoid confusion in some instances).

Lupa is the author of several books on pagan and magical topics from Immanion Press/Megalithica Books. Hir first book, *Fang and Fur, Blood and Bone: A Primal Guide to Animal Magic*, is a groundbreaking work that revolutionizes the practice of animal magic. S/he followed this up with *A Field Guide to Otherkin*, the first book completely dedicated to the study of the Otherkin community. S/he also cowrote *Kink Magic: Sex Magic Beyond Vanilla* with Taylor, presenting a guide to utilizing the altered states of consciousness inherent in BDSM and fetish play for practical and metamorphic magic. S/he is a contributor to both *Magick on the Edge: An Anthology of Experimental Magick* and *Manifesting Prosperity: A Wealth Magic Anthology*, as well as the editor of *Talking About the Elephant: An Anthology of Neopagan Perspectives on Cultural Appropriation* (Fall 2008) and *Engaging the Spirit World: An Anthology of Shamanism, Totemism and Other Animistic Practices* (tentative 2009).

When not writing, Lupa creates ritual tools, jewelry, and other sacred artwork out of bones, fur, leather, feathers, beads and other such things (and is in the process of writing a book on the topic). S/he also enjoys hiking and other outdoor activities. Spiritually, s/he is in the process of developing a formalized neoshamanic practice, called therioshamanism, based on over a decade of diverse experiences. S/he is currently pursuing a Master's degree in counseling psychology with an emphasis on ecpopsychology.

Lupa may be found online at http://www.thegreenwolf.com, http://www.kinkmagic.com, http://lupabitch.wordpress.com, http://lupabitch.livejournal.com and http://therioshamanism.com. S/he moderates http://totemists.livejournal.com. Hir email address is whishthound@gmail.com, and s/he welcomes constructive feedback, reviews, and chances to talk shop.

Did You Like What You Read?

Fang and Fur, Blood and Bone: A Primal Guide to Animal Magic
by Lupa
ISBN 978-1-905713-01-0/MB0101
$21.99/£12.99 paperback
This is like no other book on animal magic! Totems, familiars, and animal sacrifice are just a few of the topics in this controversial text. Not for domesticated magicians.

Ecstasia: A Practical Introduction to Transcendental Music and Dance
by Julia R. Zay
ISBN 978-1-905713-10-3/MB0119
$21.99/£12.99 paperback
A guide to ecstatic dance based on Mediterranean traditions. For novices, ritual performers, and those who simply enjoy music and dance.

Magickal Progressions by Moonsilvered
ISBN 978-1-905713-16-5/MB0117
$21.99/£12.99 paperback
Do you know somebody who's interested in magical practice, but not sure where to begin? This thorough introduction is one the reader will return to again and again.

Sekhem Heka: A Natural Healing and Self-Development System by Storm Constantine
ISBN 978-1905713-13-4 / MB0114
$21.99/£12.99 paperback
Egyptian healing techniques and Reiki are elements of this dynamic system for healing on all levels of the self, created by the author.

Find these and the rest of our current lineup at http://www.immanion-press.com

Breinigsville, PA USA
14 March 2010
234160BV00001B/103/P